T0322150

Coming of Age

Coming of Age

How Adolescence Shapes Us

LUCY FOULKES

THE BODLEY HEAD

LONDON

1 3 5 7 9 10 8 6 4 2

The Bodley Head, an imprint of Vintage, is part of the Penguin Random House group
of companies whose addresses can be found at global.penguinrandomhouse.com

First published by The Bodley Head in 2024

penguin.co.uk/vintage

Typeset in 12/14.75pt Bembo Book MT Pro by Jouve (UK), Milton Keynes
Printed and bound in Great Britain by Clays Ltd, Elcograf S.p.A.

The authorised representative in the EEA is Penguin Random House Ireland,
Morrison Chambers, 32 Nassau Street, Dublin D02 YH68

A CIP catalogue record for this book is available from the British Library

HB ISBN 9781847927293
TPB ISBN 9781847927309

Penguin Random House is committed to a sustainable future
for our business, our readers and our planet. This book is made
from Forest Stewardship Council® certified paper.

'I am rescuing her from teenage hell. Do you know the
wounds from adolescence can take years to heal?'

Cher Horowitz, in the film *Clueless*

Contents

Author's note

While all the stories in this book are true, some names and identifying details have been changed to protect the privacy of the people involved.

Introduction

The power of adolescence

Imagine you have agreed to participate in a research study about human memory. On the way to the university psychology department you anticipate being asked to memorise a series of shapes that appear on a computer screen, or maybe remember a list of words – the usual sort of exercise. But when you get there, the researcher ushers you into a small, windowless testing room, and you see there is nothing on the table except a ballpoint pen and a few blank sheets of white paper. The researcher hovers behind you – these rooms are always too small to talk face-to-face – and gives you the instructions. It's simple, really, she says. You just need to write down the ten most important memories of your life to date.

Whenever adults are asked to do this, something consistent happens. The memories that people report most often are from their adolescent and early adult years – from the ages of ten to thirty.[1] The effect is found regardless of how old the participant is when they take the test: it applies to eighty-year-olds as much as it applies to thirty-five-year-olds. This is the so-called 'reminiscence bump', and it's one of the most robust findings in human memory research. It's a surprising phenomenon, because everything we know about memory suggests that recent events should be the ones we remember best, while details about earlier memories should fade. But when it comes to life moments that are important to us, it's the teenage years and twenties that really count.

There are a few rather mundane explanations for the bump. One is that your brain is functioning at its prime during those years, so anything that happens in that time is stored in your memory in a particularly effective and long-lasting way. Another is that those years involve a lot of firsts – first love, first time driving a car, first time living away from parents – and that simply because of their novelty, these events leave a bigger mark in the mind. This is all true, but there is another explanation: the period of life captured by the reminiscence bump, particularly the ages of ten to twenty, is fundamentally about figuring out identity. We remember events from those years, in other words, because they make us who we are.

I'm talking here about *adolescence*: the period of development that starts with puberty, when a flood of hormones triggers significant psychological, physical and neurological changes across the mind and body, and ends when the person has transitioned away from the family unit and taken on their own adult roles and responsibilities. Of course, identity-defining events and relationships happen from the moment we're born, and continue to happen into adulthood. But adolescence is distinctly important for a number of reasons. For starters, thanks to the extensive neurological and cognitive development kicked off by puberty, adolescents are biologically driven to seek out the kind of identity-defining experiences that are most memorable.

Many of our adolescent memories involve our friends, for example. Why is this? As we will see in the following pages, adolescents care enormously about what their peers think of them, which drives a lot of the clichéd teenager behaviour that is so familiar: the self-consciousness, the cliquey friendships, the intense romances. They are often mocked for this, but it actually makes good biological sense: to survive beyond the family and integrate with a new social group, it's wise for an adolescent to spend a lot of time thinking about whether people approve of them and whether or not they fit in. Adolescents adjust their own behaviour and even their thoughts to fall in line with their peers, because this is what is needed to achieve the safety and sense of belonging that comes with being part of a group. As a result, experiences with peers are particularly salient and powerful at that age, forging formative memories.

Growing up and leaving the family unit isn't just about finding friends, it's also about finding a mate, which means adolescents are generally very driven to have romantic relationships and sexual experiences. Arguably, that's the whole point of adolescence. Again, this biological imperative means adolescents end up having some intense, identity-defining experiences of sex and love – often, as we will see, at a very young age indeed. Lastly, adolescents are biologically driven to take risks, because this enables them to explore the world and establish their independence, and again build relationships beyond their immediate family. So you can see how all these logical, necessary, primal drives mean that as adolescents we wind up in the kinds of situation that make for powerful, self-shaping memories, ones that we all recall in detail even many years later.

This isn't just about biology. To add fuel to the fire, the biological drives of adolescence kick in at the exact time that a monumental shift occurs in the outside world too. In many countries around the world, right around the time of puberty, children leave the cosy safety of primary (or elementary) school and start secondary (or high) school, which means a complete change in their social world: a whole new group of peers and much less time with adults. Back in 1961, the sociologist James Coleman wrote that, with the move to secondary education, adolescents are 'dumped into a society of peers',[2] and that's as true today as it was then. In the early years of school, a child's social world is constrained and predictable: they spend most of their time in a small, familiar group of peers. They are closely monitored by teachers – and often a single teacher for most of the day, who knows the social dynamics of the class well. Outside of school, any peer socialising is typically organised and supervised by parents or other adults, and activities are generally structured, like playing games or sports. Parents tend to know the names of their children's friends, and often know the friends' parents as well.

With the shift to secondary or high school, everything changes. The pool of peers is suddenly huge and unfamiliar, and very rapidly, the socialising is organised by the children themselves, not the adults. Socialising outside of school shifts to being unstructured and unsupervised. This is the age of parties, of meeting up in town, of hanging out in the park late at night. Parents soon don't know the names of all their children's friends, or indeed any of them, and they often don't know who their child is with at any one time. Within a year or so of starting secondary education, the walled containment of childhood socialising has been entirely blown apart. In their new social context, adolescents are not just deeply biologically interested in friends, sex and risk, they also find themselves in a perfect setting to act on those interests. Like journalists dropped into a war zone, adolescents are landed in the very place that interesting stuff is going to happen. In fact, you couldn't design a better combination of factors that would allow big-hitting, memorable events to play out.

The stories we tell

But even so, this still doesn't quite get to the heart of why adolescent memories can become so deeply cemented in our minds. To fully grasp this, we need to recognise that adolescence is the first time people are able to tell *stories* about what happened to them. I'm not talking so much about the stories people tell others – the ones they might share in the pub or at work, for example – although those are certainly stories too. I'm talking about the stories people tell *themselves*, those internal narratives we all have about who we are and what happened to us and why. Many psychologists have puzzled over the question of how we create a stable identity – how we answer that vexing question of who we are, especially considering we can behave so differently across time and in different contexts. Somehow, we need to create a sense of what psychoanalyst Erik Erikson called 'self-sameness' – some sense that, despite how differently we can behave and feel, the person we are right now is essentially the same person we were yesterday, a month ago, years ago, and the same person we will continue to be in the future.[3] And the answer, at least partly, is that we create stories about ourselves.

This means that, consciously or unconsciously, we tend to rearrange our experiences and memories into logical narratives. While the reality of experience is noisy and filled with randomness, these narratives have a clear beginning and a defined end, and everything in between has a coherent order and some sort of relevance or meaning. For example, when reflecting on why we were fired from a job, we might begin the story in our mind not with our first day in the office but when we had that first minor disagreement with our boss. Likewise, when remembering a failed romantic relationship, the beginning might be the first moment of significant connection – a late night conversation, a first kiss. Whatever the beginning, the stories we tell then focus on the characters who do noteworthy things rather than the countless people whose paths we may have crossed. We home in on the moments that are significant to the outcome we have in mind, while the infinite mundane ones tend to be filtered out. The end is always a meaningful point too, a logical place to end the story: the day you had the meeting about the redundancy or the day your partner walked out, and the impact this had on you, making you the person you are today.

Stories are important because they allow us to make sense of ourselves, to weave a thread between things that have happened in the past and in the present, and to predict what might happen to us in the future. Stories make actions and events *meaningful*, and save us from thinking the things that happen to us are just a series of random, unconnected accidents. In this sense, stories aren't simply tools that we use to understand ourselves – they become our very essence. Dan McAdams, a psychologist who researches how we form and maintain a sense of personal identity, argues that our entire sense of self is a story that we tell ourselves and others: 'We are all storytellers, and we are the stories we tell.'[4]

In his early work, McAdams used the analogy of a novel. He said that a person's identity was 'a big story, an integrative autobiographical project, a personal myth . . . If you could literally see it (and read it), it would look like a bound novel. You would see or read the chapters, and you would likely focus in on particularly important, self-defining scenes . . . like high points, low points, and turning points.'[5] He later refined his thinking, stating that the key stories of a person's life are not orderly chapters that progress in a straightforward way as they do in a novel, and that a better, more realistic metaphor of our identity might be an anthology of related stories – more like a short-story collection with a single author. He reasoned that, just like a book of short stories, our life narrative is made up of individual stories each with their own mini plot lines – but put together, they share overarching themes, a related overall tone. And of course, they all share a main character: you. There are other people in the chapters, parents and friends and lovers who are vital to the story, but they are relevant only because of their impact on you. They are supporting actors; you are the lead.

But we do this throughout our lives, which might make you wonder why stories about adolescence are special. After all, the things that lead to powerful adolescent memories continue to drive us across our whole life: we continue to care deeply about how other people feel about us, and we continue to be motivated by sex and interested in risk-taking – to different degrees, depending on who we are. Part of the explanation is that storytelling is cognitively demanding stuff – for example, to tell a story about yourself you need to be able to remember multiple different events and the order in which they happened, understand people's motivations, and reflect on common threads between different experiences. You can do all these things to a degree in childhood, but it's in adolescence that these skills really come online – that we have the cognitive machinery, so to speak, to write it all down in the storybook of our minds.

The second part of the explanation is that much of the adolescent stuff happens *first*, relative to adulthood, and that matters. In adolescence, so much of what we experience is still completely new, and you don't yet know who you are. It is the first time you start asking the question, 'Who am I?', and you look around yourself for evidence: from the things you do, from the way people treat you, from the relationships you have with others. Because your brain has little else to go on, it seizes upon this evidence *and it doesn't let go*. Like tattoos etched onto fresh skin, the relationships and mistakes and events we go through in adolescence all leave marks that last.

Adolescent memories then colour how we interpret everything else that happens to us afterwards. Just as early chapters in a book will shape how a reader perceives the main characters for the rest of the story, our own early chapters define how we understand our later selves. For example, as we will see in this book, if we are bullied in adolescence, this shapes how we interpret other people's behaviour towards us as adults. If we are popular at school, this shapes how confident we are that people will like us. If we are dumped unexpectedly as a teenager, this can affect our ability to trust partners in romantic relationships, sometimes forever. Memories from the adolescent years are like footprints in wet cement, indelibly shaping the adult you ultimately become. That's what this book is all about: understanding why adolescents behave the way that they do, and why the resulting memories continue to affect us even decades later.

Puberty

Importantly, this is not a book about the biological process of adolescence – but biology is an essential part of the story, so it's important to understand what's going on in this respect. At the start of puberty – the biological event that marks the start of adolescence – a hormone called gonadotrophin-releasing hormone (GnRH) is released from the hypothalamus, deep in the brain. GnRH is heavily suppressed during childhood, but puberty removes those brakes.[6] Suddenly, high levels of GnRH travel from the hypothalamus to the pituitary gland, which itself then secretes its own set of hormones. These then travel to the testes and the ovaries (the gonads), triggering a process of growth and development involving testosterone and oestrogen that, all being well, sets the individual up to be capable of sexual reproduction. In parallel to all this, the adrenal glands are also releasing hormones, which trigger many of the physical changes associated with puberty, like the growth of pubic and facial hair. These hormones also cause the glands in your skin to produce more oil, which can lead to spots and acne, and more sweat that can lead to body odour.

As the body transforms, so does the brain. For example, pubertal hormones affect the body's circadian rhythm – the internal body clock in the brain – causing a 'delayed sleep phase'.[7] This means that the time at which adolescents become sleepy at night (and thus the time they want to wake up in the morning) is shifted later by a couple of hours, relative to children or adults. The world around them doesn't take this into account, though: adolescents still need to start their day at the same early time that children and adults do, which means there is a problematic mismatch between the sleep that

adolescents need and the sleep they are able to get. (Observe an adolescent's sleep pattern at the weekends or during the holidays to see
what their body really needs.) The fact that most adolescents are
chronically sleep-deprived is a major public health issue, given the
significant effects that sleep deprivation can have on a person's physical and mental health.[8]

The internal body clock is just one tiny brain system impacted by
puberty and adolescence. Other extensive changes happen in parts of
the brain involved in emotions, reward and higher-level thinking
tasks like decision-making, reflecting on social relationships and
understanding ourselves.[9] In adolescence there is not much change in
some brain regions such as those involved in visual or auditory processing; the development occurs in regions that will enable the
individual to seek out all the experiences they need to mature into
adults. In other words, changes to brain structure and function propel
adolescents' desire for close friendships, sexual relationships, self-
understanding, and exciting, risky behaviours.

This biology underpins everything we will see in this book, but
we will be exploring how all those biological changes manifest at
the level of *psychology* : how pubertal changes to the brain and body
affect how adolescents think, feel and behave. I'm an academic
psychologist and have spent a great deal of time conducting this
kind of research: measuring and learning about adolescents' behaviour in a scientific lab, using questionnaires and computerised tasks
to see how this age group differs from children and adults. Looking
at adolescence through the lens of psychology is the best way to
understand why the adolescent years matter so much to us, and why
these memories grow roots so firmly in our souls – in other words,
how adolescence shapes us.

Understanding ourselves

At its heart, this is a book about stories. Alongside the scientific
research, it contains throughout real people's memories of their
own adolescent years, as expressed by them in their own words.

These serve to illustrate the broader points being made but their presence is more important than that suggests. It is no exaggeration to say that the interviews I conducted, from which these passages are drawn, have transformed my understanding of my own subject. It was only by hearing other people reflect on their own teenage memories that I truly learned what adolescence is and why it matters so much.

One of my interviewees was Georgia, now twenty-five. Georgia grew up in a village on the outskirts of Bournemouth with two older brothers, and went to a mixed comprehensive school with a wide catchment area – 'so we had people coming in from more rural areas, deprived areas, affluent areas – it was a very mixed bag'. She responded to my advert, posted on social media, in which I asked people to share their memories of adolescence, to tell me about a decision she made when she was fourteen that ultimately changed her life. As is the case with many stories in this book, Georgia's revolved around a particular friendship group:

Originally, I became friends with them because we were in the same form, and I guess we just gelled at some level right from day one. We all had stuff going on at home, and I think that solidified those friendships because we all could relate to each other. For the other girls, there were parents who were divorced and their mums were working full time. For one of them her dad left when she was pretty young. For another, her mum got cancer and she was just really, really ill and her dad wasn't around. It was things like that. For me, my mum is in recovery now, but she was an active alcoholic at the time. She went into rehab twice during my adolescence, and my dad was in the army, so he worked away and wasn't at home very often. So obviously, there was a lack of supervision for me and confusion about why I was experiencing negative things at home and how that reflected on me, I guess. Lack of supervision was probably the main common theme for all of us as a group.

The lack of supervision affected things a lot. And a lot of us had older siblings, so there was definitely that influence too. I would go to some of the girls' houses and their older brothers would be there

smoking and drinking. There were no parents around and the older
brothers were tasked with looking after us. As we started to get into
the middle of secondary school, age fourteen or fifteen, for some of
the girls [spending time with older brothers] became really problematic. Associating with older boys, you know, as we were maturing . . .
there were issues there that I was not comfortable with at all. I still
think it's too early [to have sex], like I did at the time. But what they
were doing was a thing for people to talk about. Other people in the
school . . . they didn't respect it, but it was like, 'Oh my god, yeah,
that's what they're doing at this age.' It was notable. So, you know,
even though they weren't good things that we were doing, the group's
behaviour stood out and people were intrigued by it. It was all novel.
I guess it was just a thing for people to talk about.

Until this point in our interview, Georgia had been describing some
very common adolescent phenomena, ones that we will examine
throughout this book: that similar teenagers flock together; that
teenage girls often have sex with older boys and men; that teenagers
who do risky, adult-like things can become 'famous' in the microclimate of their school. What made Georgia's story distinct, though,
and really rather remarkable, is what she did next.

She found that she felt increasingly distant from her friends and
uncomfortable with what they were doing. In particular, the group
had begun to bully and intimidate other students. 'I realised I was
getting mixed up in stuff that really wasn't me and didn't feel morally
acceptable', she told me. 'Despite the fact that we all had what you
could call justifications or reasons for our behaviour, our behaviour
was still unpleasant.' Again, this situation is not unusual: many teenagers find themselves in friendship groups that make them unhappy
or uncomfortable. But few decide to leave. The costs involved in
walking away from the protection of a group – even a flawed,
unpleasant one – are just too great. Georgia decided to take the risk:

I don't remember exactly the conversation where I told them I was
leaving. But I remember it all happening within like a week, or a
matter of days, where I just had to say to them explicitly that this was

going to happen, that I wasn't going to be friends with them anymore.

I was really lucky, in a way, because it coincided with the second time that my mum went into rehab. When she came out, it was different to the first time. I felt that the process had been different for her and it seemed to have worked – and it did, because she hasn't drunk since then. And I think she was a bit of a role model for me. Her bravery to do that made me think you can go through tough things, and it won't be easy, but what's at the other side will be so much more worth it. So I think, yeah, my mum doing that gave me a role model to be brave. And it also just removed some of the negativity or the fuel I had for being angry, I guess. It wasn't easy, repairing that relationship with my mum. But it definitely gave me the space in my mind to fix things [at school].

But once I'd left that group, there was absolutely no one. I remember, after I'd done it, I had absolutely no one in the school, because obviously everybody disliked me for being friends with that group. And then [those girls] started bullying me. I remember, say, I went to the toilet and they followed me into the toilet, and they'd be banging on the doors and doing things like that. Or if they saw me in the corridor they would shove me into the walls, they would throw stuff at me in lessons. I kept my head down for a long time. I found that the library was the only place where I could go. And if they tried to do anything like that there, the librarian would be on it and she would actually do something. So that's kind of how I ended up studying and working hard, because I was hiding in the library.

Over the course of this book we will explore why being different or standing up for yourself is so much riskier when you are a teenager, and why the costs to your physical and psychological safety can have consequences for the rest of your life. For Georgia, however, the risk ultimately paid off. After about six months of bullying and ostracism, something happened that, she says, changed her life forever:

I managed to get picked up by this group of girls who could see that it was getting pretty awful. At break times, they would invite me to sit with them, and just being able to have that safety of sitting with them . . . It allowed me to get to know people, and people to get to know who I really was, and everything sort of improved from there, really. I really trusted them. If, for instance, one of the horrible girls walked past us and said something like, 'Ugh, why are you sat with her?', the new girls would say something like, 'Oh, she's actually very nice.' They would actually stick up for me, proactively stick up for me and defend me. So I felt really secure in that . . . and then the girls' comments didn't hurt as much. And I think because I was reaping the rewards and doing better at school, my predicted GCSE grades went up. Getting friends who are actually nice and good, and doing so much better with my school work . . . it just started to become much clearer that [leaving the first group] was a good decision. I always reflect on it, honestly, as the best decision I ever made. I think my life would have taken a very different path if I'd stayed with them.

Like Georgia's, many of the stories in this book will involve painful experiences, challenging relationships and feelings of fear, insecurity and loneliness. Adolescence is rich with such emotions. But what is less talked about, perhaps, and what I hope to convey, is how adolescence is also full of courage and connection, a time of extraordinary friendship, affection and love. Georgia's story contains both, but the real reason I share it here is to illustrate something more fundamental than that.

Notice that Georgia's story has a defined beginning – the girls being put in the same form group at school – and a defined ending, when Georgia is established with her new friends. Along the way, it has two distinct turning points: the moment she decided she needed to leave the old group, triggered by her mum's own bravery, and the moment she was picked up by her new friends. She is recounting the facts of her past, but at the same time she is organising them into a narrative. In other words, this is a story – in this case, one that results in redemption, of something bad ultimately leading to something good – that in some way explains who she is today. As we will see, many of the stories we tell ourselves about our adolescence are stories with turning points or realisations, stories that somehow explain who we are by describing how, through a particular experience, we came to be. In other words, they are origin stories, and we tell them partly because it helps us make peace with difficult events in our lives, and partly just to understand who we are. In this particular case, all the elements were there: by sharing with me what happened in her teenage years, Georgia told me an exemplary identity-defining story.

Georgia is typical of my interviewees in another sense. Like her, all grew up in the Western world, mostly in the UK. Accordingly, the research I describe primarily focuses on Western populations, with teenage participants largely from the UK, Europe, Australia and the USA. In my own work as an academic in the UK, I have also focused on teenagers growing up in this context. This means that the adolescence we will explore in this book is a Western one, and that's important to note, because adolescence is to some extent a culturally-bound phenomenon. That's not to say it doesn't exist elsewhere. Across the world, puberty happens: there is a biological transformation in young people's bodies and minds that begins somewhere in late childhood or the early teenage years. And even in very disparate cultures, including the most remote communities, there is usually at least some distinct period of social transition between being a child and being an adult.[10] Nonetheless, any individual's adolescence is significantly shaped by all sorts of aspects of the society in which they live: its demography, geography, economics, politics, religion and culture. For example, adolescents around the world vary significantly in terms of when they are expected to start earning income, how and when they should find a spouse, and how much freedom they have to express their political opinions. This means that while many aspects of development covered in this book are universal — almost everywhere, for example, adolescents have a penchant for taking more risks[11] — it is also the case that the modern Western adolescence is just one version of adolescence, just one route that humans can take to transition from a child to an adult.

One universal truth, though, is that humans are storytellers. Whenever they were born and wherever they grew up, people gravitate towards stories as a way of making sense of who they are and what has happened to them. And across many different cultures, when people are asked to share important memories about themselves, something consistent appears: the reminiscence bump. There are some variations in the exact ages, and some variations in the content of memories – for example, one study found that white Americans are more likely to recount memories that cast them as a central character, focusing on their own needs and perspectives, while Chinese participants were more likely to convey memories that placed them in a wider group context.[12] But broadly speaking, research demonstrates that people across many cultures show the same pattern: events that happen in the teenage and early adult years seem to be universally important to a person's sense of self.

For some people, the outsized and defining significance of adolescence is no big deal. In all likelihood, these people enjoyed a relatively comfortable adolescence after a loving, secure childhood. The teenagers with supportive parents who were generally available to lend a listening ear, and who provided a safe, stable home. The teenagers who had fun with their friends and were respected by their classmates; who fell in love with someone who loved them back; who managed to sidestep the landmines of bullying or other abuse. In short, the fact that your adolescent years can linger in the mind won't be too troubling for those who *enjoyed* them. For that minority – which does exist – learning about the psychology of this age period should hopefully be a nourishing and worthwhile exercise in self-understanding.

But such a wholesome adolescence is rare. Many people, like Georgia, harbour memories of adolescent experiences that ultimately turned out well but that nonetheless left a painful scar. Even people who were relatively lucky in their adolescence will find that happy memories are interspersed with ones they'd rather forget: things that happened that confuse or upset or shame them even now. Almost everyone has teenage memories that they would rather not share, and some people have closets full of them. Too many adults struggle to come to terms with how they behaved or were treated in their formative years. For these people understanding the psychology of adolescence is a more essential, and more therapeutic, exercise. Appreciating *why* teenagers do the things they do can help people understand the young people in their lives today – but, perhaps most importantly, it can also help people understand themselves.

Through this understanding comes compassion, for others and for ourselves, and indeed forgiveness. This matters because teenagers are often derided and stereotyped. The common narrative about teenagers is that they consistently behave in all sorts of stupid, selfish, short-sighted ways. They are rude and sullen because they have no respect for others; they become pregnant because they don't care about consequences or think of the future; they drink too much and take dangerous drugs because they think having fun and impressing their friends is more important than staying alive and because they don't understand that society's rules might exist for their own benefit. For teenagers in the last decade or so, two new narratives have been added: they are defined by an epidemic of mental health problems and, relatedly, they are all addicted to their phones, with social media enabling a new suite of baffling, problematic behaviours. Now, we are told, teenagers obsess over their popularity online, send naked photos to each other, and spend every spare moment playing harmful video games or watching porn.

All these stereotypes have roots in a version of the truth. Teenagers do take more risks than other age groups, teenagers today do report more mental health problems than previous generations, and smartphones have enabled versions of socialising and gratification that can genuinely cause problems. But to remain only in the realm of stereotypes and moral panics entirely misunderstands *why* teenagers behave the way they do. Social media is simply a new avenue through which age-old adolescent behaviour is expressed and explored, and today's adolescents are not uniquely vulnerable to mental health problems – this time of life has always been a period of risk; symptoms of these disorders are best seen as extreme manifestations of psychological phenomena that adolescents have always experienced. To understand why today's adolescents use social media or develop mental health problems, then, we need to actually talk a little less about this specific generation, and a little more about what has always gone on beneath the surface at this age. When we delve deep into the fundamental psychology of this period – the changes that all adolescents are going through and the challenges they face – it becomes eminently clear why teenagers use social media the way they do, and why mental health problems can develop at the extremes.

When we go beneath the headlines and the stereotypes, we can also begin to respect adolescents more. Even behaviours that look foolish or selfish at first glance are usually just a surface manifestation of a far more complicated truth, and that applies to an adolescent thirty years ago or a hundred years ago or today. Teenagers have always been utterly underestimated, and relegating them to caricatures dismisses the significance and nuance of their behaviour. Perhaps most importantly, when we use the same caricatures as a lens to understand our own past, we dismiss and misunderstand ourselves. This book, then, is a call to take teenagers more seriously, and that includes the teenagers we ourselves used to be.

Although adolescence is a brief period compared to the full extent of a human life, it can loom larger in our memories and matter more, for better or for worse, than any other. The aim of this book is to explain why and so to provide clarity and reassurance: for anyone who is trying to support a teenager today, but equally, for anyone trying to understand themselves. Ultimately, reflecting on our adolescence and how it affects our adult life also means celebrating our former selves: the wild and fragile person that helped us become who we are today.

1. The paradox of popularity

It was a bit like *Lord of the Flies*, the William Golding book. It did get a bit like that, in terms of the bullying, the survival-of-the-fittest hierarchical social structure. Where if you showed any vulnerability, you became a target. It seemed that the culture at the school – and I'm sure this is the same for most schools the world over – was stratified into the cool crowd at the top, then you had the inbetweeners or whatever, and then you had the more geeky people. And if you were geeky and nerdy and perhaps not so good socially as well, and not physically big and good at sports and more robust . . . then you were seen as a lower rung on the social strata. It was quite primitive stuff really, quite chimp-like in a way.

Alex, now forty-eight, is telling me about his teenage years spent at an independent all-boys school near London. And he's absolutely right: the strict social hierarchy he describes is indeed the same for most schools, certainly throughout the West. Many of the interviewees for this book brought up this hierarchy, unprompted, and told me their place in it. One interviewee, for example, described herself and her friendship group as being 'socially adept nerds – not popular, but not at the bottom either'. This is testament to the fact that of all the things that shape us in the teenage years, social status is one of the most important. And social status is decided and defined within the context of school.

As social ecosystems go, school during adolescence is uniquely all-consuming. Younger children spend more time with their parents; adults have multiple pockets of friends, family and colleagues in different social settings. But for teenagers, school is the setting of almost all the social relationships and interactions they actually care about. Our place in the hierarchy is the context for so much of what happens to us in adolescence, for better or worse, and it therefore deeply affects who we become. And it is categorically different from the adult world. As psychologist James Youniss and his colleagues write, adolescent peer culture is not 'an immature and warped version of adult society' but 'needs to be studied as a complex social organization' on its own terms.[1]

The social structure of school and the roles and relationships pupils hold within it are remarkably consistent and predictable, and will no doubt be familiar to most of us. Adolescents generally don't float around their year group untethered, hanging out with different people at a whim. They assemble into *cliques*: friendship groups of between around three and ten adolescents, usually, wherein each member would knowingly consider and describe themselves to be part of the group and would be recognised as such by onlookers.[2] Cliques emerge within the first few months of secondary school. To state the obvious, group members tend to be similar in some way, as we saw with Georgia's initial friends in the previous chapter, and they spend time together: they sit together at lunch, hang out together outside of school and, these days, would share exclusive social media interactions, such as a group chat on WhatsApp. Of course, there are always some exceptions: some adolescents don't belong to any cliques, some manage to successfully navigate multiple group membership right from the early years – but broadly, this is the social set-up for many adolescents up and down the country, and indeed around the world.

This simplified description captures what cliques are in broad terms but not their real significance: what they do and the power they wield. In the words of psychologists B. Bradford Brown and Christa Klute, cliques are 'instruments of socialization and social control, sometimes providing social support and other times engaging in ostracism and ridicule'.[3] When young adolescents leave a clique, it is rarely a straightforward process. They either leave voluntarily and face harsh consequences, as we saw with Georgia in the previous chapter, or they are intentionally ejected by other members – in a process known in the academic literature as 'deselection' or 'peer group pruning'.[4] Likewise, new members join only because they are *allowed* to join, with the process usually overseen by the core members of the group. There is no paper trail, of course, but the process of belonging to an adolescent friendship group is really no less formal than beginning or ending employment at a place of work.

Over the first year or two of secondary school, and sometimes within a matter of weeks, cliques begin to assemble themselves into different levels of a social hierarchy, just as Alex described. The cliques who rise to the top are, as you would expect, the ones whose members have certain specific markers of social status, even when they are only eleven or twelve years old: they're socially skilled and generally grow up to be conventionally attractive (more on that in the next chapter). These are the adolescents who, over the years, engage in more risky behaviour like drinking alcohol and having sex, and they exert a great deal of influence, in the classroom and outside it. Critically, these adolescents have *visibility*, as Georgia highlighted in the last chapter. Those lower down the social hierarchy know what high-status students are doing, what they're wearing, who they are hanging out with.

So far, so obvious. But what is interesting about these high-status teenagers is that while they are the 'most popular' in the school, they are also consistently disliked. Researchers seeking to identify which students fit into this top tier can reliably find out who they are by (privately) asking adolescents the question: *Who is popular in your class?* There is generally a high level of consensus across classmates about which these teenagers are. But when researchers ask *Who do you like the most?* they end up with a fairly different list of students. So distinct are these two categories, in fact, that researchers have come up with two different terms: being well liked is known as having 'sociometric popularity'; the counterintuitive, popular-but-not-liked phenomenon is known as 'perceived popularity'.

It is pretty easy to spot which teenagers are sociometrically popular because they behave the way that anyone who is widely liked behaves: they help, support and care for others. They're friendly and fun to be around. They don't act as bullies. They are respected, and lots of people want to hang out with them. The more interesting group – psychologically – are the perceived popular ones. Research shows that these teenagers tend not only to be risk-takers, they tend to be very socially strategic, sometimes in a cruel way: aligning themselves with other popular peers and rejecting those who might harm their own social status. But according to one theory, the perceived popular teens have one trait above all in common: they conform to the stereotypical appearance and behaviours associated with their gender.

Gender conformity

The extent to which you conform to gender stereotypes is one of the key factors in defining your social experience at school, and thus your entire adolescence. The theory of how this relates to popularity was devised by psychologists Lara Mayeux and Margaret Kleiser and focuses solely on cisgender boys and girls – i.e. those whose gender identity, whose innermost sense of which gender they are, aligns with the sex they were assigned at birth – but it has obvious implications for transgender and non-binary teenagers (a subject we will return to later in this book). Broadly, they argue, boys who look and behave like boys are expected to tend to have more perceived popularity than boys who don't, and the same applies to girls who look and behave as girls are expected to. The researchers term this the 'gender prototypicality theory of adolescent peer popularity' and they devised it in 2020, so this is recent stuff, not some relic of the past.[5]

Anyone familiar with the genre of the American high school movie will recognise the phenomenon. We might call it the 'jocks and cheerleaders' theory of perceived popularity. What is interesting – if perhaps depressing – is that the academic research entirely backs it up. For boys, gender prototypicality is partly about attitude: a certain nonchalance, an emotional toughness (sadly, one of the most socially damaging things a teenage boy can do is cry in front of his peers). But it is also about physical prowess, about size and strength, which is why Mayeux and Kleiser say that 'athletic ability is perhaps the most consistent attribute of popular boys in published research, making a strong appearance in virtually every study of popularity to date'.[6]

Sportiness as a key part of popularity came up many times in interviews for this book. Consider Alex, from the start of this chapter, who recognised that his athletic ability served as a form of protection for him:

> Being really good at sport seemed to help me. I was lucky. I'm a sensitive person, so you would have thought I'd be a natural target, you know, because I wasn't a more thuggish type. But I was lucky. I think I was saved by the fact that I was very good at sports. For some reason, being good at sport seemed to sort of mean that you were respected.

It is perhaps obvious why, for adolescent boys particularly, being sporty brings all kinds of benefits. Typically it involves entry to an exclusive social circle, a team, which offers all sorts of opportunities for bonding, social integration and status. In fact, research shows that expectations around gender prototypicality make it harder for boys to form emotional bonds with each other, which is the basis of so much friendship among girls; sports teams therefore provide a useful acceptable context in which boys can make friends.[7] Being sporty also tends to mean being physically fit, a key marker of conventional attractiveness, and it often means being physically bigger and stronger, an age-old signal of social status – and a particular advantage in schools where disputes between boys easily escalate into physical fights (or threats of them). Being sporty is essentially a shortcut to saying 'I am masculine', and that in itself, according to the theory, is what helps confer social status and popularity. Throw in being conventionally attractive and you have a recipe for a 'popular' teenage boy.

Research shows that adolescents who don't conform to typical gender norms are more likely to be unpopular and bullied, especially if they are boys. In particular, boys who do not display 'enough' physical or emotional toughness are more likely to be bullied and ostracised by their peers. In a 2007 study, researchers asked fourteen- to seventeen-year-olds to read brief descriptions of fictional characters and rate how 'acceptable' they thought they were (i.e. how much the participant would personally like and welcome this person).[8] The

descriptions were of either boys or girls, and the researchers system-
atically adjusted the extent to which the character followed gender
norms in either how they dressed or the activities they engaged in.
For example, a 'gender non-conforming' boy was described as being
a member of the local ballet company or wearing nail polish and eye-
liner; a 'gender non-conforming' girl was described as playing on the
football team or never wearing make-up or dresses (yes, these are clichés, but that was the point). The sexual orientation for each character
was also given. Participants were asked to rate the acceptability only
of the characters with the same gender as them.

The researchers found that it was the extent to which the characters conformed to gender norms rather than sexual orientation that
seemed to matter. Whether straight or gay, individuals who were
non-conventional in their appearance and mannerisms were rated as
less acceptable than individuals who conformed to gender conventions. Interestingly, the authors found that the boy characters who
presented themselves in more feminine ways were particularly
harshly rated if they were straight rather than gay. In other words,
teenagers are relatively more accepting of a gay teenage boy wearing
nail polish than with a straight teenage boy doing the same, because
it fits with a simplified rubric of what different people are allowed to
do and look like.

In the gender prototypicality theory, the rules for girls are slightly
different. Sport matters to an extent – popularity often goes hand in
hand with playing netball or hockey (and in the US, cheerleading) –
but gender prototypicality for them is inevitably more about
appearance. As a perceived popular girl, you can get away with being
rubbish at sports if you are conventionally pretty and have what is
deemed to be the right body, which usually involves being slim. I
recently contributed to a study that ran focus groups with sixteen- to
eighteen-year-old girls to ask them about the different pressures they
were experiencing at school and beyond.[9] Many of them talked about
the pressure they felt to look a certain way, which was essentially
being 'pretty and skinny' but also maintaining and presenting their
body in a certain way, for example by wearing make-up and remov-
ing their body hair, and this was compounded by ideals promoted on

social media. For all our attempts to diversify the kinds of bodies that are accepted and celebrated in society, it seems nothing has changed among teenagers for decades.

Popular teenage girls focus on and invest time in their appearance in stereotypical ways: styling and dyeing their hair, wearing make-up, and having clothes and accessories that are considered fashionable and cool. This sort of investment in one's appearance is stereotypically feminine, hence why it comes into the gender prototypicality theory. Being socially sophisticated is also important for girls, more so than boys. Both sociometrically and perceived popular girls tend to be kind and cooperative, although as we know, for some girls these behaviours will be intertwined with (or entirely replaced by) more aggressive, tactical social strategies such as social exclusion and gossip. Some of the girls who are truly good at maintaining their high social status will have a mixture of prosocial and antisocial traits, and be sufficiently skilled at subtly using relational aggression tactics so that many would indeed still consider them to be kind and cooperative at the same time.[10]

Again, I suspect much if not all of this will be (sadly) familiar to most readers. The question is *why* behaving in gender-typical ways is so strongly associated with popularity. Why is conforming to these conventions so admired and revered by so many adolescents? The answer likely comes down to biology. We have discussed so far that adolescence is all about establishing your identity and fitting in, but evolutionarily speaking, it's also about finding a mate. The primary function of puberty is to develop a child's body into an adult one that is capable of having sex and making babies. According to Mayeux and Kleiser, the thinking is that, in part, teenagers ascribe popularity to gender-prototypical teens because they are the ones assumed to attract more sexual partners – which, thanks to brain development and hormones, is something most teenagers really want.[11] This is why teenagers give social status to teenagers who are most likely to be fancied.

There's more to this than sex, though. This is also about following rules. We may think of adolescence as a time when people challenge authority and convention, but the reality is that teenagers are fundamentally conservative. When it comes to being popular in the early years of secondary school, those with emerging status see what worked for older year groups, or older siblings, and they adjust their behaviour to follow suit. Those with more precarious social status then observe their newly-anointed popular classmates and do their best to follow the example being set for them. This is how any culture is passed on and how it perpetuates itself: by establishing social norms, by being – in the literal sense of the word – conservative.

When you can't follow the rules

The trouble is that some adolescents aren't able to play by the rules of the game. There are wide variations in physical appearance, sporting prowess, and willingness to engage in gender-stereotypical behaviours. Some adolescents may actively choose to define themselves against the norms – they may not *want* to achieve mass popularity. But there are others who yearn for popularity or social acceptance at school and find it eternally out of reach. By definition only a minority can enjoy elite social status, so the feeling of striving and failing to achieve popularity is likely the norm. (In the long run, though, this may be less unfortunate than it first appears, as we shall soon see.)

A more challenging experience is that of young people who struggle to follow the social rules because they don't fully recognise or understand them in the first place – or understand them in a literal sense but find them immensely difficult to implement. One group who are particularly vulnerable to this issue are autistic adolescents. Autism is a form of neurodivergence that has a wide-ranging impact on how a person thinks, feels and behaves, particularly with regard to social interaction and communication. Autistic people also tend to show repetitive, restricted behaviours, such as highly-focused interests and a desire for sameness, and particular hypo- or hypersensitivity to noise and other sensory stimulation.[12] There's huge variation from person to person in terms of how autism impacts the individual, but among this variability, something consistent is found: while the Wild

West of secondary school is difficult for almost everyone, it's even harder for adolescents who are autistic.

It's often thought that autistic people are uninterested in social relationships, but this is a myth. Studies have shown that plenty of autistic adolescents badly want friendships and meaningful connection with their peers, they just generally find it more difficult. For example, one 2017 study asked twelve- to eighteen-year-olds to answer questions about how lonely they felt.[13] Some of the participants were autistic, some of them had another neurodevelopmental condition, attention deficit hyperactivity disorder (ADHD), and some had neither diagnosis. The researchers found that the autistic young people reported significantly more loneliness than both the young people with ADHD and those with neither diagnosis – but there was no difference in loneliness in seven- to eleven-year-olds who had been divided into the same three groups. This suggests there is something specific about autism, and autism in adolescence, that makes social relationships more difficult and thus makes these years lonelier.

The heart of the problem is that the very nature of being autistic makes it harder for individuals to follow the social norms dictated by non-autistic people – and we will see throughout this book how important these are in adolescence. Consider, for example, the differences in how autistic people often express themselves during social interactions. An autistic person might use less eye contact, or they might use different gestures or body language, or they might have more difficulty with the seamless back-and-forth turn-taking of a typical conversation. They might struggle to read between the lines of some social interactions, for example to recognise when someone is lying or joking with them. None of this is a problem, as such – it's just a different way of communicating – but as we will see, being 'different' in even a minor way in secondary school immediately increases your odds of being socially rejected. Similarly, the highly-focused, specialised hobbies and topics that an autistic adolescent might love usually deviate from the acceptable interests endorsed by the wider peer group – which risks the individual being marked out as unacceptable, too.

Secondary schools are also typically loud, crowded environments. Research shows that autistic adolescents are particularly likely to find the unstructured, less supervised aspects of secondary school difficult – like the journey to and from school, lunch and break times, and the transition between classes.[14] That's not surprising when you think about how autistic people experience the world. For example, a defining trait of autism, which also crops up in anxiety disorders, is an *intolerance of uncertainty*. Autistic people can find unpredictable or unknown situations extremely negative and anxiety-provoking. Often, they manage this by trying to stick to specific routines, which can work well at home. But in the social melee of the school canteen or the school bus, things are inherently unpredictable – as well as being physically uncomfortable (too much noise, not enough personal space) in exactly the way that autistic people can find overwhelming.

The upshot of all this is that many autistic adolescents expend enormous amounts of mental effort trying to stay calm and fit in at school. Essentially, this means trying to hide the fact that they are autistic – a practice known as *camouflaging*.[15] This can be conscious or unconscious, and might include suppressing repetitive hand movements, forcing themselves to make eye contact, following rehearsed scripts about how to engage in conversation, or mimicking phrases or gestures that they see other people use. There is some evidence that autistic girls are especially likely to camouflage, which may partly explain why autism in girls often goes unrecognised.[16] The trouble is, even if a young person 'succeeds' at hiding the fact that they are autistic, camouflaging is exhausting. It also has consequences for identity development: some autistic adults report that they have camouflaged so extensively it's difficult to explore or understand who they truly are.[17] And sadly, even with the best efforts, camouflaging often isn't successful – autistic adolescents are consistently more at risk of being bullied than their non-autistic peers, often because they are deemed 'different'.[18, 19]

This isn't to say that social acceptance in a mainstream school is impossible for autistic adolescents. This group of young people vary enormously, and many find meaningful, self-affirming friendships within or beyond school, with friends that appreciate who they are.[20]

In addition, many young people see being autistic as a positive and integral part of their identity, and report pride in being different to others.[21] Hopefully, this will become increasingly common. In the past two decades, there has been the emergence of the *neurodiversity* advocacy movement, which argues that the social differences long ascribed to autistic people are a perfectly valid, albeit minority, way of interacting with others – and that these are only deficits when society expects autistic people to think and behave the way non-autistic people do.[22] But the reality is that, despite positive progress in this area, secondary school can remain a hostile and exhausting climate. Many autistic adolescents must continue to navigate daily life in a school full of predominantly non-autistic students who consider conservatism critical for social acceptance and mark any deviation from this as a threat. In other words, the experiences of these young people are a potent reminder that the rules of adolescence are rigid and unforgiving, for everyone, and sometimes it's just impossible to keep up with the game. And here we begin to approach the reason why no one actually likes those perceived popular teens, the ones who regulate the rules in the first place.

Why no one likes perceived popular teens

There aren't many films and books about sociometrically popular teenagers, probably because, by definition, their kind and reasonable nature is never going to make for great dramatic tension. But there are a lot of perceived popular characters in films and books, and one thing is clear: they are rarely portrayed in a positive light.

The 2003 film *Mean Girls*, for example, follows sixteen-year-old Cady Heron as she joins an American high school, after many years travelling round Africa with her zoologist parents. At first, she makes friends with Janis, who dresses in grungy clothes, and her friend Damien, who is gay. But soon, Cady is spotted by three of the school's queen bees – Regina, Gretchin and Karen – who see that she is conventionally attractive and take her under their wing. These girls are pretty, dress fashionably and get lots of attention. Cady switches allegiances, and rapidly moves up the social ranks. Feeling abandoned, Janis lashes out at Cady late one night outside a party, and she shouts at her from a slow-moving car: 'See, that's the thing with you plastics. You think everyone's in love with you, but in reality, everyone *hates* you.' The finale of *Mean Girls* is a satisfying fall-from-grace for the main character Regina George, in which her bitching about the other people in her school is finally revealed.

The film *Bring It On*, about popular cheerleaders, opens with them singing a song that includes the lyrics, 'I'm wanted, I'm hot, I'm everything you're not' and 'Don't hate us 'cos we're beautiful, well we don't like you either, we're cheerleaders.' Films like these suggest that popular teens are disliked because they are mean, most obviously, but also because they are envied and because they make everyone else feel bad about themselves and their appearance. This all chimes with intuition. But the reasons why popular teens end up disliked are actually a little more nuanced than this.

Chloe, now thirty-one, first got in touch with me to talk about her best friend from her teenage years, Natalie. Tragically, Natalie died by suicide when they were both twenty-seven, and Chloe contacted me because she wanted to share her memories of their friendship. 'I love her eternally and think about her every single day,' she said when she first got in touch, 'and I will always remember her as my very best friend.' Later in the book, we will return to their story, and the adventures and serious risks they took together. But when I first spoke to Chloe, and asked her to give me a little bit of background about her adolescence, it became clear that she was squarely in the 'perceived popular' camp:

> Even now if I see people from when I was at secondary school it's like . . . everybody knows me. I've got quite a unique name as well, which makes me more knowable. Yeah . . . I'd say I centralised myself. It was important to me to be cool. And I had an identity of being a bit of a rebel.

Chloe tells me how, at school, other students knew what she and her friends were up to. They were judged by their peers, often in a harsh way – which she refers to as 'negative press'. For example, she told me how common it was to see graffiti about her on school desks – usually saying, in her own words, that she was a 'slut'. I asked Chloe how this made her feel:

> I suppose in a lot of ways it did make me feel like shit. But also, do you know that Lady Sovereign song, with the lyrics 'Love me or hate me, it's still an obsession'? I was riding round in cars with boys with that song on dead loud, singing along to it, I knew every single word and I still do. And I very much connected with that. I felt like . . . I did feel like a celebrity. I didn't want bad publicity, but, you know, it was all publicity, I guess.

This perfectly captures how perceived popularity is about visibility, and about how that visibility can be intoxicating. It also tells us important things about why popular teenagers are often not much liked by their peers. We can see from Chloe's description how popularity can easily go to a teenager's head, and make them seem arrogant, showing off, flaunting their higher status in a way that highlights their classmates' lower status. Even if they are not deliberately showing off, the visible social success of a popular student can easily induce feelings of jealousy and resentment from their peers.

It is also well established in the research literature that popular teenagers tend to be more aggressive.[23] When I say aggression here, I'm not necessarily talking about overt, physical aggression – although there are certainly some young people who fight and bully their way to the top using their fists, particularly boys. But popular teenagers also engage in *relational* aggression: the more subtle practice of using tactics like spreading rumours and excluding others from social events or group chats on social media. The latter approach may be especially effective as a means of establishing and maintaining social power, precisely because it is relatively subtle. In the words of psychologists Antonius Cillessen and Amanda Rose, engaging in relationally aggressive behaviours such as spreading rumours 'affords one a degree of anonymity and therefore the opportunity to strategically hurt other people while hiding the appearance of being mean'.[24]

Similarly, some popular students successfully lessen the impact of their aggressive behaviour by combining it with acts of prosocial behaviour, doled out at the right times in the right amounts – 'deploying cooperation and beneficence to mitigate damage arising from the forceful attainment and exercise of power', in the words of psychologist Amy Hartl and colleagues. In their 2020 study of US seventh graders (twelve- to thirteen-year-olds), these researchers found around twelve per cent of students (both girls and boys) used this 'bistrategic control' approach to achieve high social status.[25] This group were rated by their classmates as the most 'popular' students in school, scoring more highly than the popular students who used either prosocial or aggressive strategies alone.

There are other factors that contribute to why high-status students end up disliked. A 1985 study led by sociologist Donna Eder, in which she coined the term the 'cycle of popularity', suggests that less popular classmates may dislike perceived popular ones because at some point they have been personally rejected by them.[26] Eder conducted an ethnographic study, which involved observing the adolescent pupils at an American high school. She and her colleagues sat in the canteen at lunchtime for over a year, gradually speaking to different students, observing interactions and learning the ins and outs of the different cliques and friendship groups. This study focused on girls in sixth to eighth grades (ages eleven to fourteen). The researchers observed that a handful of girls acquired social status early on – generally because they were considered pretty or wore fashionable clothes. A fast track to such status was becoming a cheerleader, which essentially guaranteed a seat (literally) at the table of popular students; even being a friend of a cheerleader was a quick route to this table. Over two years, the researchers noticed that these high-status girls were increasingly disliked by the other students. These other girls had often attempted to be friends with the popular girls at first, or actually *had* been friends with them, but had been crowded out or ejected from the clique. In some cases, these girls had been pushed out for purely practical purposes: there are only so many hours in the day, and only so many friendships that one popular girl can maintain. 'Popular girls do not necessarily dislike less popular girls,' Eder wrote. 'But they may ignore less popular girls because they simply do not have the time or energy to maintain friendships with all the girls who would like to be their friends.'

Being socially rejected like this in adolescence is a powerfully painful experience. Being spurned by one of the emerging cool students, especially one who you might have initially been friends with, is painful twice over. You not only lose a potential friend, but you lose the opportunity to be popular yourself – since being friends with someone of high status is itself a fast-track route to social status. And you haven't just been overlooked, you've been tested and deemed inadequate. The researchers concluded that, over the two years, there developed a 'cycle of popularity' – although the term *trajectory* may be more accurate – 'in which feelings towards popular girls moved from positive to negative, eventually making them some of the least liked individuals in the school'.[27]

Perceived popular teenagers are genuinely very good at engaging in strategic, sometimes cruel social behaviour, but to dismiss all high-status teenagers as the selfish caricatures we see in films is missing something important. As Chloe says, it is like being a celebrity, and that comes with heightened challenges: rejecting someone's friendship can inspire far more intense feelings of dislike than would otherwise be the case. Your behaviours are subject to continuous scrutiny and judgement. Many people will want to see you humiliated and being high-status means you have much further to fall. It is pressurised at the top. And a lot of the time, it is mere genetic chance that elevates a teenager to the echelons of high status. Importantly, having such status doesn't necessarily make for an easier or happier adolescence, and in the long term it may even lay the foundation for problems that less popular adolescents won't face.

When Mean Girls grow up

The TV series *Friends* is almost three decades old but it remains hugely popular, especially among those who are old enough to have watched it when it first came out, which was when many of them

were adolescents. In one episode, Monica bumps into Chip Matthews, who had been the most popular boy at her high school.
Monica, who never experienced such popularity, is initially very
excited when he asks her out. But on the date, it soon becomes apparent that Chip hasn't progressed very far since leaving school. He still
lives with his parents and still has the same job, working at the local
cinema ('I can get you free posters for your room,' he says). He then
tells Monica that he bumped into another classmate recently, and
gave him a wedgie. 'Isn't he an architect now?' Monica asks. 'Yeah,
they still wear underwear,' he replies. When she gets home, she tells
Rachel: 'You know how I always wanted to go out with Chip Matthews in high school? Well, tonight, I actually went out with Chip
Matthews in high school.'

There is a folk understanding that the social power experienced by
popular teenagers doesn't extend beyond school. It even has its own
phrase: to 'peak in high school'. But what is the reality for the Chips
and cheerleaders of this world when they hit adulthood?

There is some evidence that being popular at school sets you up
extremely well for your adult life. However, this tends to apply primarily to the teens who were actually well liked – the 'sociometrically
popular' ones. Researchers have shown that teenagers who were sociometrically popular at school tend to have better mental health, better
physical health and more success in education and work as they grow
up, relative to their unpopular classmates. One study found that
thirteen-year-olds who were more liked at school were more likely
to have better outcomes in adulthood, including being more likely to
go into further education after school, less likely to experience
unemployment, less likely to experience economic hardship and less
likely to develop a mental disorder.[28] The relationship between sociometric popularity and later outcomes wasn't explained by a number
of other possible factors, such as the adolescents' socioeconomic
status or cognitive ability, which were statistically controlled for in
the study.

Of course, it may be that being liked isn't necessarily *causing* the
later benefits: it's just that the attributes that make some teenagers
particularly likeable in the first place, such as being friendly or

extraverted, are ones that also set them up for better outcomes later on. But another explanation is that being well liked in school gives you access to all kinds of material and social 'resources', which then benefit you as you navigate growing up. The more an adolescent socialises, the more likely they are to have social support when they go through a difficult time. They also have access to more useful information (for example, being part of a study group could provide helpful information for boosting exam grades). They also have more opportunities to learn about the world, to try out new things, and to develop social and psychological skills, like coping strategies, that might benefit them later on. These resources then shape the teenagers' expectations, ambitions, behaviours and choices for the life ahead of them – which then affects the decisions they make and how they think and feel about themselves.[29] It is this chain of linked events that ultimately leads to those beneficial outcomes in adulthood.

It is the same process (in reverse) that means that teenagers who are not well liked – those who are bullied or otherwise lonely or rejected – can be negatively affected as they grow up. Later in this book, we will see how being bullied in adolescence is particularly damaging, and how being regularly assaulted or humiliated, as is the case for these students, can have a long-term negative impact on a person's sense of self-worth. Indeed, being bullied is associated with a significant increased risk of just about every mental health problem possible, including an increased risk of suicide, even decades later.[30] But even being merely lonely is problematic. Anyone with lower social status in adolescence, particularly those with few friends, will have less access to the resources that so benefit their peers: they have less social support, fewer networking opportunities, and fewer chances to learn about the world. Importantly, lacking social status at this time of life shapes how you see yourself, sometimes forever. As we know, it is in adolescence that you form your sense of self, and you do this largely by looking to what other people think of you and how they treat you. Just as being popular leads to an upward spiral of psychological and social resources, being unpopular can lead to its own linked chain of events that affect how people see themselves long into adulthood.

But in the cases of Chip Matthews and cheerleaders, we are not dealing with sociometric popularity. To understand the long-term effects of perceived popularity, we need to think instead of the kinds of trait that these individuals tend to have: for example, their tendency to show more aggression, particularly relational aggression. In adulthood, if you are very skilled at subtly engaging in relational aggression, you can continue to use it to your advantage, and if this is the case, the high social status you achieved in secondary school will likely be maintained. But if your relational aggression is noticed or exposed or tips over into pissing everyone off, or if you also have high rates of physical aggression, then the opposite may happen. Romantic relationships will be fraught and short-lived, friendships will be full of conflict, and colleagues won't trust you. What is tolerated or even admired in the microclimate of school – giving someone a wedgie – is likely to be considered unacceptable in the outside world.

As previously noted, perceived popular teens also tend to be risk-takers. One study found that teens who had perceived popularity when they were fifteen or sixteen were more likely than their peers to be drinking heavily and having sex two years later.[31] This may be because they're invited to more social events, so they literally have more opportunities to drink alcohol and have sex and do other risky things, or it may be that these teenagers were hard-wired to be risk-takers to start with and that helped them achieve high status, since risk-taking is often admired by adolescents, for reasons we will come to in the chapter after next. But risk-taking can, by definition, have drastic lifelong consequences, and can spell disaster for these teenagers as they grow up. Risky sex can lead to unwanted pregnancy, and drinking alcohol can lead to poor physical and mental health, physical assaults or serious accidents, all of which can affect your life opportunities in the long term.

A 2014 study followed a group of 184 adolescents in the US from age thirteen to twenty-three, and found that participants who engaged in more risk-taking behaviour at age thirteen (measured as minor delinquent behaviour, early sexual behaviour and alcohol and marijuana use) were more popular with their peers by age fifteen – but that this success was short-lived.[32] By the age of twenty-one to twenty-three, these participants were more likely to have problems with alcohol and substance use, more likely to engage in criminal behaviour – and more likely to be considered bad friends by their peers. Even if you manage to avoid these outcomes, the tendency to take risks may begin to work against you because risk-taking behaviours in adulthood aren't quite so cool: excessive gambling, extramarital affairs, reckless decisions at work. A hunger for risks is admired by peers in high school because it often involves doing things that appear grown-up for the simple reason that they are prohibited to young people. In adulthood this gets flipped on its head: repeated risk-taking as an adult is usually seen as rather immature.

The power of friendship

We've talked a lot about the negative side of cliques, hierarchies and friendship groups – about how they are tools of social control, about what it feels like to be trapped in the wrong group. And adolescent friendships can certainly be full of jealousy, conflict and arguments. But they can also be wonderful. And while it is true that being socio-metrically popular at school does seem to lead to better outcomes in adulthood, sometimes all it takes for an adolescent to feel accepted and to experience all the accompanying benefits is a single friend.

Friendships matter so much at this time because they create the opportunity for self-development. They are the ideal context for the fundamental adolescent task of exploring and understanding who you are. At their heart, adolescent friendships are love stories, and so it should be entirely unsurprising that the very closest friendships also involve periods of tension and difficulty. But it also means they can be some of the most profound and beneficial relationships of our lives. Part of the power of friendship groups, as we will see time and again in this book, is that they offer the opportunity for social acceptance and, when necessary, social protection. They offer the opportunity for *fun* too, which often seems to be overlooked when adolescence is discussed – with the right friends, these years can become an exhilarating, unrestrained experiment in learning how to have a good time. At the end of the Stephen King short story *The Body* (and its film adaptation,

Stand By Me) the narrator sums it up perfectly: 'I never had any friends later on like the ones I had when I was twelve. Jesus, does anyone?'

Vicky, now thirty-five, grew up in Florida in the US with her parents and five brothers. Like Georgia in our last chapter, she found herself in the wrong friendship group in her early teenage years. At elementary school she was, in her own words, 'always one of those kids who was on the periphery of the cool kid crowd. Like there were the cool, cool kids in the centre, and then I was right on the edge, because I was never confident enough or outgoing enough to be right in the middle.' In primary school, this strategy worked out fine, she told me: she was 'a chameleon kid', able to go along with whatever was happening around her. But with a new group in secondary school, she no longer wanted to be in that position.

At first it was just like, okay, I've been here before. I can just be the periphery cool kid, just do my thing. I realised pretty quickly, though, that this was a slightly different group. They were way more socially advanced than I was. I remember overnight it was boys, overnight it was make-up, in a way that was jarring to me and just so unfamiliar. I had brothers at home and my mom always said, 'You don't need to grow up too fast.' That was her thing. She wasn't anti-boys or anti-make-up, but she was more like, 'Give it time. It'll happen.' And these girls were on the fast track to that type of thing. That was where I started to realise, 'Oh, hang on a second. I'm not comfortable with the acceleration, how fast everything was going.' I felt like the train was leaving the station without me.

At the same time, I was doing really well in school and loving my classes. I was just really nerdy and really loved talking about what I was learning, and that just wasn't something I was getting from this group. They weren't willing to get deep into the science projects like I was. And I was also in our school band. These kids were not in our school band. So I just didn't feel like I had the connections that I was really seeking. All I was getting was a seat at the lunch table. And I remember having this thought, going back after Christmas break, where I thought . . . I'm just over it. I just can't do it. I'm so uncomfortable with trying to figure out this whole dramatic social positioning thing. So I literally just moved lunch tables one day. It wasn't some big dramatic thing you see in the movies where someone walks across the lunchroom and everyone's staring. No, nobody cared. It wasn't a big deal because I was already on the periphery. Nobody cared about the quiet, nerdy girl leaving.

What makes Vicky's story very different from Georgia's is that Vicky didn't leave her friendship group because they were behaving badly. They weren't bullies, and there was minimal risk of them turning on her. As she says, they barely even noticed her leave. She also wasn't leaving them for the great unknown: she had already identified where she wanted to go. In a fairly impressive feat of self-understanding and self-determination, Vicky had spotted a friendship group across the canteen that she felt would suit her much better. It was a group of girls who she knew vaguely from band practice, and they welcomed her in. Immediately, she found her home – a place where she could finally, comfortably express who she was:

There was another group of girls who were so weird and so funny. They were laughing all the time. Every time I looked at them, they were just laughing and it looked so fun. On that first day I just started talking to them about whatever we were doing in band and then instantly it was like . . . I don't even know how to explain it. Like a huge sigh of relief. Like I could just be myself. It was so nice because they were hilarious and goofy and they were just themselves. And they accepted me, just because. There was one girl who was way smarter than I was – she's a doctor now – and so she was really into academics. And we could participate in projects and things in a way that we could bounce ideas off each other. It was just nice to have other people like me. I think I was seeking a calmness, you know. My life at home was happy, but it was chaos. My brothers at that point were aged eight to eighteen. So it was chaos. Our parents were busy and I think I was seeking a calmness.

One time when we were fourteen, I had four of [my new friends] over to my house and we painted our faces like monsters because Halloween was right around the corner. I thought it was really fun. It was a weird thing to do. I mean, I guess maybe some people would think that's not age-appropriate, but it was appropriate for us, you know? To me, it felt like the first group of girls were on an accelerated path towards adulthood in a way that I was just not ready for. With the new group, I think all of us were not quite ready to be teenagers yet, or we were just getting there but we still needed to be kids for a little bit longer. In the end, I found the group that was growing up at the right speed for me.

Like Georgia, this decision to change friendship groups changed the course of Vicky's adolescence and therefore, ultimately, her whole life: it wasn't dramatic, she tells me, but it was 'a pivotal moment' in her life. It taught her a value that remains important and relevant to her even now: of listening to her instincts and being authentic to what she likes and what matters to her. It's a lesson that has guided many decisions at work, she tells me, and one that she is keen to pass on to her infant son. But it's also a lesson for us all, about the power of friendship, and the importance of finding people similar to you in adolescence, who accept you and enable you to explore and under-stand who you are. This is an aching, overarching need we all have in our teenage years, and the struggle to get there lies at the heart of many of the chapters to come.

The social world of adolescence takes place primarily in the intense microcosm that is secondary school. We've seen that it has a strict social architecture, established early and often rigidly enforced, made up of various cliques at different levels of the pecking order. We've seen that your position in the hierarchy affects how you see yourself, even many years later, and we've also seen that it is finding some decent friends, among the stress of it all, that might matter the most. This is the setting of many of the adventures, misdemeanours, excitement and trauma that we will explore in the rest of the book – the world in which the drama unfolds. Now we're going to turn our attention to the lead character: the adolescent as an individual. And what matters a great deal, for better or worse, is what that character looks like.

2. Image is everything

At the start of secondary school, it would never be, 'Rebecca and Amy', it would just be, 'The twins'. I really remember a comment in Year 7, this boy said, 'Oh, but they're just the same. So it doesn't matter if we ask one of them, they're both the same.' It really offended me, but I don't think he even comprehended what he was saying. Everyone just kept calling us the same and thought that whatever they'd asked me would automatically apply to my sister, and whatever they asked her would mean I'd be happy with that. It would be things like, 'What class do you want to take?' or the idea that, if one of us is invited to something, we must be invited together. We were never seen as different. And I remember the frustration of being like, 'But we're not the same,' or having someone talk to me thinking I'm my sister. And some people do that as a genuine accident, that doesn't really bother me. But yeah, at the start of secondary school, no one made any effort to try and tell us apart and just assumed we were the same person. And we started to realise quite early on that we're actually very different people.

I'm talking to Rebecca, now thirty, about being an identical twin. Her story captures why this is such a distinct challenge in the adolescent years. When you're an identical twin, you have the same task that everyone else does in adolescence: to manage the fact that a complex sense of self is emerging, to observe the many things that are happening to you and how you react, and somehow, from all this, establish a stable sense of who you are. But you must also figure out who you are *as distinct from your twin* – someone you are likely to be similar to in many respects, not least your appearance. In fact, the psychologist Dale Ortmeyer refers to the 'we-self' of identical twins: that in parallel with having their own self-concept, they share 'a psychological unity . . . of two personalities to some extent functioning as one'.[1] This poses a challenge for twins in childhood to an extent – most twins will remember the frustration Rebecca describes starting very early – but it becomes considerably more important in adolescence, when the question of our identity takes on such urgency, and the cognitive ability to reflect on who we are improves significantly. It must be exceptionally difficult and frustrating to try to express your identity, and to understand who you are as an individual, when people keep mistaking you for someone else.

Rebecca decided she had to take action.

> I went through a phase of wanting to look different to my sister, so every single day I used to get up at 6:00 in the morning and curl my hair just so I didn't look similar to her, even though we shared a room and it used to really annoy her. If I didn't have my sister, I wouldn't have bothered doing that. But I just needed to make sure I had something that differentiated me and her when we go into school so people could think, 'Oh that must be Rebecca because she's got curly hair.'

But Rebecca didn't just want to *look* different to Amy (and be seen to look different). She wanted people to recognise her personality as different, too. At the start of secondary school, they were both 'incredibly shy', she tells me, never putting their hand up in class, never speaking up in social groups. The obvious way to distinguish herself from Amy, then, was to pretend she was confident.

> I remember vividly there were times when we were in a group and people were talking to us and Amy was being particularly quiet, and I remember thinking in my head, 'Well, we can't both be quiet, so I'm going to have to talk.' I remember thinking, 'One of us needs to be the more confident twin' – I hated this feeling that we were both such shy kids. I didn't want to be seen as shy, even though I was. It was too embarrassing for us both to be like that. It's almost like I let my sister take on how I was actually feeling, and I'd put on this kind of brave front to be like, 'Oh no, look, we can't be just the shy twins in the corner. One of us needs to talk.' And it started to work. As soon as someone started to recognise, 'Oh, that must be Rebecca, because

she's slightly more confident or she's slightly more outspoken or just less shy,' I ran with that.

The experiment had significant consequences for them both. Rebecca found herself increasingly 'obsessed' with how her peers viewed her, while Amy was less bothered, and they ended up in different social circles as a result. Rebecca navigated her way into the popular crowd, where she made friends but frequently worried about what they thought of her and whether they were leaving her out. Amy, on the other hand, stuck with a smaller core of close friends. The two of them didn't hang out together much, and only found their way back to each other once their school years were over, after Rebecca lost touch with the popular group of friends. (They went on holiday without inviting her: a potent example of the cut-throat membership policies of these groups.) Once school finished, Rebecca and Amy became 'inseparable', she tells me, and they still are today. While there were some clear benefits to Rebecca's confidence experiment – it forced her to confront her social anxiety, she says, which made her genuinely more confident in the long run – she has regrets. 'I still have moments where I feel bad for seemingly prioritising popularity over my own sister.'

While identical twinship is fairly unusual – around 1 in 250 births are identical twins[2] – what Rebecca experienced was a heightened form of a universal challenge that we all face in those years – and appearance lies at its heart. Figuring out your identity is an internal process; your appearance is how you present that identity to the world. That's what this chapter is about: what you look like as a teenager powerfully shapes people's understanding of who you are, and this leads teenagers to do sometimes extreme things in an attempt to change the narrative.

This will come as no great shock, but research shows that looks take up a lot of head space for teenagers: they spend a lot of time having appearance-based conversations with friends, comparing their appearance to that of their peers, and they experience teasing and bullying as a result of what they look like. In line with what we would expect based on the gender prototypicality theory, the work of psychologists Diane Jones and Joy Crawford confirms that 'peer appearance culture' in girls is largely about being skinny: 'The cultural ideal of thinness has glorified low body weight as a central attribute and has become a defining feature of feminine beauty.'[3] This thin ideal is particularly pervasive among white Western adolescent girls: for example, a recent review found that young Black women in the United States are more likely to describe the ideal woman's body as being curvaceous or hourglass-shaped rather than thin, or to report receiving conflicting messages about what body shape is most desirable.[4] But whatever the specifics, the point is that there is always an ideal to strive for, and it can involve being the right height and having the right size breasts and the right amount of body hair and darker or lighter skin, and a particular face and a little bit of muscle tone but not too much. In short, being a teenage girl with a socially-approved appearance is about fitting into many narrowly-defined boundaries, defined by one's specific society and culture, most of which are not remotely under your control. Just as we saw in the previous chapter, adolescence involves navigating an extensive series of rules, which are policed rigorously, governing what is and isn't acceptable – and what you look like is one of their key concerns. With the advent of social media, research suggests that the advertising and endorsing of these rules has only become more intense.

Boys, too, are subject to 'peer appearance culture', though they talk about it less. While being skinny is all-important if you are a girl, it can work against you if you are a boy. For boys, Jones and Crawford say, muscularity is the dominant ideal. When it comes to appearance, this is the main topic of discussion, and boys will tease and bully one another for a lack of muscle mass and attempt to correct this via exercise. But God forbid you should lean the other way: for both girls and boys, being overweight is one of the most frequent reasons why adolescents are bullied.[5]

When beauty ideals are painful

The way teenagers evaluate each other's bodies can affect how they see themselves – indeed, the worth they assign themselves – forever. I am certain that everyone remembers at least one specific thing that someone said about their appearance in adolescence that continues to affect how they think of themselves today. Maybe it was said repeatedly, maybe it was said literally once in a pretty off-hand manner – but it stuck. Unsurprisingly, then, some teenagers go to extreme lengths to adjust their appearance.

Beth, now forty-four, grew up in Manchester. She is mixed race – her dad was West African and her mum is white British – and she wrote to me to tell me about her adolescence, and more specifically, her hair. In her teenage years, Beth spent a lot of time with her three cousins on her mum's side – all slightly older than she is, and all white. She spent most weekends with them, getting the bus to their house and hanging out in their bedroom, 'listening to music, smoking pot and all this kind of thing'. She tells me her cousins were into rock, indie and grunge music. Critically, they also all had long straight hair and a floppy fringe, just like the icons of that musical era. Which meant Beth really wanted long straight hair and a floppy fringe too:

My afro hair had other ideas. At some point, my mum agreed that I could have my hair chemically straightened. I sat in the hairdresser's chair with the chemical paste on my head for as long as I could bear before the itching and burning became unbearable. They finished the treatment and blow-dried my hair straight, but when I got home, it was still frizzy and nowhere near as straight as I'd wanted. So we went back to the hairdressers, the same day I think, and they applied more of the straightening treatment. The second dose absolutely ripped my scalp to shreds. I can still remember the feeling now. It was incredibly painful for days after, covered in lumpy scabs and horribly itchy. It was pretty disgusting. My hair never went properly straight and I have never had a fringe that lasted more than about half an hour.

I think, weirdly, going back thirty years, I probably would never have articulated it . . . I didn't really recognise that the inability to achieve the hair I wanted was anything to do with race. I mean, it was what I look like, but I never quite articulated it that clearly that my hair was like this because I'm mixed race. There was never a thought of wishing I was white. It was just wishing I could make my hair look how I wanted it to look. And wishing my body was built more like a white person . . . you know, thinner thighs, a flatter bum.

As we talk, I ask about her hair now – which she wears in a natural, curly bob – and she tells me that not only has she made peace with it, she likes it now. Like so many adolescents, she was desperate to look like her idols, both family and celebrity, and it is only in adulthood that she has gradually learned to celebrate her 'difference':

> In my thirties I finally stopped chemically treating my hair, and these days I'm happy, and even proud in fact, to wear my hair naturally. I'm forty-four now and I just finally feel like I've grown into being happy with who I am and not having to make any excuses for that or change any of that. And being the me that I am is acceptable in the place that I am now in life – you know, personally, family and professionally. It's all good. Becoming a mother in particular had a big, positive impact on my self-esteem and identity. My three mixed-race children are all beautiful and unique and visually different to one another in amazing and wonderful ways. I'm working hard to help them to believe that. I impress upon them often how beautiful they are and say to each of them how their skin is the best colour – even though their skin is all different colours to each other.

For all of the attempts made to increase the visibility of minoritised ethnicities in recent years, the current research tells us that adolescents of colour still face a more complicated challenge in forming their identity, especially if they are in the minority at their secondary school – a subject we will return to in more detail at the end of this chapter.

For other teenagers, the adolescent obsession with their appearance can morph into something altogether more dangerous – and very occasionally fatal. The symptoms of the three main eating disorders overlap, and vary from person to person, but typically anorexia involves severe food restriction, leading to an extremely low body weight; bulimia involves a pattern of binging followed by purging, for example by self-induced vomiting; and binge eating disorder involves binging episodes in the absence of purging. A common thread among all eating disorders, though, is that they are accompanied by a very distorted body image. Sufferers often harbour very negative feelings about their weight and shape, they misperceive themselves as overweight, and their body image has an undue influence on their sense of self-worth.[6,7] Anyone can develop an eating disorder at almost any age, but the vast majority of eating disorders begin in adolescence.[8]

It would be an oversimplification to say that eating disorders are caused by adolescent body dissatisfaction, itself caused by living in a culture obsessed with thinness. Many teenagers are unhappy about their appearance, are bombarded with the message that certain body shapes have more value, and engage in some form of unhealthy restrictive eating, but very few develop a full-blown eating disorder. Indeed, decades of research now demonstrate how genetics, brain structure and function, thinking styles, family dynamics and traumatic life events can all play a role in the development of eating disorders.[9] But at the same time, it is not unreasonable to see some kind of connection between the image concerns and dieting behaviours that are common among teenagers and the warped, all-encompassing psychology of eating disorders. And here we find a critical explanation of why adolescence is such a period of risk, not just for eating disorders but for many mental illnesses.

It is now well established that, if a person is ever going to develop a mental illness, it is most likely to begin in adolescence. This is true the world over: the same pattern has been found in low-, middle- and high-income countries.[10] To use the example of eating disorders, this is because they are an exaggeration and distortion of what is, at one level, a typical adolescent process – in this case self-consciousness and unhappiness about a changing body. Why this occurs in some teenagers and not others is hugely complex, but to simplify dramatically, among the minority of teenagers who develop a mental illness, innate biological vulnerabilities combine with particular environmental circumstances to derail what are otherwise the common and in fact necessary biological and psychological changes of adolescence. Neuroscientist Tomáš Paus and colleagues described this phenomenon as 'moving parts get broken'.[11]

The same is true of social anxiety disorder. This is characterised by an intense concern about being judged by others and that social interactions will lead to humiliation, embarrassment and rejection or will cause offence. Like eating disorders it begins almost exclusively in adolescence – it has even been referred to as the 'prototypical adolescent disorder'[12] – and that is because, again, it is effectively a gross exaggeration of something entirely normal at this age: as a teenager, it's natural and even useful to spend quite a lot of time thinking about how you're coming across to others. Again, the cause of the exaggeration is far from straightforward but often teenagers whose social anxiety develops into a disorder have been bullied, humiliated or rejected by their peers.[13] (As we will see in Chapter 4, bullying is a risk factor for almost all mental disorders.)

The clothes on your back

Only a minority of adolescents will experience a mental disorder, but all will be concerned to some degree with how they appear. And while our bodies are very hard if not impossible to change, the clothes we wear are highly flexible and adaptable. The fact that we get to exercise some choice over them makes them all the more important as a signifier of our identity. For those who wear a school uniform, the devil is in the detail: how short your skirt is, how you carry your bag, the way you tie your tie, the kind of coat you wear. Preparation for a non-uniform day at school can be an extremely lengthy exercise in deciding how to present yourself not only to your friends but to your wider peer group too.

Clothes give clues about your gender and sexual orientation. They can tell people your religion and what kind of music you listen to. They can sexualise your body and make you look older than you really are. They can be a means of hiding your body altogether. They are a way to advertise that you reject social convention or to make a political statement. Teenage clothing can be the difference between social acceptance and admiration on the one hand and total ridicule and ostracism on the other. As marketing academics Maria Piacentini and Greig Mailer write: 'Clothes have the dual function of ensuring that young people are dressed in a socially acceptable way (often conforming to the group norms), but also in marking their individuality in order that they may be attractive to others.'[14] In other words, clothes map onto the two key tasks of adolescence: figuring out your identity and fitting in with your peers.

Depending on the context, one of these drives might take priority over the other. If you are being bullied or have low social status among your peers, your number one priority might be to look as unremarkably conformist as possible. In these cases, teenage clothes are not so much an expression of self as an attempt to be socially safe – as a 'tool for social survival', in the words of marketing academics Katja Isaksen and Stuart Roper.[15] Consider this quote from a fifteen-year-old boy, in a 2004 study by Piacentini and Mailer exploring what teenagers think about branded clothes:

> I'd prefer to have [branded clothes] because it makes you mix in. You don't want to be any worse than what your friends have got and you don't want to be any better so you just get the same logos as your friends just to keep up with them . . . I wouldn't want to stand out of the crowd; I just want to be part of it.[16]

We see this everywhere – groups of teenage friends often seem to have a uniform (if you're not sure, look at their shoes). The art is generally to find a balance between looking sufficiently similar but to avoid being identical. To wear exactly the same outfit would be embarrassing: exposing the truth that everyone is just trying to conform, revealing that you were trying too hard to fit in. The goal is to project a confident individual identity that just so happens to also be socially acceptable, and a common solution is to wear the same brand or style of clothes, but not exactly the same item.

Even if you don't have a fragile social status in adolescence – in fact, even if you're very popular – the pressure and desire to wear the right brands to avoid social ridicule is intense. But for many adolescents, this can present a significant problem: fashionable, branded clothes cost more. Teenagers may be a marketer's dream, but according to Isaksen and Roper 'the dream is unlikely to take into consideration the financial and psychological nightmare that may be inflicted upon the adolescent and his/her family as a result of advertising messages'.[17] Parents find themselves in the maddening situation of standing in a shop where they can see another pair of trainers or a jacket that will do the job perfectly well, for far less money, but their child insists on having the branded version. The reason is often that they want it to feel *safe*.

The desire to have the right clothes is likely to feel especially urgent for those who can least afford them. The fifteen-year-old quoted above was interviewed as part of a study conducted in 2004, in which researchers Piacentini and Mailer spoke to two groups aged twelve to seventeen about how they felt about clothes. All the participants were from Glasgow, but half went to a comprehensive school and were from more deprived backgrounds, while the other half went to private school and had wealthier families. The researchers found that, for all the teenagers, clothes were deeply important as a means of self-expression and in determining how others viewed and treated them. When asked if branded clothes were important to them, the students from the comprehensive school generally said that they were a means of fitting in and being accepted, even if they weren't personally too interested in them. Students from the private school, on the other hand, were less likely to view branded clothes as important. It was as though because everyone could afford those clothes, they weren't the same indicator of wealth or status, and so had less social value. When the interviewer asked if the private school participants would be impressed if someone came into school with a brand-new pair of expensive trainers or a top-of-the-range jacket, a twelve-year-old girl replied, 'In my opinion, I think that makes him look quite sad that they've went to all that trouble just to come to school.' A seventeen-year-old boy, also at the private school, agreed: 'I do try and shy away from brands and what not, it's just advertising how much money you've got, which I don't think is necessary.'[18]

For others, having limited money to buy the right clothes not only affects an adolescent's ability to fit in or project an identity, it can fundamentally affect their ability to *build* their identity and sense of self at all. Some researchers have argued that clothes and other possessions are so fundamental to our understanding of ourselves and how others view us that they are effectively part of us – our 'extended self'. In support of this idea, another study by Isaksen and Roper, in 2008, assessed groups of thirteen- to fourteen-year-olds from two schools in the north-west of England: one from a particularly afflu-ent area and one that 'borders on a notoriously poverty-stricken council estate'.[19] They found that the adolescents from the second school were more likely to endorse statements such as, 'It is import-ant that others like the products and brands that I buy,' but also statements such as, 'I spend a lot of time wondering about what kind of person I really am.' The researchers found a relationship between these two variables: participants who cared more about having branded things had 'lower self-concept clarity'. What this study can't tell us is whether there is a causal relationship between income, the desire for branded products and self-concept clarity. However, the authors speculate that low-income adolescents may be trapped in a 'vicious cycle', in which those who are least able to buy branded clothes want and depend on them the most for their sense of self.

In England, where these teenagers were from, *relative poverty* is high – i.e. there is a greater discrepancy between the wealth of the richest and the poorest, as compared to other countries. Relative pov-erty can be defined as having fifty or sixty per cent less than the average household income in that country, but it can be also be defined more broadly as the relative deprivation from socially-defined neces-sities, the things that are considered requirements for a 'normal' lifestyle. In countries like England, living in poverty as a teenager doesn't only mean not having enough, it means not having enough *in a society where other teenagers do*, and this feels far worse.

Choosing a look

This doesn't make clothes straightforward for wealthier teens. Even those who do have the money to choose their clothes must face the question, 'How do I want others to see me?' and, ultimately, 'Who do I want to be?' We have seen how clothes can act like an invisibility cloak, especially branded clothes, as a form of social protection. But for some adolescents, particularly those with some social standing and a bit of available cash, clothing is not only about fitting in but also about standing out. Most adolescents want to look at least a bit different to their peers, as an expression of their developing individual identity. And at a time when they don't know exactly what that identity is, that can mean cycling through a lot of different looks. This is what happened to Alex, who we heard from earlier, who spent many years experimenting with the image he wanted to portray.

I definitely went through some quite radical changes in identity and so did friends. Music was very tied in with it. I remember carrying a vinyl – it was vinyl in those days, and tapes – and walking around the playground with it. Like as a badge to say, 'This is who I am, because I like this band.' I wanted to make sure that everybody saw me walking along with my record of this band, so they knew I was identifying with that particular tribe. I think it was about exploring different aspects of myself, or trying out a way of being, like trying out a hat to see if it fits. I remember going through a phase where I was a bit of a punk, almost – I had dreadlocks and my head shaved on the back and sides and I was into being very alternative and very anti anything conventional. Almost like I wanted to embody the rejection of convention – of the establishment and conventionality. Then I remember going through a phase where I shaved off the dreadlocks and had a very neat crew cut. And I started dressing in denim jackets and shirts. And that was when I was getting in to the jazz scene. A lot of jazz musicians were wearing suits, and I thought I wanted to be a bit more like that. Then I went through a phase when I was at music college where I wanted to be a really straight kind of guy . . . very hard working and serious about my music. And then I realised that wasn't me either.

Then in my twenties I started to look at the different identities I tried as a teenager, and realised that they were different aspects of me. I started to realise that, you know, some of the types of music that I had rejected I actually still really liked. Or some of the attitudes and ideas I had in one phase of myself I started coming back to. I think there was a phase I went through where I was trying to incorporate the different selves that I'd explored and find a way to make them into my adult self.

Psychologists would refer to Alex's carrying a vinyl record under his arm as an example of 'identity signalling'.[20] It's something we do throughout life – driving a sports car, reading an intellectual book on a train, placing political signs in our window. Clothing is one of the most obvious and commonplace examples. In adolescence, identity signalling can shift frequently as the person figures out who they are and how they want to be seen. In adulthood, it tends to stabilise. As I interview him for this book, I notice what Alex is wearing now: a plain navy T-shirt and jeans. I comment on how he is no longer dressed in such a way as to stand out as a member of a particular tribe, and he says that experimenting with his look was very much confined to his adolescent years:

> I don't know how conscious it was [to stop identifying with a specific tribe], but there was definitely a day where I suddenly thought, 'Oh my God, I don't think I can be this person anymore. I need to be a different person.' I think it was to do with maturing a bit. Maybe the need to rebel had been played out enough, you know, the fire was dying down. It was like, 'I think I've done that now. I think I've really, really shocked my parents now with my haircut and my clothes, I think I've worked that through my system.'

Subcultures

We have seen the many ways in which adolescents are socially conservative and conformist in relation to their peers. But as Alex demonstrates, some adolescents also have a powerful need to rebel against convention, often in relation to the adult world. As Quentin Crisp wrote: 'The young always have the same problem – how to rebel and conform at the same time. They have now solved this by defying their parents and copying one another.' One solution to this dilemma is found in *subcultures*: groups that define themselves as specifically distinct from the main culture in some way. Joining one is to conform to a particular kind of non-conformity, usually expressed, at least in part, by the clothes that you wear. Why do some adolescents end up in these alternative subcultures, while others do not?

Kate, now thirty-nine, was, in her own words, a 'mosher' in her adolescence. This involved dressing unconventionally (for example, black jeans, band T-shirts, radical make-up, and long hair for the boys), meeting up with other 'alternative' people at the skatepark outside of school, and listening to punk and nu metal music. She continues to identify with this subculture as an adult, though she now considers herself a 'metalhead', the more common current term. For Kate, the journey into the world of subculture began at her secondary school in Yorkshire, when she felt a creeping sense that she didn't fit in:

I'm from a middle-class family . . . well, middle-class parents who had working-class parents. I would say we were 'new money'. And I went to private school, which was difficult, I think, for my parents – my dad particularly found that a very hard decision because he was quite interested in left-wing politics. He was a doctor, but he came from a working-class background and he carried a lot of his working-class values with him. Me and my sister both had a bit of a sense of difference at school, because I think socially and culturally we didn't necessarily fit. At our school it tended to be kids who had a lot of wealth, privilege and a particular kind of politics that didn't really sit with my family. And I can remember feeling very strongly that I didn't really fit in there particularly – or maybe that I didn't even fit in anywhere. You know, I sort of had that sense of being a bit at sea. You're forced together at school aren't you, pretty much. I wasn't horribly bullied or victimised or anything like that but equally, I wasn't popular. I had one or two people that I would hang out with but I think that was based on the idea that none of us particularly had other people to hang out with. So we stuck together. But that was about it really. So I wasn't really relating to my peers, but I also wasn't necessarily relating to anybody else either.

It was against this backdrop that Kate became aware of an alternative crowd, the moshers who hung out at her local skatepark, and began to spend time with them. The alternative music and alternative scene, she says, were very helpful, giving her access to 'a different group of friends, different people, different interests'. She started listening to the same music as them and dressing like them outside of school. At school, where she was required to wear a uniform, her peers didn't know of this aspect of her identity until one particularly memorable day:

> I remember in my mind it felt like a very important decision [to become a mosher] and I can remember telling my friend at the time. We were quite different people, and I can remember telling her, you know, 'I'm going to become a mosher.' It was like coming out! She was like, 'Don't worry, I'll still support you.'
>
> We had uniforms at school, and the coming out moment, if you like, was on one of these occasional non-uniform days. And she was like, 'What are you going to wear, your secret mosher stuff?' As I suppose a lot of teenagers find, on non-uniform days everyone wore exactly the same. At the time it was Adidas and Kappa tracksuit bottoms or washed blue denim jeans. Everyone seemed to have the same pair, even from the same shop, you know, it had to be from the same shop. And so ironically it was a uniform even though it was a non-uniform day. So that felt like a binary choice for me: do I kind of 'come out' almost in that moment? What I ended up wearing was something pretty pathetic, like some corduroy trousers or something. But it was different to what everyone else was wearing.

Typically, teenagers who affiliate with alternative cultures are, as you'd expect, the ones who feel they don't fit with the mainstream culture, or who have been actively rejected from it by their peers. The subculture offers an alternative route to the same thing: that crucial sense of social belonging. Kate's decision to wear something different that day was a deliberate choice – and that taps into an important theory about alternative cultures in adolescence. Teenagers who adopt alternative subcultures often consciously do so to regain some control. By dressing in a radical way, they are embracing a *chosen* difference – i.e. a difference that is dictated by them, and not their peers. As social work academic Paula Rowe wrote in a study that asked young people why they became metalheads:

> The results show that metal was vitally important when participants felt vulnerable to bullying and exclusion by popular peers at school. But crucially, the young 'metalheads' were able to disrupt power relations at school by embodying 'chosen' heavy metal identities as a strategic response for countering 'unchosen' marginal school-based identities . . . Metal youth, as self-described outsiders, were able to . . . enter into social relationships on their own terms, protecting themselves from social threats to their mental health and well-being in the process.[21]

One young man in this study, reflecting on his school days, described how he was already feeling different from his peers because he had less money than them. He was from a working-class, single-parent family, and attended an all-boys private school on a scholarship:

> [The early years of school] were the most depressing time of my life, it was an all-boys Christian school and it was a rich school, everyone was talking about me coming in poor. They'd spend up big at the canteen and I had a crappy Vegemite sandwich to last me the whole day . . . The drawback is you go to good schools and you're that odd one out. An example is I had to wait ages for a Super Nintendo when PS1 and Xbox were reigning supreme. It sounds pathetic but at a young age that really fucks with you, it was the only way to fit in, without it you're just fucking gone. I was the weird kid sitting in the corner alone 'cos I didn't wanna go out and get picked on.

For this boy, his relative poverty had significant social consequences. The social ostracism he experienced escalated into verbal and physical bullying. As a way to protect himself, he decided to adopt a metalhead identity. For him, this offered quite a literal sense of safety:

> I told once [about the bullying] and it got worse after that so I thought fuck it, I need some way to deal with it myself . . . I started growing my hair as long as I could and I'd wear Slipknot shirts and draw band logos on everything and write Slayer on my arm, you get instant respect . . . All through the senior years I barely spoke a word, I would've been voted most likely to come back with a gun and shoot everyone . . . You think about bashing them, but if you can just intimidate them and get them to pull back, then you've won, you've got 'em . . . It was a way to shield myself. It's just like a defence thing . . . I mean being metal is intimidating for some people . . . come on, you've got a dead corpse on your shirt! Yeah, in a way it's reflecting, 'Don't talk to me.' Not that you'll do any harm, but you've had enough bad experiences, you just don't wanna deal with it anymore. This is a way to kind of keep people at bay, just a way to deal with the shit at school.

Not every metal teenager feels like this, of course – not everyone was bullied, or takes on the persona to protect themselves, or fantasises about hurting the people who've excluded them. But this sense of a division between the subculture and everyone else, and the protection it brings, is pervasive. 'There's this real thing you get about "outsiders being together" in metal,' Kate tells me, 'this idea that people who are socially rejected by other people come together to find metal.' Kate was never bullied, but she still talks about a strong sense of division between 'us' and 'them' – something that still holds today, in certain contexts. For example, she tells me about a controversial moment in 2016 when the celebrity Kendall Jenner, who became famous for appearing in the reality TV show *Keeping Up with the Kardashians*, decided to wear a T-shirt referencing the thrash metal band Slayer. The true metalheads weren't happy about it:

A lot of people essentially felt it's like appropriation. As though they were saying to her, 'You're taking something that is not only important to us but that doesn't apply to you. Because you're one of these popular people, you're not in that social reject group. We've been marginalised and upset by people like you so you're not allowed to do that.'

When teenagers choose what clothes to wear, they are trying to control their image and therefore their identity: managing how they will be seen by others, establishing a sense of protection, inverting a power imbalance. But there are particular circumstances where the pressure to fit into mainstream norms is far greater, or where it is much harder to attain control. Later in this book, we'll see how trans and non-binary adolescents navigate the decision about when and how to demonstrate their gender identity to other people. Here we will return to a subject we touched on earlier: skin colour and its relationship to minority ethnic identity.

Ethnic identity development

For teenagers who are white and live in predominantly white areas, skin colour doesn't factor much into how they understand themselves or think others understand them. Indeed, some researchers have argued that, in many Western countries, being white is seen as such a prevailing norm – i.e. it is the most visible identity, the one given the most space and attention – that white people rarely view being white as a relevant part of their identity at all.[22] But for adolescents of colour in such cultures, skin colour looms considerably larger in the process of forming their identity. Like everyone else, adolescents of colour are in the process of figuring out who they are, a process that involves incorporating other people's views and assumptions about them into their identity. But in addition they face a whole other set of assumptions about them, *society's* assumptions, based on their skin colour or ethnicity, assumptions that invariably include stereotyping and prejudice.

Priya, fifty-three, is a second-generation Sri Lankan woman who went to an all-girls school in London in the 1980s. Of the 125 girls in her year, she tells me, there were five South Asian girls (including herself), one East Asian girl and one Black girl. Everyone else was white. In her childhood she remembers being shouted at in the street, and spat on, and called racial slurs. In secondary school there was nothing so explicit – but she nonetheless learned early on that her ethnicity and culture were things that she should downplay or hide:

The two other South Asian girls in my class were more 'obviously Asian', you could say – you could smell the cooking on their clothes, and they used coconut oil in their hair. And they definitely got snide remarks, which acted like a warning to me: don't be too Asian. There was a feeling that there was a way to be normal. And if you were Asian, you were already a little bit away from that, so you had to try harder. I guess it's the idea of difference, you didn't want to be too different . . . so then I definitely started turning down anything that was 'too Asian'.

To conform was everything. I wanted the same shoes that every-one else had, and I wanted the same clothes. I pushed down my interest in South Asian politics and culture, I never wore clothes with 'ethnic' prints. I had to be wrestled into a sari for weddings. And, out-side the home at least, I pretended that I didn't like spicy food. In primary school, I remember we had a lesson about culture or some-thing, and there was talk about how people in Britain used to eat mutton. And I immediately said, 'Oh, we eat mutton!' because mutton curries are a really big part of South Asian food. And the teacher said, 'How do you cook it?' And I suddenly realised I'd have to say the word 'curry' and I kind of clammed up and went, 'Oh, you know, just plain.' I couldn't say anything else because I didn't want to share that difference with my class. In the early days of secondary school, I brought some delicious food in from home and there were enough negative comments that I never brought in food again from home. In fact, that habit of not ordering curries in restaurants persisted long into my university years.

This is a version of what so many teenagers do: to avoid being different, they look around to their peers, observe what rules are being policed, and try to follow them closely in order to avoid being ostracised or mocked. For Priya, her skin colour immediately marked her out as different – and there was nothing she could do about that. So to achieve some control over her image, she ensured rigorous conformity in all the areas where that was possible. But when this involves diminishing your ethnicity, you face a distinct challenge: a rupture between the image you are cultivating at school and the long-established identity you have at home.

For Priya, as for so many other teenagers like her, there was only one solution: to maintain two identities. At school, she would embody the identity that was accepted among her peers, and at home she would embody the one that was accepted, and indeed required, by her parents. This meant a lot of lying: lying to her friends about what happened at home, and lying to her parents about what happened at school.

> The habit of lying to my parents became so deeply ingrained in me. I lied about what we talked about in school, about what films I watched at my friends' houses, about what we were doing. I developed a habit of lying about the most trivial things, something which I only stopped in my mid-twenties. I was trying to pretend that I was the person they wanted me to be. But that inability to be myself . . . it definitely held me back. Having to remember the person you are pretending at any one time doesn't make for a smooth adolescence.

Gradually, things got easier: Priya went to university, made close friends, and experienced the kind of social and personal freedom she never had as a teenager. She met her future husband, moved to London, and began what would become a successful career as a radio producer ('I found a job I seemed to be good at and that really, really helped.'). Priya tells me that, for ethnic minority teenagers today, the world outside the home is probably easier now than it used to be – norms are shifting, racism is considered less acceptable. But within the home, she says, teenagers of first-generation immigrants in particular must still be up against it, since the culture in which they are growing up will always be very different to the culture in which their parents grew up. As Priya says: 'I think when you have a culture clash or a culture gap between parents and kids, it's really hard to connect across the generations. Because everyone around you has the age gap issue with their parents, you know. But you're the only one that has this huge extra challenge.'

How skin colour and ethnic identity affect a person's adolescence will depend on countless different variables. Each person will be affected differently, depending on their particular circumstances, their personality and their parents' personalities, the culture of the school, the historical context, and so on. Priya's story, like all the stories in this book, is ultimately unique. Even so, there are common threads – among adolescents of colour but adolescents more generally too. The most consistent theme is that being an ethnic minority in a predominantly white society means being *different*, and being different as an adolescent is hard.

In this book so far, we have explored the hierarchical and rigorously normative social world where adolescence takes place and the effort that adolescents will expend to try and fit in. We have seen how, when an adolescent is particularly different to their peers, for whatever reason, they often adjust their behaviour and appearance to conform, to try and pass as something they are not. Alternatively, they can try to accept their difference to one group of peers by fitting in somewhere else – for example by aligning themselves with an alternative subculture, finding kinship in the joint act of rejecting the mainstream. Either way, we have learned that much of how adolescents present their appearance and image is about trying to keep themselves *safe*. But we haven't yet spent much time considering what adolescents actually do, what they get up to with their friends. What's the game all about? Our route into the subject of adolescent

behaviour begins with a concept we have touched on already, something almost synonymous with adolescence itself: risk-taking. At
first glance, risk-taking seems very much at odds with trying to keep
safe – but look a little deeper, and something rather more surprising
emerges.

3.   In defence of risk-taking

On the night of Saturday, 11 November 1995, Leah Betts took an ecstasy tablet.[1] She was at home having a party with her friends, around thirty of them, celebrating her recent eighteenth birthday. After taking the drug, she then drank a huge amount of water – around seven litres in ninety minutes. She was possibly following common advice that you should drink lots of water after taking ecstasy, because the drug significantly increases energy levels and therefore brings a risk of dehydration. But she drank far too much, and the volume of water in Leah's body meant that the level of sodium in her blood became dangerously low. The drug also reduced her ability to urinate, compounding the problem. This led to swelling in her brain, and she collapsed. Leah was taken to hospital, where she remained in a coma for five days before her life support machine was switched off. The swelling had caused irreparable damage to her brain. She died fifteen days after her eighteenth birthday.

Leah's parents were in the house, in another room, at the time of the incident. While Leah was in hospital, they decided to release a photo of her in a coma to the press, in order to raise awareness about the dangers of recreational drugs. A generation of teenagers, myself included, will remember that image. The message was widely promoted in UK schools, and aligned with the 'Just Say No' campaign run in the 1980s and 90s in the US as part of its so-called war on drugs. Still today, the official story that adolescents are told by their parents and teachers is that recreational drugs are dangerous, often lethal, and to be avoided at all costs.

For some, this message will be followed resolutely. But many, many other teenagers will take drugs anyway, in spite of these warnings. Not only that, but they will also try out all other kinds of risky behaviours, including binge drinking, driving too fast, having unprotected sex and engaging in criminal behaviour such as vandalism and

theft. Of course there are some teenagers who are extremely risk-
averse, particularly those who have high levels of anxiety, as we will
see later in this chapter. But on average, adolescents take more risks
than children and adults, and this pattern is found pretty much the
world over: across countries with widely different cultures, the propensity to take risks follows an inverted-U pattern across the life
span: gradually increasing from around the age of ten, peaking in the
late teens and early twenties, and then declining again.[2]

True to the stereotype of a perceived popular teenager, Chloe,
whom we met in Chapter 1, engaged in a lot of risky behaviour, usually with her best friend Natalie by her side:

> For example, when I was fourteen, I broke my ankle so was off
> school. Natalie knew where my spare key was so she let herself in, and
> she woke me up with a spliff and a bottle of alcopop. The school rang
> me but I said I hadn't seen her. Then another time we went to Skeg-
> ness together for a day out and got tattoos together. She got one
> first. And there was no way I was not going to get one after she got
> one. I thought that was the coolest thing ever. So I wanted one too. I
> didn't realise that I could get a tattoo that young, but once I knew that
> I could go to Skegness and get one, then I was getting one.
>
> [Those years] involved having sex with lots of people, taking lots
> of drugs, truanting from school, going out in cars with much older
> men. Where I'm from is quite a small place, so I had friends that were
> three or four years older than me, and then they had friends that
> would be four years older, and then they had friends, you know, so it
> was easy to meet older people. And everyone smoked weed in our
> social circle. We would be buying weed off these guys, we were
> always looking for some. Honestly, I think weed is so central to the
> story for me. I was always looking for somewhere to smoke weed. I
> never wanted to be at home because I wanted to be out getting stoned,
> and if it was winter, I wanted a car to sit in or a house to sit in or
> something. So that's how I would meet older boys. Oh my God, it's
> so cringe now, thinking that someone with a car was cool . . . but
> that's what it was like.

When me and Natalie were in Skegness, we met some men and Natalie disappeared off with one of them to a hotel for sex. We missed our train home because she wasn't back. I was waiting at the station and she got there just in time for the last train home but we argued and she ran off. I had to phone the police because I couldn't find her. We found her in the end and she was safe, but the pattern continued like that for another thirteen years.

In terms of volume and extent of risk, Chloe's adolescence is probably up at the extreme end of the scale, but she and Natalie certainly aren't the only fourteen-year-olds engaging in these behaviours. So what is it that drives teenagers like them to such reckless-seeming, dangerous activities, when the consequences could be so dire?

Why do adolescents take risks?

The most basic level of explanation is that they simply have more opportunity, especially compared to children. They are supervised less by their parents, they go to parties, they are offered drink and drugs for the first time, they are able to drive for the first time. Most of the time, their parents haven't disappeared because they are neglectful or uninterested, they are simply out at work. We saw all this with Georgia in the opening chapter, who described how various parental circumstances meant she and her friends were often unsupervised, or left with older siblings. It was certainly a relevant factor for Chloe, whose adolescent years involved a rather specific combination of a school renovation, a single parent out at work, and living in a convenient place:

It was a really strange time at my school because, when I started in Year 7, there was the old school from the 1970s with temporary buildings that would get shut down when it was too cold because the boiler would break. And then when I was in Year 8, they started to knock it down and rebuild a new school. And this created a situation where the school was getting smaller before it was getting bigger, so we would sometimes go to buildings on another site, with a fifteen-minute walk in between that was through a park. There was a little side alleyway where you went off to the park. And it meant that there was a lot of opportunity for truanting. There was a lot more freedom within my school than there probably ever would be at any other normal school.

I also lived just the other side of that park, so I could just scooch across there and go home. Also my mum worked full time and I lived just with my mum, so that made my house a bit of a hotspot for truants. And then also as they were knocking down the school and then building on our field, we ended up being allowed to go to the park at lunchtimes because there wasn't space for all the students at school. But obviously that park then made it possible to go into the town centre or you could leave to go off to my house. So there was a lot of opportunity to get away from school and I was right in the thick of it, I was like essential . . . If anybody wanted to skive school, they would ask me because I would have somewhere that they could go.

But opportunity is a circumstance, not an explanation. After all, if it were merely a case of opportunity, adults would take an ever-increasing amount of risks as they become more and more independent, but risk-taking declines in the early to mid-twenties.[3]

Perceived invulnerability

On one level, what drives risky behaviour is obvious: the possibility of reward. What makes something a risk is that it has an unknown outcome, and at least one of the possible outcomes is bad. There must also be the chance of a good outcome – we wouldn't bother doing it if there weren't. So to understand why adolescents take so many risks, we need to understand what they stand to gain from risky behaviour and what they stand to lose, and how that is different from adults. Or rather, what do they *think* they stand to gain and lose?

One possibility is that adolescents don't understand the extent of the risk that they are taking. They either don't understand the potential loss involved, or don't think it applies to them. This is termed the theory of 'perceived invulnerability', and is the confident logic behind all those campaigns and initiatives (like Leah Betts' parents sharing her photo) that aim to highlight the dangers involved in risk-taking.[4] The hope is that, if only we could explain to teenagers that certain behaviours can have bad outcomes, then they would no longer do those things.[5] However, there's little scientific evidence that adolescents don't know about these bad outcomes.

In fact, one well-known 2002 study found that adolescents actually *over*estimate the likelihood that bad things will happen to them, particularly young adolescents.[6] The participants were aged between ten and thirty. The researchers gave everyone a list of scenarios and asked them to decide how likely they thought the bad outcome would be, from zero per cent to one hundred per cent, if they personally were in that situation. For example, they were asked how likely they would be to die if they were outside during a lightning storm, to have an accident if they cycled home from a party after drinking, and to get an STI after having unprotected sex (although the questions about sex were not asked of the very youngest group).

The researchers found that as age increased, the percentages decreased. The adults gave the lowest estimations that something bad would happen, and the adolescents, especially the youngest ones, considered their personal risk to be pretty high – maybe even excessively so, in fact. This makes sense, in a way. As people grow up, they start to see for themselves that the bad stuff doesn't always happen. They see that plenty of people take drugs and not only don't die but can actually have very positive experiences (and everything in between). They see that many people can have unprotected sex and live to tell the tale, and with no baby in sight either. They learn that newspaper stories and films don't tell the whole story. Gradually, over time, people adjust the perception of their personal risk. If anything, then, adolescents are even more aware of the potential negative consequences of their actions than adults are. So what about the potential gains?

Sensation seeking

In the equation of risk, if the gain is sufficiently compelling, it will override any true consideration or conceptualisation of the possible loss, and one of the gains is simple: risk-taking can be thrilling. There is a personality trait, *sensation seeking*, which describes the tendency to do things that give us novel, intense and complex physical and psychological feelings. All of us fall somewhere on the spectrum of sensation seeking throughout our lives, but across the board, sensation seeking tends to temporarily increase in adolescence, with a peak around ages twelve to fifteen.[7] One of the most obvious examples of sensation seeking occurs when adolescents choose to take recreational drugs. Of course, this can occasionally have disastrous consequences, as highlighted by the story of Leah Betts. But many people who decide to try drugs learn the secret they weren't told by their parents and teachers: for all the side-effects and comedowns and consequences, some of them very serious (and indeed fatal), drugs offer a potentially exhilarating physical and psychological experience.

Josie, now aged thirty-eight, went to a 'pretty rough' secondary school in Glenrothes, Scotland. Her adolescence began unhappily, where at school she hovered uncomfortably on the fringes of her friendship group – a tale we've now heard many times:

> My best friend at school was very popular, we were in what you would class as the popular group. But I was not one of the popular kids. I was bullied in that group. I was pushed about quite a lot. I was like the dogsbody. I would be the one that would be sent off to do things. Like one time, I went and stole four boxes of fricking hair dye from the local chemist because I got pushed into it. I wouldn't have wanted to do that, oh my God. There were times when the girls would come to the door and I would say to my mum, 'Just tell them I'm grounded,' so I didn't have to go. And she did that for me. Yeah, that was probably quite a hard time. School wasn't great.

Josie decided to leave school aged sixteen, and moved to Dundee to study drama at college. She had been a risk-taker to an extent before that – with her school friends she was already smoking and drinking – but it was in Dundee, she says, 'when things really exploded'. She met a new group of friends and, like many teenagers trapped in problematic groups at school, was finally able to be herself. It just so happened that her new friends were very into taking drugs. She remembers spending time in the flats of drug dealers, seeing scales on the side and mushrooms 'drying on top of this guy's TV'. It snowballed quickly, and soon she was taking them regularly herself, staying out till 4 a.m. the night before college or work, taking drugs into clubs for her dealer friends. She is very lucky, she concedes, that no harm came from it, and that she never ended up addicted.

When I ask her why she first tried drugs – and it was ecstasy the first time – her answer is immediate: 'It was because of a guy. I fancied him and he was a manipulative arsehole.' But what is most interesting is to hear why she carried on, why she kept coming back for more:

> I just kinda got into that scene and enjoyed it. I kept going with it and I got in with some wild groups. And do you know what, it was really exciting. I thought I was the shit. Like, look at me, getting free stuff, doing free things. Just partying. I look back on that and think, I don't want my kids doing that, but it was great at the time. I think anybody who tells you different is lying. Don't get me wrong, the comedown the next day and the feelings and all that are hellish. There's always going to be the bad at the end of it. But in the moment of doing all these things it felt great. I loved it. I do reminisce about that and think, oh man . . . I couldn't do it now – I wouldn't do it now, I've got kids – but it was good. It was great fun.

Here, Josie is perfectly describing how people take risks, and take drugs in particular, because it can feel very good – and they come back for more because they are seeking that rewarding sensation.

Sensation seeking ramps up in adolescence for good evolutionary reason. If you are going to become a successfully functioning adult, you need to learn what is and isn't safe, and figure out how to make those judgements – and this fundamentally involves taking some risks. Sensation seeking therefore partly increases in the teenage years because it drives more independent, exploratory behaviour. If parents and other adults try to put up too many roadblocks in an effort to prevent these behaviours and so prevent their teenager coming to harm, they can inadvertently stunt this process of exploration and independence – which leads to all sorts of problems, as we'll see later.

Dual systems model

It's also possible that, when something feels good, adolescents don't have sufficiently strong 'brakes' in their brain to stop themselves from doing it, even if it's potentially dangerous. This is best captured in a theory of adolescent risk-taking known as the *dual systems model*.[8] This theory states that there are two key networks in the brain that are relevant for adolescent risk-taking. The first is the *cognitive control system* located in the frontal regions of the brain, which is responsible for the kind of sophisticated thinking that sets humans apart from other animals: decision-making, planning, inhibiting impulsive reactions, that kind of thing. The second is the *socioemotional system*, buried deeper in the more ancient regions of the brain, which is responsible for emotions and the experience of reward. The dual systems theory states that, during adolescence, the cognitive control system develops more slowly than the socioemotional system. This means that the emotional drive to take risks, and the rewarding feeling you get from it, becomes much more powerful, and the control system that usually dampens down and manages these urges is not strong enough. The upshot is lots of emotional, reward-driven, risky behaviour – like saying yes when a guy you fancy offers you a little pill.

Scientific evidence for the dual systems model is mixed. Some studies have found that at least some adolescents show this mismatch in brain development between the two systems, while other studies haven't.[9] It may be that the dual systems idea is more relevant for some types of risk-taking than others. Specifically, researchers think it's particularly relevant for impulsive risk-taking, the kind of behaviour that happens in the heat of the moment – what is known as *reactive risk-taking*. But not all risk-taking is like this. Crucially, plenty of teenagers actively choose to do potentially reckless things, sometimes considerably ahead of time.[10] This *reasoned risk-taking* is premeditated and calculated, and it's critical for understanding the complexity of adolescent behaviour that, on the face of it, can seem so stupid. In the words of psychologist Julie Maslowsky and her colleagues, some adolescents are 'capable of channelling their maturing cognitive abilities and their drive for novel sensations into behaviours that achieve a desired benefit'.[11] Peek behind the cognitive curtain, and you'll see that these teenagers aren't reckless at all.

Peer influence

A crucial thing to note is that, in general, adolescents don't take risks on their own. Adolescents take risks with their friends. In a famous psychological study conducted in 2005,[12] participants were divided into three age groups: mid-adolescents (thirteen- to sixteen-year-olds), late adolescents (eighteen- to twenty-two-year-olds) and adults (twenty-four years and older). They were invited to a research lab to play a driving simulation task, which measures the player's propensity for risk-taking. The object of the game is to get a car to move as far as possible, as quickly as possible, without crashing. Throughout the game, traffic lights appear, which cycle from green to amber to red, just as in real life. If the participant's car is still travelling when the light turns red, they will crash, which costs them valuable time. But waiting at a red light costs time too. Each time the light turns amber, then, players must make a decision: whether to play it safe and wait, or to take a risk and drive. Importantly, in this study, each participant played the game twice. One time, they played in a room on their own. The other time, they played the game while two people of the same age stood over them, watching how they played. (It was randomised as to which version each participant played first.) The people watching were told that they could call out advice about whether the player should stop the car or keep going. The researchers found that all three age groups took more risks (i.e. drove through more amber lights) when their peers were watching them, an important reminder that adults aren't immune to the effects of peer influence. But the effect was much more pronounced for the adolescents, especially the youngest group. The thirteen- to sixteen-year-olds were most affected by having two same-age peers watch over them, taking considerably more risks in front of peers than when they were alone.

This peer effect has now been established in a number of other studies, measuring risk-taking in various different ways, and there are a number of explanations for the finding. One theory is that the presence of friends creates a 'hot cognition' situation, which leads the adolescent to experience powerful feelings of stress, excitement or other heightened emotions that overwhelm their capacity to weigh up risk and make careful decisions (this is relative to 'cold cognition' situations, where decisions can be made more sensibly because the person is under less emotional strain).[13] But some of this comes back to the biological purpose of adolescence. From an evolutionary perspective, it makes sense that adolescents are wired to feel good taking risks around friends. Taking risks with others allows the opportunity to develop independence while also fitting in with and being protected by a tribe. If it feels good, they will be more inclined to do it and therefore reap these benefits. It can be exhilarating when teenagers try reckless things with their friends – and it helps them grow up into an independent adult at the same time.

More than that, risk-taking signals to *everyone else* that the teenager is making strides towards being a grown-up, independent adult. Risk-taking behaviours are often part of what psychologists call *pseudomature behaviour* – teenagers' attempts to appear older than they really are. They are either things that adults are allowed to do but adolescents aren't (like smoking and drinking) or that involve rebelling against the law or some other form of adult approval or rule (like vandalism or truanting from school, or even simply defying uniform regulations). In other words, risk-taking says, 'I'm independent and grown up, and I don't listen to adults,' and it's a highly successful strategy in winning the approval of others, as we've seen. This helps to explain another interesting phenomenon: adolescents tend to avoid doing precautionary things that could help keep them safe, even when those behaviours involve little effort and are eminently reasonable – for example, wearing a bicycle helmet, a seatbelt or sun cream. It is often deeply important for adolescents to reject, and be seen to reject, these adult-endorsed safety behaviours.

Avoiding social risk

We've seen that the equation of gain and loss is significantly different for adolescents as compared to adults. If anything, adolescents over-estimate the possibility of bad outcomes, but what they stand to gain is so much greater still. In addition, there is another element here: what they stand to *lose* from *not* taking risks, which turns the whole equation on its head.

Time and again in this book, we have seen and will continue to see that when teenagers rebel against their peers, they are taking a mas-sive risk. Which tells us that, when a teenager conforms to their peers, they are actually being risk-averse. When the behaviour at hand is itself risky (e.g. smoking, bullying), then the teenager is making a trade-off between a health, legal or moral risk on one hand and the social risk of ostracism on the other. What might look like risk-taking behaviour, in other words, is actually an attempt to avoid a risk of a different kind – a 'social risk'.[14] As cognitive neuroscientist Sarah-Jayne Blakemore has written, 'the social risk of being rejected by peers outweighs other potentially negative outcomes of decisions, such as threats to one's health or the prospect of getting caught'.[15]

In 2020, I contributed to a study, led by Jack Andrews, that dem-onstrated how concern about taking a social risk changes with age.[16] To do this, we devised a list of health risk behaviours (such as 'Eat food that has passed its sell-by date' and 'Cross a main road when the crossing light is red'). These weren't extreme risks, because we wanted them to be things that many people of different ages had been exposed to. We also devised a separate list of social risk behaviours (such as 'Defend an unpopular opinion that you believe in' and 'Admit that you listen to a singer or band that none of your friends like'). All the social risks essentially amounted to being different from your friends, which as we've seen can lead to the very negative consequence of social exclusion and criticism. We then asked participants aged eleven to seventy-seven to rate how concerned they would be about taking these different types of risks.

We found that for both types of risks, concern gradually decreased across age – adolescents were more worried about all of it than adults. But the rate of this decline was especially steep for social risks. Across age, concern for social risks dropped off pretty rapidly – meaning adolescents were really preoccupied about the possibility of being different from their peers, whereas adults weren't that fussed about it. This confirms what we already suspected: branching out from your friends, standing up for yourself or saying no are really daunting things to do when you're young, and I suspect this is because the consequences are so much worse then.

The myth of peer pressure

So far, I've avoided using the phrase *peer pressure*. When it comes to risk-taking behaviours, the truth is that on the whole adolescents play a far more conscious, autonomous role than the clichés of peer pressure might have us believe. We've already seen a number of reasons why – sensation seeking, group safety, forging independence, pseudomature behaviours that enhance one's social status. In fact, in 2000 the social work academic Michael Ungar interviewed forty-one teenagers about what they do with their friends and concluded that, when participants go along with what their friends are doing, it's usually a willing, deliberate decision.[17] The title of the paper is 'The myth of peer pressure' – Ungar concluded that teenagers adopting the behaviour and appearance of peers was a 'consciously employed strategy to enhance personal and social power'.

This was demonstrated in a study conducted back in 1996, investigating why teenagers start smoking cigarettes.[18] The researchers asked twelve- to fourteen-year-olds to complete questionnaires and take part in focus groups to discuss various aspects of teenage behaviour, including smoking. They concluded that the idea of a teenager being pressured against their will to start smoking was often not accurate. They said: 'Data from this study lead us to reject definitions of peer pressure as one way and coercive, and assumptions about adolescents as socially incompetent and vulnerable.' The teenagers in their study, they argued, made their own decisions about whether they wanted to start smoking or not. If they didn't want to smoke, 'they avoided particular social situations and contexts associated with smoking behaviour, or chose non-smoking friends or, if necessary, dropped friends who started to smoke'. Teenagers were not entirely at the mercy of what their friends were doing – they could make their own mind up about what they wanted to do. In fact, the researchers argued that teenagers who start smoking have already to some extent made up their mind that they *want* to start smoking, and they then seek out the kind of social situations where smoking is more likely to happen. In the words of the authors: 'We hypothesise that pupils who are ready to smoke knowingly hang out with peers who will facilitate their entry into smoking behaviour. They are neither surprised nor upset by the offers of cigarettes that follow.'

Birds of a feather flock together

When two teenage friends like Chloe and Natalie engage in risky behaviours together, you might conclude that one of them must be explicitly or implicitly influencing or pressuring the other. But what makes things rather complicated for researchers (and indeed parents) who are trying to understand peer influence is that teenagers who are similar tend to gravitate towards each other in the first place – the idea that 'birds of a feather flock together'. In Chloe's case, she said that she and Natalie 'were both probably damaged in similar ways, and looking for similar things'. And evidently, they were both prone to taking risks. This phenomenon is known as *selection effects*, and it's key to understanding influence between friends. When teenage friends drink alcohol, shoplift or get tattoos together (or do something more benign like play video games), part of the reason is that they were both inclined to do these things anyway, and indeed that's what led them to be friends in the first place. However, teens might flock together in the early days because of their similar personalities and desires but *then* influence each other over time. This is known in psychology as *socialisation effects*: part of the reason why friends behave in similar ways to each other is because, as the friendship deepens, they influence and encourage each other's behaviour in a dynamic, often reciprocal way.

A host of studies have shown that both selection and socialisation effects are important for understanding all kinds of things that teenage friends get up to. Both processes explain why friends tend to engage in similar levels of substance use (including alcohol, recreational drugs and smoking), and why friends tend to show similar attitudes and behaviours relating to sex, such as if they use condoms or if they've had sex at all.[19, 20] Both processes are relevant for antisocial behaviour too, including bullying, as we'll see in the next chapter, but also for committing crime more broadly: teenagers who have a tendency towards antisocial behaviours gravitate towards each other, and then influence each other to behave increasingly badly once they're friends.[21]

Interestingly and importantly, selection and socialisation effects might be relevant for mental health symptoms, too. For example, there is evidence that adolescents who are prone to depression tend to have friends who are prone to it too.[22] Many studies have also found that friends are relevant when it comes to self-harm – i.e. the deliberate destruction of one's own bodily tissue, most commonly by cutting the skin with a blade, often done to provide relief or distraction from negative thoughts and feelings.[23] As with many mental health problems and risky behaviours, self-harm most commonly begins in adolescence: one study, reporting on data from nearly 600,000 participants across forty-one countries, found that the average age of onset was thirteen years.[24]

Around half of those who self-harm only do it once or twice, but it's a concerning behaviour, because the adolescents who persistently self-harm are more likely to also have thoughts of suicide, attempt suicide, or engage in other harmful risky behaviour like excessive alcohol use.[25] This means it's important to predict who might end up self-harming, and a clear risk factor that determines if any one adolescent will self-harm is whether they have a friend who is already doing it.[26] The trickier question, for both depressive symptoms and self-harm, is whether vulnerable teenagers are simply drawn to each other anyway (selection effects) or whether they actively influence each other (socialisation effects), and while there's some support for selection effects, the research has proved inconclusive so far.[27, 28] With the jury still out, the research continues: because if adolescents can influence each other to have more mental health problems over time, or to escalate existing distress into physical self-harm, then friendship dynamics will be a key focus for treatment and prevention work.

When it comes to risk-taking, all this is important because it tells us that teenagers with friends who are a 'bad influence' on them do not necessarily feel unhappily trapped in the friendship or experience any pressure from them to engage in risky behaviours. In fact, sometimes, a friend's risk-taking can be so extreme that it actually leads to reduced risk-taking for some adolescents. This was highlighted by Chloe:

> To be honest I think I was the more sensible of the two of us. Natalie was much, much more vulnerable than me. So even though I was vulnerable and putting myself in stupid situations, she was putting herself in worse ones. And I actually feel that watching some of her mistakes – because I identify with her so, so closely – I was able to see what was happening to her, and it stopped me. There's the potential that I would have taken many more serious risks and may not even be here. I put myself in a lot of fucking hairy situations when I was younger that I shouldn't have done, and I look back and think, 'How the fuck did I get out of that alive?' But I did hold myself back because of some of the risk-taking that she made. And so I could have taken things further. In some respects, because of her, I didn't.

So Natalie actually helped Chloe put on the brakes when it came to her own risk-taking. But this didn't exactly make them risk-averse, and this kind of information won't comfort a parent who is worried about what their teenager gets up to with friends. Unfortunately, when a teenager develops a friendship with someone prone to risk-taking, this presents the scenario that every parent worries about: their child is affiliating, willingly, with another teenager who will mean they end up in all sorts of potentially vulnerable or dangerous situations, perhaps far more so than if they'd never met each other. It can be hard to accept that both teenagers are probably active agents in this risk-taking. Indeed, it might sometimes be more palatable for a parent to blame the friend in this situation, to avoid recognising that their child, too, might want to be doing this stuff anyway.

When parents thwart risk-taking

Sadly, when an adolescent risk goes wrong, it can go really, really wrong. Teenagers making risky decisions can end up disfigured, disabled, with a criminal record, or with a child to look after while they're barely out of childhood themselves (more on that in Chapter 6). For good reason, then, there are whole industries and fields of research dedicated to reducing the severity or consequences of adolescent risk-taking: encouraging them to have protected sex by handing out free condoms, or dissuading them from smoking with gruesome images of diseased lungs, or incentivising slower driving with black box speed recorders and reduced insurance premiums. All of these efforts work on the principle that you cannot eradicate risky behaviour entirely, but that you can put protections in place to reduce the potential harms, and they have undoubtedly saved lives and averted countless other bad consequences.

At the same time, adolescents need the opportunity to take risks. The whole point of this age period, after all, is for children to gradually learn how to be independent, and making some mistakes is an essential part of that process. Parents must therefore figure out how to put boundaries in place without eliminating risk-taking altogether, because that brings its own negative consequences. When an adolescent is consistently denied the opportunity to make their own decisions, try things out for themselves, or have the freedom to develop their own social relationships, psychologists refer to this as *overprotective parenting*. Developing autonomy – literally, the state of being self-governing, of making your own decisions – is an essential task of adolescence, and overprotective parents thwart this process.

Heather, now fifty, got in touch to tell me about the restrictions her mum placed on her as a teenager. Heather grew up in the West Midlands, and went to an inner-city, mixed comprehensive school, which covered a wide demographic of students ('At the end of school, some people went to Oxbridge and some people went to prison,' she tells me by way of illustration). At home, she lived with her parents, her two older brothers and their golden retriever dog. In her words, it was a typical lower middle-class family set-up, and in childhood it was straightforward and predictable: 'If dad wasn't home by 5 p.m. and we weren't having tea by 5.30 p.m., that would have been very unusual,' she tells me. But once Heather hit her teenage years, problems started to emerge:

> My mum was very strict. About everything, about just . . . having a life. About going out, or going out without having really early curfews. It was about where I was allowed to go, what I was allowed to do. She was worried that I would get pregnant, that I'd have a teenage pregnancy. I think that was always what it came down to. One hundred per cent. Or that I'd drop out of school or . . . I don't even know. Just something terrible. But that's what would be terrible in her world, that my life would go off the track, off the conveyor belt that I was on. And that I was going to do something by being with the wrong people or just going to the wrong places.

Maybe this all sounds pretty normal. As we'll see in Chapter 6, it's very common for parents to feel uncomfortable about the prospect of their teenager having sex, and reasonable for them to be worried about unintended pregnancies. Plenty of parents place some degree of restriction on what their teenager can do: who they hang out with, where they go, how late they can be out. But evidently Heather's mum took this to the extreme, and Heather was essentially unable to see her friends at all except at school. The anger she still feels about this is palpable.

> None of this happened in school. When I was in school, we were this tight little group moving around together. It was when we wanted to meet up outside of school. For example, there was one time when it was the last day of term and all my friends were going around to somebody's house after school. And as far as I can tell, and I still would say this, for no reason – it wasn't late at night or anything – I just wasn't allowed to go. I had to come straight home from school. And I made up some lie about why I couldn't go, rather than saying, you know, 'My mum won't let me.'
>
> And the thing that really frustrated me – this is the fundamental bit that still really frustrates me – was I just felt like my parents didn't trust me. My mum was always very, you know, 'Oh, it's not you. It's other people I can't trust.' But it felt like it was about me. And this is the infuriating thing: I didn't even want to do the thing my mum was worried about. I was definitely the last of my friends to have sex. I was probably the oldest virgin in town. When my friends started having sex, I was just like, 'Oh, my God, are you insane?' I wanted to say to my mum, 'That isn't even what I want to do! We're aligned on this. The thing I want to do is just go to the nightclub with my friends and dance.' She was stopping me doing something that I didn't even want to do anyway.

This is the sad irony of overprotective parenting. In an attempt to shield their teenager from any form of harm, overprotective parents rob them of the opportunity to develop and deepen social relationships, to explore the world for themselves, to make healthy, acceptable mistakes and learn from them. And this can cast a very long shadow indeed. For Heather, the impact on her social life is apparent decades later:

> I know, intellectually, that I have some really, really close friends who I can call on, rely on, who really support me. I know that, for a

fact. And I have numerous different groups of friends. I'm a sociable person, I love meeting new people and I'm curious about people. I get energy from people and I really enjoy that. But at the same time, it can be really easy for me emotionally to feel like, oh, but they're not my real friends, are they? Or to think the relationships are one-way. It bemuses the hell out of my husband. He's just like, 'How can you possibly think that? Your friends think this, your friends think that, your friends adore you. They love spending time with you.' But I will still have one of my crises where I say, 'Oh my God, I haven't got any friends and nobody likes me.' Maybe it's about trying to manage being in more than one group. Maybe it's partly that. But it's also not feeling secure in a friendship group. I think, 'Yes, I'm here, but if I wasn't here, the friendship group would still happen. I just wouldn't be in it.'

In adolescence, Heather learned a lesson that has evidently stayed with her: her friendship group could carry on perfectly happily without her. Repeatedly preventing an adolescent from meeting up with their friends has other damaging effects, too. An inevitable, necessary step in establishing your own identity is to extract yourself from the identity given to you by your parents and family, and the only way you can do this is by spending time away from them, discovering the world either by yourself or with friends and so seeing yourself through a different lens. Part of this process involves hiding parts of yourself from parents: true independence is impossible if they continue to know every single thing about you. Going out with friends or shutting yourself in your room are simple, important ways of building this new boundary. Of course adolescents might withhold information from their parents because they're worried about being judged or getting in trouble. But if a parent insists on keeping constant tabs on their teenager, this essential means of identity development becomes difficult or impossible.

It's hard to say whether new technologies make this balance more complicated to achieve. In Britain, eighty-eight per cent of children have a smartphone by the time they are twelve years old,[29] and many parents understandably want to protect them from harm on social media and the internet more broadly, and solve this by monitoring what they do on their phone. There are even apps that can help with this, which can block certain websites and remotely manage screen time, scan all the words the child sends and receives in emails, messages and social media posts, and alert the parent if it finds anything that might indicate issues like bullying, self-harm or sexual content. For younger children, it is entirely reasonable to take such precautions. But what happens as these children get older?

In the past, parents could not have access to all the things that teenagers talk about and do with their friends. But now that these interactions and relationships are increasingly played out online, parents who closely monitor their adolescent's phone use are theoretically able to witness or know about all of it. Smartphones now have the functionality for parents to physically track their child, so they know exactly where they are at all times. Again, this makes sense from a safety perspective, especially in younger children. But where does it stop: if you track your child's location when they are twelve, and become comfortable with this, how do you ever make peace with turning off the app?

The marketing spiel for one app states that, 'As a busy parent, reading every text message, post, and email just isn't realistic'[30] – as though the optimum situation is indeed one in which every exchange can be monitored and checked, the only problem being lack of time. But at some point, adolescents need to be able to have private conversations. At some point, a difficult, delicate transition must take place between a situation in which challenging online interactions or 'inappropriate' content require parental intervention and one where such things must be navigated alone, as part of growing up. When this takes place will vary depending on the content: a seventeen-year-old might need the space to exchange intimate messages with a romantic partner, but still need parental advice if, for example, they are sent an anonymous threat. Likewise, adolescents will at some point need to have the kind of adventures outside the home that mean ending up somewhere spontaneous and not necessarily parent-approved, and there will therefore be a blurry point at which the location tracking should probably be turned off for good.

In a minority of cases, overprotective parenting is part of a wider pattern of abuse that deprives a child of typical loving experiences and healthy, normative development. Most commonly, it's a misguided expression of love: a completely understandable attempt to protect the child from dangers that the parent doesn't fully understand, and a simple continuation of the role they've played in their child's life to date. Often, it comes from fear, and a lack of understanding about what a teenager needs. Consider what Heather tells me about her mother's own upbringing:

> The conclusion I come to more and more as I get older is about my mum's own childhood. My mum was the youngest of two, and when she was three, her five-year-old sister drowned. And so she was effectively brought up as an only child by parents who went, 'Right, we're going to wrap you up in cotton wool. And we're going to keep you away from the world. We're not going to teach you how to swim. We're not going to let you go near water. We're going to make you really frightened of water. We're going to make you frightened of all of these things in life.'
>
> And somehow, aged sixteen, she met my dad. Someone who looked like David Bowie and was super cool and who messed up his A-levels because he was just too naughty, bright but naughty. I've got two older brothers, I'm the youngest of three, and we're all quite loud. And I think my mum was just like, 'I don't know how I landed in this family and I don't really know what to do with you.' It was confusion and unfamiliarity and I just think she didn't know what to do. She was fearful. Fearful and out of her depth with us.

The cost of anxiety

Adolescents need to take some risks and they need at least some freedom to do so if they're to figure the world out for themselves. But a small proportion of teenagers face a hurdle: teenagers who experience high levels of anxiety – in some cases, badly enough to warrant a diagnosis of an anxiety disorder. It's important to emphasise just how crippling an anxiety disorder is: teenagers with these diagnoses are held hostage by relentless and overwhelming worry or panic that endures for months or years. The specific focus might vary – in social anxiety disorder it's about being judged by others; in generalised anxiety disorder it's widespread worry; in panic disorder it's a repeated cycle of panic attacks and the fear of panic attacks. But a common thread in all these disorders is that the anxiety is disruptive enough to affect the person's daily life – for example, stopping them from going to school or socialising with friends. This interference with daily functioning is the critical feature that sets apart anxiety disorders from the kind of worry and stress we all feel in varying degrees from time to time.

Researchers have found that adolescents who are prone to anxiety consistently avoid taking risks. One psychological task commonly used to assess this is the Balloon Analogue Risk Task (BART).[31] Participants are presented with a balloon on a computer screen and told that each time they press a button, they will inflate it by a small amount. The bigger they make the balloon, the more points they will win, which translates into more take-home cash. But if the balloon bursts, the participant loses all points and any potential money. As you might expect, anxious young people consistently inflate the balloon less than their non-anxious peers, which is taken as evidence that this group tends to be more generally risk-averse.[32]

We've seen what a problem it can be when parents prevent teenagers entirely from taking risks; in the case of anxious teenagers, the obstacle to appropriate risk-taking may be themselves. This means that anxious teenagers might actually need to be encouraged to take some risks. Interestingly, there's some evidence that anxious adolescents have *more* of a propensity for certain real-world risky behaviours, particularly alcohol use. This may be because drinking makes them feel more relaxed or more able to face anxiety-provoking situations.[33] But this is not true of the day-to-day risks that allow us to explore and practise our independence: getting public transport alone, sitting exams, going to social events.

Sometimes, their anxiety is so debilitating that a young person needs much more than gentle cajoling. In the case of an anxiety disorder, this is true by definition. That's when support from a therapist can be helpful, particularly cognitive behavioural therapy (CBT). A fundamental principle of CBT is that people who are struggling with anxiety should gradually practise doing exactly what makes them anxious.[34] The technique is called *graded exposure*, which means devising a step-by-step plan of challenges that gradually increase in terms of how anxiety-provoking they are. The idea is that the person gradually works their way up the list, practising relaxation and coping techniques as they tackle each step, and staying there until they feel comfortable to move to the next challenge.

The key principle here is that when someone avoids what makes them anxious, their anxiety is relieved in the short term, but at a cost of being maintained or even exacerbated in the long term. This is because when a person does something anxiety-provoking, they learn two things. First, that the thing they fear might not be as bad as they thought. Second – and I think this is the most important one – they learn that they can cope, even if something is hard. Research shows that people prone to anxiety routinely not only overestimate how bad things will be, but also underestimate how well they will cope if something bad does end up happening.[35, 36] When they do find themselves in situations they feared, anxious people consistently cope better than they thought they would in advance. If teenagers (and adults) avoid anxiety-provoking situations, they will never learn these two lessons – so the anxiety never reduces.

In recent years, there have been huge efforts to destigmatise mental health problems, including anxiety and anxiety disorders, with some success. At the same time, as awareness grows, teenagers are increasingly citing anxiety as a reason to avoid certain activities, like giving a talk in front of their class or sitting their exams in an exam hall. We would do well to consider that, excepting a minority of cases (such as autistic adolescents), being given permission to not do the things that make them anxious could ultimately be genuinely problematic for these students in the long run.[37] Of course, the solution isn't to force young people to do things that terrify them either – lots of support might be needed, possibly via a therapist. But as we seek to raise awareness about mental health, and seek to support the teenagers who experience anxiety, we mustn't lose sight of the value and importance of risk-taking.

Over the first four chapters of this book, we've seen how so many adolescent behaviours are shaped by peer influence: the friends they keep, the clothes they wear, the risks they take. Almost every moment of every day, the way that adolescents think, feel and behave is influenced by what their peers are up to. Peers exert their influence even when they are not physically present: even in the safety of the family home, a young person may be reluctant to do certain things because they imagine that their friends or classmates might disapprove. All of this is driven by an exceptionally powerful need to belong and an equally powerful fear of standing out or being rejected. None of this is necessarily a problem: being susceptible to peer influence in adolescence is often just part of the journey towards becoming a self-assured, well-adjusted adult. But peer influence is also crucial for understanding one of the most troubling and formative aspects of adolescence: bullying.

4.   The psychology of bullying

The novel *Heaven*, by Mieko Kawakami, is written from the perspective of a fourteen-year-old boy. We never learn his name, only that, because of his lazy eye, his bullies give him the nickname 'Eyes'. The story centres on the secret friendship that he develops with a girl in his class, who is also targeted by her classmates. At one point in the novel, the narrator is dragged into an empty classroom by the bully Ninomiya – a clever, good-looking student with high social status. Ninomiya and his friends tell the narrator to stick a piece of chalk up his nose and then take it out and draw something on the blackboard – 'something that would make them shit their pants'. Our narrator stands there paralysed, so Ninomiya changes tactic, telling him instead to eat three pieces of chalk, while his friends watch and laugh. The narrator obeys the instruction:

Thus far I had been forced to swallow pond water, toilet water, a goldfish, and scraps of vegetables from the rabbit cage, but this was my first time eating chalk. It had no smell or taste. They yelled at me to chew faster. I closed my eyes and broke the chalk apart inside my mouth, focusing on chewing, not on what it was. I heard it crunch. The broken pieces scraped the insides of my cheeks. My job was to keep my jaw moving and to swallow, so I swallowed. Chalk coated the inside of my mouth.

I did this for all three pieces. One of them yelled, 'Lemonade! Lemonade!' and brought me a plastic cup streaked with paint and full of a dirty milky liquid. Chalk dust dissolved in water. Pushed against the wall, cup pressed into my face, I drank it all. As the liquid travelled down my throat, I felt the urge to vomit, and the next thing I knew I had thrown everything up. Tears and spit dripped from my nostrils and my eyes – dry heaving, both hands on the floor. One of the guys asked me what the hell I was doing and stepped back, but he was clapping. Cheering. They pressed my face into the mess and said, 'Clean it up.' Everyone was smiling, laughing.

Too often, the term 'bullying' gets dismissed as something mild or playful, or part of the inevitable rough-and-tumble of growing up, but it's far more than that. It's chronic, relentless abuse: a campaign of targeted cruelty, exclusion and humiliation against a vulnerable individual. For some people, it is the defining story of their adolescence.

Even one experience like the one described above could be traumatic enough to increase your risk of mental health problems for many years afterwards. Victims of bullying, by definition, experience this abuse as a regular occurrence. In fact, the constant anticipation of cruelty is part of what makes bullying so damaging. In one study, a thirty-five-year-old man who had been bullied at school summed it up thus: 'I remember a constant feeling of distrust and anticipation of what would happen to me today, again. I knew it would and I knew it would be horrible, I just didn't know what exactly.'[1]

Why do people become bullies?

To understand why bullying happens, we need to look at it from the point of view of ringleaders like Ninomiya. Their behaviour is more than just aggression or violence. They aren't just losing their cool when they feel threatened or frustrated. It is a repeated, deliberate action, which indicates that it has some predictable and beneficial consequence for the bully. Research shows that young people who bully tend to particularly care about social status: for example, they report that they like making others do what they say.[2] Note also that the majority of bullying incidents at school – as many as eighty-eight per cent – take place when there is an audience of other peers.[3] Bullying, then, is a means of gaining, demonstrating and sustaining social power. Through public acts of physical intimidation and, crucially, psychological humiliation, bullies advertise that they are higher up the social hierarchy. Once that status has been achieved, the bully then continues their behaviour as a way of maintaining their position.

Of course, bullying is only one way of achieving social status, so the question then becomes why some young people end up going down this particular route. One of the many proposed explanations is that some adolescents learn bullying at home.[4] According to the *family systems theory* of behaviour, first introduced by psychiatrist Murray Bowen in 1966,[5] an individual's behaviour cannot be understood in isolation and its causes only become apparent in the context of their family unit, the web of interactions and relationships that they inhabit at home. Applied to bullying, family systems theory suggests that young people who become bullies have parents or siblings who have been abusive towards them, or they have learned that behaving like a bully at home leads to benefits (or both). Either way, the home environment has taught the child that physically or psychologically tormenting other people is a way to get results or to make themselves feel safe, so they then bring that approach to school and apply it to their peers.

In a similar way, some young people become bullies because they themselves have been a victim of bullying at school. They learn how it feels to be treated as weak, and then learn to mimic their own bully's actions on other people as a way of elevating and protecting themselves. Perhaps unsurprisingly, this subgroup of young people do not entirely transition away from being victims, instead falling into a role where they are both a bully to some peers and a victim to others – the so-called 'bully/victim'.[6]

Other explanations focus more on the individual's psychology than their environment. One theory is that people who bully have a limited capacity for two key feelings that help to inhibit bullying behaviour in most people: empathy and guilt.[7] There is evidence that even in children as young as three, those who show particularly low levels of empathy and guilt are more likely to end up bullying when they are older.[8, 9] It is perhaps unsurprising that these young people often have parents who show similar traits. This means that the young person may have inherited these propensities genetically but also that they are likely to be on the receiving end of callous behaviour at home and may learn it as a viable social strategy that way.[10]

But understanding why one young person might end up as a bully doesn't explain why bullying is quite so prevalent and so difficult to control. To understand this, we need to widen our perspective beyond only the bully and their victim, because thinking of bullying as a relationship between two people is to miss its most important feature. As the scene in *Heaven* highlights, bullying is a group activity. It doesn't just involve a victim and a bully; there is almost always an audience. In fact, the group dynamics of bullying are so well established that research has identified a number of roles, a number of characters, that consistently appear.[11] There is always a ringleader like Ninomiya, but there are several other key roles, and they cover every single person in the classroom – *everyone* plays a role in bullying. Most enable the bullying to happen: they either directly encourage it or take part in it (these are the *reinforcers* or *active supporters*) or they disengage from it, passively allowing it to happen (*outsiders*). The vital final group – the *defenders* – are the adolescents who intervene to stop the bullying and support the victim. Every character's behaviour is shaped by the behaviour of other people in the class.

Freddie, now twenty-nine, shared with me his experience of being bullied in adolescence. Freddie grew up in East London and was bullied for almost all of his school life, between the ages of seven and sixteen. This means it started in primary school and continued in secondary school – because, he tells me, he was already vulnerable by then: 'Kids can sniff a victim like sharks can sniff blood from a mile away.' The bullying was verbal, physical and carried out online (Facebook had just started around that time). The secondary school he went to was a large state school in a deprived area – 'one of the roughest schools in the borough' – and he tells me that homophobia and Islamophobia were rampant, as was sexism, and girls were 'treated a lot like property by a lot of the boys'. This environment helps to explain why, after an initial couple of years being bullied by one group of peers, he was ultimately bullied by almost everyone in his year group:

> It was like being in a prison environment. It was dog eat dog. A lot of people were doing what they could to survive. Looking back, I think some of the kids who bullied me or picked on me were just nasty people, but others were doing it as a way for them to survive. It was fear of the lead bully. You've got to be a physically strong or mentally strong person to stand up to someone in that environment. Or you need to have enough social status yourself to not feel anxious about standing up for someone who has no social status themselves and risk that loss of your own social capital.
>
> There were a few girls who stood up for me, and I'm still friends with them today actually. They are by-and-large the only people I'm friends with from secondary school. They were very strong girls that the boys didn't fuck with, put it that way. Even the boys who bullied me were scared of them. So the girls who were in that position were able to defend me. But that was rare.

The power of norms

Throughout our lives, in every situation, we look to others to understand what the 'normal' thing to think or do is, and we usually follow suit. The idea of social norms took on great importance during the Covid-19 pandemic: there became an established norm to wear a mask on the London Underground, for example. Once a norm starts to dissipate – once an individual looks around the carriage and sees other people aren't wearing masks – they will likely soon stop wearing one themselves. As we have already seen throughout this book, in adolescence, social norms reign supreme – and this is true of bullying, too. The process of bullying begins when a ringleader selects a victim. But bullying is *maintained* when that bully–victim dynamic is witnessed by the rest of the peer group. This sets off a complex series of events in which the whole class (and sometimes the whole year group) may eventually come to see it as normal that that particular adolescent is victimised.

Research consistently shows that before they are bullied, victims are already in some way isolated, insecure or physically weaker than the bully.[12] Since the goal of bullying is usually to establish or maintain social status, it makes sense that bullies target those who already have lower social status. As described by psychologist Christina Salmivalli, selecting weak victims 'enables bullies to repeatedly demonstrate their power to the rest of the group and renew their high-status position without the fear of being confronted'.[13] In 2019, psychologists Robert Thornberg and Hannah Delby asked thirteen- to fifteen-year-olds to describe their experiences of witnessing bullying and why they thought bullying happened.[14] As described by one participant, all it can take to become a victim is a single comment:

> For example, if you kind of gave a wrong answer to a question in the classroom, they would like to bring that up for weeks afterwards . . . or if you just said something ordinary at lunch and they thought it was something wrong to say, then they would bring that up and stand in your way and say, 'No, you can't do this,' or get other people to dislike you by going behind your back and kind of saying mean things and intentionally making the person feel excluded.

Thornberg and Delby sum up this process as 'victim constructing'. Having decided who is uncool, different, or otherwise vulnerable, the bully then promotes that message through 'name-calling, rumour-spreading and social exclusion, meaning that the victim is further labelled as deviant and stigmatised'. And just as the victim is deemed to have broken certain norms, the whole peer group must then follow a new norm: agree with the bully and ostracise the victim, lest you end up a target yourself. The situation is not unlike an authoritarian state, in which extreme violence inflicted on a few individuals instils such fear in the whole population that everyone starts policing each other, for fear of having the violence turned on themselves.

Except that, in secondary schools, not *everyone* obeys these rules. In every year group, there is a rare handful of students who are aware of these social norms but decide to defy them. These are the 'defenders' that I already mentioned – and understanding this small group is key to understanding how to reduce bullying.

Rejecting the norms

In Chapter 1 we met Alex, who went to an all-boys boarding school and spent much of his teenage years experimenting with different styles of fashion and music to figure out his identity. These experiments might give you a clue that Alex is an example of someone who was confident enough to make up his own mind about what social norms he wanted to follow – and this extended to who he wanted to be friends with at school:

> I started out in the cool crowd for the first few years, but I didn't really like a lot of them. And I started to find out that a lot of the people who were the more geeky and nerdy science types would often be much more interesting than the people in the cool crowd and the rugby players, you know. So I would find I'd be having fascinating conversations with a lot of these people. And I really liked them. And I just thought, why is it when I talk to someone who's supposed to be 'lower status' in terms of this bullshit hierarchy, everyone would then go, 'Ugh, I saw you talking to so-and-so. Why were you talking to so-and-so? He's a twat.' And I'd go, 'Well, he's actually really interesting and I like him.' And they'd say, 'Ugh, you dickhead, how can you like him? What a dickhead you are.' And you just think, God, this is awful. Why do we even have a hierarchy? Those were the sort of thoughts that were going through my head in adolescence, you know, 'Why?' Questions about human nature. Why am I in this nineteenth-century authoritarian structure, where even the teachers are quite bullying? It just seemed very close-minded, very odd.
>
> But I felt as adolescence progressed, the status hierarchy thing seemed to intensify. Age fourteen to sixteen seemed to be the worst

period where it got very intense in terms of everyone wanting to be top dog. And there was a lot of conflict and a lot of bullying. They would often rule using humiliation and bullying and brutality. It was pretty horrible, really, to see it happen. And I just thought I'm really finding these people boring. I didn't have anything in common with them. I thought, there are loads of other people in the school I'm finding really, really interesting, and I don't want to be part of this bullshit hierarchy that these people seem to be imposing. And it was the people at the top that seemed to be imposing it.

The scene that Alex describes isn't especially rare, but much rarer – because it is so socially risky – are the teenagers, like Georgia in the opening chapter, who defy its conventions. As with Georgia, Alex's decision had significant consequences:

Because I stepped away and I started mixing with whoever I wanted, I was then viewed with suspicion. I think people looked at me and thought, 'I can't fit you in one of the boxes. This is difficult, therefore I'm finding you difficult and I'm finding you threatening.' And then because I was quite creative, I was interested in lots of different things, different music, reading lots of different things, there was a phase where everyone would go, 'You're a weirdo. You're just a weirdo.' All that stuff started. And it was hard, you know, it was really hard. It was really upsetting.

I think the path I chose was quite a painful path because it did involve people turning on me. But I think there's just an aspect of my character that's very bloody-minded and was very like, 'You know what, sod everyone else, I'm just going to do what's right for me.' But there were also huge anxieties as well. It was both. There was a lot of, 'God, maybe they'll think I'm a dickhead,' and all that sort of stuff – that was there, definitely. My adolescence was full of anxiety, like everyone else's is. But I think there was this underlying kind of bloody-mindedness that seemed to be stronger.

The whole experience helped me work out that I really don't like hierarchical status-orientated thinking. I really think the idea that some people are better than others is one of the worst ideas that humans have ever come up with. That is something that I took into adulthood – I thought, I do not want to subscribe to that in adulthood. I think that was something I was determined about by the end of school. That's a value I definitely left with, you know.

Research shows that, to effectively reduce bullying, action must be taken at multiple levels. This is referred to as a *whole school approach* and might include involving parents, facilitating mediation between bullies and victims, punishing the bullies, and/or monitoring any bullying 'hotspots' in the school (unsurprisingly, most bullying incidents take place in unsupervised spaces).[15] But a key component of these interventions is to change the behaviour of the 'bystanders', i.e. anyone who witnesses the bullying. Research confirms that in private, many bystanders feel like Alex: deeply unhappy and distressed about the bullying that they see. This means that in theory, these students are an excellent group to target to reduce the problem: they already have the right *attitude*, all they need is encouragement to *behave* in a helpful way.

There are ways to do this that show some degree of effectiveness – for example, making all students aware of their role and improving reporting systems – but it's hard. Realistically, only a small number of students will be able to take the social risk involved in standing up to bullies. One 2010 study of ten- to fifteen-year-olds found that the students who defended victims tended to have high levels of empathy and a strong belief that they could bring about change (so-called 'self-efficacy') – but the ones who defended the most had both these traits *and* high levels of perceived popularity, i.e. high levels of social status themselves.[16] Even if their actions aren't enough to eradicate the bullying, interventions by such students can be incredibly powerful and comforting for victims. Remember the girls who intervened to help Freddie, the ones that even the boys 'didn't fuck with': like many others in his position, Freddie remembers their kindness more than a decade later.

Adolescent peer influence involves prosocial behaviour too

This is no easy task: to identify the relatively small number of students in each school who have high levels of empathy, self-efficacy and social status and expect them to take action in all bullying incidents. But there is something else that can be done, something more subtle. Again, it relies on the power of social norms. Just as adolescents can be influenced by their peer group to behave antisocially, they can be readily influenced to behave prosocially, too.

In 2016, I ran a study with a group of my colleagues in which we asked 755 participants from all over the world, aged eight to fifty-nine, to complete a simple task on the computer.[17] During the task, the participants were shown a list of prosocial behaviours – acts intended to help another person that most of us have the opportunity to do. Our list included 'Raise money for charity', 'Carry a friend's bag for them', and 'Care for a family member when they're ill'. Participants were asked to rate how likely they were to perform each act on a sliding scale from 'Not likely at all' to 'Very likely'. Participants were then shown average ratings, supposedly from other participants but in fact randomly generated, and given the opportunity to change their first answer. We wanted to see whether younger participants were more likely to change their answers relative to adults, and they were: children and teenagers (eight- to eighteen-year-olds) all significantly changed their answer after seeing the average participant rating, whereas adults kept their answers the same.

This study had an important limitation – we were asking about *hypothetical* behaviour, rather than measuring actual prosocial behaviour, and we know from other research that what people say they would do doesn't necessarily marry up with their actual behaviour. But my finding has been supported by more recent research indicating that adolescents are indeed particularly likely to be influenced by their peers in a *positive* way. For example, a 2020 study, which looked at charity donations in participants aged eleven to thirty-five years old, found that younger participants were more likely to increase their donation if they learned that similar-aged peers had given more, compared to the older participants.[18]

This is what makes this phenomenon relevant to bullying. One study assessed over 16,000 secondary school students in Germany (nine- to sixteen-year-olds) over approximately two years,[19] and found that adolescents who were in classrooms with high average levels of prosocial behaviour in one year were more likely to be prosocial themselves two years later. (In this study, 'prosocial behaviour' included things like helping each other with school work and helping to resolve arguments.) In fact, the researchers found that the impact of being in a very prosocial classroom was particularly strong among students who exhibited *lower* levels of prosocial behaviour to start with. Quite why this might be is unclear, but what we can say is that different norms prevail in different classrooms, and that prosocial behaviour perpetuates itself and spreads over time.

We also know from a number of studies that a better predictor of an individual adolescent's behaviour is their *perception* of what their peers think and do (e.g. how much alcohol they *think* their peers drink) not what their peers are actually thinking or doing.[20] In the words of researchers Whitney Brechwald and Mitchell Prinstein: 'Social norms are in the eye of the beholder.'[21] This may sound pretty obvious – after all, we only ever have access to our own perceptions of other people. But it has really important implications for reducing problematic behaviour in adolescents, because *perceived* social norms are something that can be influenced and potentially corrected. Let's say that a teenager is reluctant to use a condom during sex because he believes that none of his peers use condoms, even though they actually do. If you could correct his misperception – via a public health campaign, or even just a private conversation – it could change his behaviour, increasing the likelihood that he will engage in safe sex.

One approach to reducing bullying has been simply to display posters in schools that highlight to students how many of their peers disapprove of bullying.[22] In a study of this technique, researchers found that before the posters went up, adolescents believed that far more of their peers had positive attitudes towards bullying than was really the case. Then the posters went up all over the schools, saying things like, 'Ninety-five per cent of students at this school believe students should NOT shove, kick, hit, trip, or hair pull another student.' (These were real statistics, based on an anonymous survey the researchers conducted at each school.) The researchers found that after the intervention, attitudes to bullying had improved and the number of bullying incidents had reduced. A year and a half later, the biggest changes had been maintained in the schools where students had better recall of the messages shared in the posters.

Other studies have found that getting adolescents to share anti-bullying information among their peers can be effective at reducing bullying, and that this is more effective than getting adults to teach the same messages. Of course, the success of this 'peer-led' approach depends very much on the adolescent who shares the message. One study found that an anti-bullying campaign run via the peer-led approach was more effective when the adolescent spreading the word was 'well connected' (i.e. lots of students reported wanting to spend time with them).[23]

The bottom line is that to reduce bullying in a school you need the buy-in and involvement of students who have some sort of established social position. In schools where the helpful high-status students are too few and far between, or where the bullying culture is too embedded or there are not enough adults willing or able to support the change, any such attempt is unlikely to succeed. The reality is that, despite enormous amounts of research investment, the best anti-bullying interventions we have still only reduce bullying victimisation by around fifteen to sixteen per cent on average.[24] Sadly, many people's adolescent years continue to be defined by this most problematic of human behaviours. For them, the only option is to cope with the aftermath – which brings us back to Freddie.

Recovering from bullying

Bullied by almost everyone in his year group, Freddie endured an exceptionally lonely and difficult adolescence. Though naturally an extravert, he 'tried staying completely quiet in class for a week or two weeks or something like that, just so people might change their opinion about me' – but it didn't work. At age sixteen, after Freddie returned from a family holiday, the bullying culminated in one of the boys in his own social group making a Facebook group with an embarrassing picture of Freddie. The boy invited the whole year group to join it and encouraged them to insult him. A few weeks later, when he felt like a 'husk of a human being with nothing left to give', he tells me he came very close to taking his own life.

It is not unusual for people who are bullied to have suicidal thoughts or to attempt suicide. This is true of adolescents not just in high-income Western countries but around the world. Researchers in a 2019 study that looked at data from nearly 135,000 adolescents aged twelve to fifteen who lived in forty-eight predominantly low- and middle-income countries, from Afghanistan to Costa Rica to Thailand, found that the participants who reported experiencing more bullying in the month preceding the study were more likely to have attempted suicide.[25] In the group of adolescents who reported no bullying, 5.9 per cent reported a suicide attempt in the preceding year; for the group that reported being bullied twenty to thirty days in a month, that figure was 32.7 per cent. Young people who are bullied are at increased risk not just of suicide attempts but of a host of mental health problems, concurrently but also many years later.[26]

In the end, Freddie made it through his adolescence, and there are shoots of hope in his story. Throughout his teenage years he was part of a cricket team, along with his best friend from outside school, where he tells me he always felt included. ('They weren't being nice to me out of sympathy or because they were forced to. They were being nice because they genuinely liked me, who I was and what I brought to the group. It was a very strange feeling to realise that for the first time,' he tells me.) He also left his secondary school after doing well in his GCSEs and moved to a grammar school for sixth form, where things began to improve considerably:

I remember really vividly, at AS level, I dropped three marks in an English exam out of a hundred per cent and all the boys were like, 'Fred, you fucking smashed that exam!' And I was so taken aback,

because people would get on to you for being academic at my secondary school, they'd call you a boffin, they'd look down on you and
essentially harangue you for it. It took me a moment for that change
of mindset to sink in and for me to realise, 'Oh right! So working
hard and being academic is actually rewarded socially here.' That
sixth form college was a really positive experience and I've still got
lifelong friends from there. I wasn't the most popular kid, but I was
pretty well liked and respected. So yeah, that was a good break from
[the bullying] and that helped me ease into university more easily.

At university, things continued to improve. He made friends and was
regularly invited to parties – 'which took quite a lot of getting used
to' – and has spent his twenties catching up on the social experiences
he never had at school. He also set up a platform, VENT, that
encourages everyone, especially boys and men, to talk about their
mental health, and regularly talks and writes about his experiences.
He tells me, in the six years since he set it up, VENT has become a
website, a podcast and a bi-annual music night. But unsurprisingly,
scars from the bullying ran deep. Freddie had eight years of therapy
to help process what happened to him, including cognitive behavioural therapy and eye movement desensitisation and reprocessing
therapy, a specialised form of treatment for people with post-
traumatic stress disorder:

> That therapy really helped me come out of what I would call a sort of
> permanent trauma or victimhood state. It was like the wool had been
> lifted from over my eyes and I could finally let go of the subconscious
> protector I had put in place that helped me survive that time. I real-
> ised all of those years were my 'lost years', because I wasn't a) fully in
> control, b) fully self-aware or c) fully healed. I think that for me was
> the biggest thing. Sadly, what [the therapy] also did was make me feel
> like I've got loads of life to catch up on. All the normal things that a
> lot of kids do during their teenage years I just didn't get the chance to
> do. It's why I could never watch the teenage TV show *Skins* because
> I'd get FOMO, fear of missing out. I've been getting to do that stuff
> now, though, in my mid to late twenties, which has been great. In

2022, I went on my first lads' holiday, for example. And I would say now I'm in the best mental state I've ever been.

Towards the end of the interview, I tentatively ask him the question that's been lingering in my mind throughout our whole conversation. I want to understand how he feels now about the boys who made his teenage years so miserable. Has he forgiven them? Until this point, Freddie has been very animated, but now, for the first time, he falls silent. Then he tells me that, since leaving school, one of the bullies had made contact with him:

The guy who made the Facebook group about me sent me an online message once a couple of years ago now, saying sorry. The way he phrased it, though, the apology didn't sound genuine and I think he was saying it to make himself feel better, to be honest. Unfortunately, it temporarily fucked me up. It triggered me so hard when I saw the message and his name on my phone screen and I was so angry. I took a deep breath, had a think and talked to a couple of mates, asking them for advice before sending anything back. I did eventually reply . . . I said something along the lines of 'Thanks for your message. I'm still actually working through what you and the others did to me. But, take this as your closure and don't contact me again,' and then I blocked him. I think that was the most polite way I could've responded. I'm still pretty proud of my response. I could have called him every name under the sun but at the end of it all, that would have just made me feel worse and I'm largely healed now. I felt sad for how his life has turned out more than anything.

Would I say I've forgiven them? It's hard to say. I want to lean towards yes, but still a part of me says no. I think I've made peace with ninety-five per cent of it. I've forgiven myself, which is the most important thing. At the beginning, there was a lot of victim blaming. I had to forgive myself for not fighting back enough. That's what I had to work through in the therapy. Also, for a long time, I felt a lot of survivor's guilt, when I've heard about so many other boys and men who have taken their own lives. That was the main thing I thought about a lot. Why did I live while they didn't? It took me a while to really process that. Because when I was going through my adolescence, I didn't see myself living past sixteen. I had a very finite view of what my life would be like or who I could be. And then when I started recovery, I actually wanted to live because I saw the greatness of life and what I could potentially do with my life. It's really weird how that mindset changes.

So, have I forgiven them properly? You know, I will be really honest and say I can't answer that question fully. I would like to say yes, but there's still part of me that hesitates. As I said earlier, I've forgiven myself, which is the most important thing.

Freddie shows us that the long-term consequences of bullying can be profound. His story offers some cautious hope, though: that with a lot of support, it is possible to overcome even the most difficult adolescent chapters to live a rich and fulfilling adult life. We will return to this idea towards the end of this book. But for now, we are going to take a look at the other end of the spectrum. We have spent considerable time thinking about peers in groups and how difficult this can be. Now we're going to look at something that involves just two people – and how wonderful it can be.

5.   First love

My parents didn't take it very seriously, and that was so unhelpful. Now, as a parent, I intend to deal with it quite differently with my children. Because at that age, it is all-consuming. You're heartbroken when it falls apart. But you can't really share that at home because no one takes it seriously. So you have to hide how meaningful it is to you, because it's bit of a joke to other people or to grown-ups . . . but for you, it's horrendous.

Tess is talking to me about a romantic relationship she had in her teenage years, now more than thirty years ago. As is so often the case, its significance wasn't recognised at the time. Tess' parents dismissed it as something trivial, the kind of transient teenage affection referred to as 'puppy love'. Maybe that's not surprising: the relationship she is telling me about lasted only six months, and happened when she was just fourteen. But this is the thing about teenage love: it is far more important and consequential than most of us realise.

In a 2003 study, psychologists David Rubin and Dorthe Berntsen asked over 1,300 adults to recall when in their life they had felt various emotions most strongly, and one of the questions was about love: 'If you have at least one memory in which you feel much in love, how old are you in the memory when you feel most in love?'[1] The participants were aged between twenty and ninety-four. The researchers found that participants in their twenties tended to report being most in love right now, but for all other age groups, the peak was at age fifteen. In other words, teenage love is exceptionally powerful, and we shouldn't be surprised when it casts lifelong shadows. In adolescence, as we will see throughout this chapter, many people experience the most emotionally intense relationships of their lives.

Early adolescence romance

The green shoots of romance generally appear around the ages of eleven to thirteen. This is not true of all young adolescents, of course – as we saw with Vicky in Chapter 1, some of them are just not interested in these experiences yet; others will have romantic experiences curtailed by their parents, religion or wider culture. But on average, and restricting our view for now to heterosexual activity, a significant social reorientation takes place at this age that encourages the emergence of romantic activity.

At the end of primary school, children are friends almost exclusively with peers of the same gender; boys and girls view each other across the parapet with wariness or disinterest. But with the transition to secondary school and the sudden arrival of pubertal hormones, interests begin to shift, and boys and girls begin to fraternise with the enemy. Like new-born lambs learning how to walk, these initial excursions are stilted and clumsy. Typically, there will be much discussion about who fancies who, and not so much actual interacting. If anyone makes it as far as an official 'boyfriend and girlfriend' relationship, these can generally be counted in weeks or even days. Young adolescents may well kiss each other – there will probably be a lot of kissing in the peer group, in fact – but they probably won't have sex. This is partly because, practically, a young adolescent couple may never even reach the point of being alone together. Indeed, a couple this age can easily reach the point of being 'in a relationship', without ever having spoken to each other at all.

This is because initial romantic interactions don't just happen *around* peers, they happen *because of* peers. In the early years, peers act as romantic messengers, relaying information about who their friends fancy to one another. Who is going to 'date' and who is going to kiss is often decided by the wider peer group, rather than any individual pair. From a developmental point of view, this makes sense: as a fragile newbie in the world of dating, the involvement of your friends provides social support, and relying on your friends to convey messages to your love interest shields you from potential embarrassment at an especially vulnerable age.

If your friends are involved, you can also be confident that you have their approval. In fact, fitting in with a peer group and achieving social status may be the real reason for the relationship: according to psychologist B. Bradford Brown, romantic relationships in those early years 'become vehicles (or possibly obstacles) to achieving these objectives'.[2] Whether you are actually attracted to a partner or whether you are compatible with them is likely to be less important than how the relationship will affect your status among your peers. As Brown says: 'Dating the "wrong" person or conducting romantic relationships in the "wrong" way can seriously damage one's standing in the group. These concerns can easily overshadow one's interest in the relationship itself . . . Some individuals go so far as to feign romantic interest in someone simply to foster their own position in the peer group; they may maintain a relationship with this person if it serves their own status interests.'[3] In other words, relationships in these early years are more like performances, acted out for an audience of peers. Each friendship group will dictate the specific social norms to which a relationship must conform: the age at which it begins, when different sexual activities should occur, but also *who* you are allowed to engage in these activities with.

The perils of being attractive

In many ways, being conventionally attractive is advantageous for young adolescents – we've already seen it's a fast-track route to being popular. But in a world where heterosexual relationships have the power to change one's status among peers of one's own gender, being especially attractive can also be risky, particularly for girls. Lauren, now fifty-four, learned this lesson when she moved to a mixed boarding school in Year 10 (age 14–15), when her parents moved abroad. (Note that Lauren was a couple of years older than the adolescents described in the previous section, but norms vary from school to school.) At this new school, suddenly and rather unexpectedly, Lauren found that she was considered attractive by the boys.

I was a very conscientious, strait-laced girl. I found friendships quite awkward. I did have friends, I did have a really good group of friends I'd left in my home town who I'd kept in touch with. And I had that solid friendship group. But in that old school I'd been this kind of geeky, glasses-wearing, spotty girl. Then I moved to the new school, and suddenly I had long, blonde hair that had been bleached by the sun because I'd been visiting my parents in a hot country. I'd started wearing contact lenses, I'd matured a bit physically, and I suddenly was perceived totally differently, as this attractive girl.

And I was just blown away by it. I couldn't quite believe it. I was just thinking, 'Wow! This is a new thing for me. This is brilliant.' And the girls seem to really like me. I was getting interest from boys, and I kissed a couple of them. They weren't actual relationships. But suddenly, the fact that I had kissed more than one boy within the space of a few weeks, suddenly it just turned and I was 'a slag' and I was persona non grata and I was awful. I was 'putting it out there', even though I'd only ever kissed them. Suddenly I was just completely ostracised and I was absolutely floored by it. I just did not understand what was going on. I misread the rules of this new school and got it horribly wrong. And because it was a boarding school and because my parents were thousands of miles away, I had nowhere to escape to. I had nowhere to go.

At one point, the girls in Lauren's year made a book in which everyone's names were listed, and everyone was invited to write comments about each other – in fact, this exactly follows the plot of the 2003 film *Mean Girls*. Lauren knew about the book, but wasn't allowed to see it or contribute. When she did eventually see it, she tells me, the comments about her were 'vile'. She spent the next two terms barely speaking to anyone, and didn't tell her family what was going on. The teachers also didn't seem to notice anything was wrong, because she continued to work hard and do well academically. 'The cruelty and fickle nature of girls' friendships at that age still astounds me,' she tells me. 'It shaped me for a long time, desperately wanting to please and be liked, to avoid that loneliness and sense of rejection again.'

Adolescent girls who are deemed attractive must walk a tightrope: being conventionally pretty and associating with popular boys offers social kudos and popularity, but if they are *too* desirable, too pretty, they become a threat within a friendship group. (Being attractive may lead to similar difficulties for teenage boys, but there is surprisingly little research into this.) What is particularly interesting in Lauren's case is that the person leading the hostility against her was another new girl, who joined at the same time as her in Year 10. 'She was the one that really stuck the knife in and was just really horrible. And then she kind of got all the other girls to think, "Oh yeah, actually, you're awful,"' she tells me. In other words, two new girls joined an existing school, which already had its established peer groups, and both were trying to find their feet and social position. It seems likely that the other new girl found Lauren's attractiveness especially threatening because Lauren's acceptance into the peer group and elevation to a high status would leave the other girl even more vulnerable and isolated than she already was. Shaming Lauren and causing her to be ostracised would have been a way to prevent this – a classic instance of 'relational aggression', which is common among this age group.

Relationships in later adolescence

As adolescents move through the mid- and late teenage years, romantic relationships begin to change shape. Getting approval from your friends still matters, but less intensely, for various reasons. By this age, adolescents start to have a more stable sense of self, so they will be slightly less reliant on peer approval and will also have a better sense of who they are attracted to. Cliques that were precarious and volatile have started to settle into more established memberships. The likelihood of being ejected from one's group gets smaller and so the risks associated with dating more widely are reduced. In addition, most teenagers will have to make peace with not being in a high-status clique, and thus acknowledge that their partner will not be either – and so the pool of potentially acceptable dating partners begins to increase.

Relationships also become more genuine. They might now last several months or even years; couples will start to spend time alone together; sexual activity begins. There will be more vulnerability and intimacy between the two partners as impression management gives way to more honest self-disclosure: the more time you spend together, the harder it is to maintain pretences about who you are. These relationships involve deeper understanding, deeper vulnerability – and deeper resultant feelings. Features of adult romantic relationships begin to emerge: empathy, compromise, trust. In other words, around the mid-teens, teenagers truly start to fall in love.

Of course, their relationships continue to differ from adult relationships in all sorts of ways. Not only will they continue to live separately, the extent to which they can spend time together at all, and how much privacy they have when they do, will be constrained by outside factors – their parents, their school schedules, their religion. They will continue to have intense friendships outside of the partnership too, more so than adults do, and they will continue to rely on their parents for at least some of their practical and emotional needs. But that doesn't make these relationships any less real. If anything, unbridled by the responsibilities and practicalities of adult relationships, teenage relationships are free to be *more* intense. Teenage lovers can focus solely on their feelings for each other – and at a time when the body and brain are wired to care about this topic the most.

Naomi, now fifty, grew up in Northern Ireland in the 1980s. This would have been a very challenging environment in which to explore teenage romance: there was a strict religious expectation that there should be no sex before marriage, as well as the constant background threat and danger of the Troubles. In spite of this, Naomi met a boy from another school, Peter, and fell in love. She explained that among Catholics in Northern Ireland who had a holiday home, it was common for it to be in the South:

So we had a holiday home. Everyone came to my holiday home when I was eighteen and Peter was part of that group. And that's where I remember just having so much fun with him. I've never laughed as much in my life. He had a girlfriend, but I remember that after that trip, I could tell that he was moving away from her and wanted to spend time with me. And then he broke up with her, and he would send me poems, mixtapes . . . there was this thrill of seeing him, and him telling me he liked me – there was a big build-up to whether or not we were dating. Everything was very, very thoughtful. He was the absolute opposite of the sort of boy my dad wanted me to be with. He was a guitarist. He was cool. He was stunningly gorgeous. He was a complete poser, and not academic at all.

But I just found total joy in him. He was very creative and we would be in the bedroom together and he'd be playing on his guitar. We weren't even doing anything, having sex wasn't even really part of our thinking. I don't remember as much of the snogging as I remember the feeling of him really, really loving me one hundred per cent, really just enjoying me, enjoying everything that I was – and me loving him. And I felt such a sense of belonging to his family. His mom could cook. My mom never cooked. They weren't well off but they had such a friendly, warm home. And, you know, his dad would give me lifts to his house and we'd have these delicious meals. And on a Sunday night, him and I would just muck around like children. Wrestle, have fun. We had our own language. We had our own words for each other. It was just bliss. It was just unadulterated fun. One time, I was babysitting a little two-year-old, and Peter came to pick me up at midnight. The parents hadn't arrived home yet, so they came in just after he'd arrived, and we were laughing so hard that they thought I was drunk. They never had me back again. But I was just enjoying myself, because we were giddy around each other, you know?

Amid all the fear and drama of teenage relationships, this simple truth often gets lost: they can provide a rare opportunity for total relaxation and fun. And when they go well, they can be a critical way for teenagers to develop an understanding of themselves. The psychologist Erik Erikson, writing in 1968, summed up adolescent love as an 'attempt to arrive at the definition of one's identity by projecting one's diffused self-image on another and seeing it thus reflected and gradually clarified'.[4] When the relationship is a loving one, the result can be a bolstered sense of self-worth that lasts forever, as Naomi shows:

> I think that relationship set the tone for the fact that I don't need to be anyone other than myself. He really loved me. And I remember him saying that no matter what happened in life, you know, he still would love me. And just the other day, I got a message from a really good friend of mine in Belfast, and she said she was in a pub and he was playing music there. And she said to me, 'He's still as gorgeous as ever.' And absolutely none of my feelings have ever changed for anyone I've ever loved. If I've loved them, I still love them. He's still gorgeous and he's still lovely. Why would I stop? You know, I never grew out of loving him.

So, why didn't they stay together longer? Why aren't they together now? Despite the power of the relationship, and the love they felt for each other, Naomi chose to end the relationship after a year. She tells me how she knew, even then, that she would never marry him:

> He just wasn't aspirational. He hated all the things that I loved about learning. And I was always ambitious for myself. The sad demise of that relationship, the death knell, was when I went to London for the summer. I met someone else, a man who was ten years older than me, and I thought, 'Wow. This man is so intelligent. And he has a PhD. And this is amazing.' And you know, I came home and . . . It's so painful to think about but I told him that I've met this guy. I was quite honest with him. I explained that I still loved him, but I wanted to explore. And he said, 'You don't want me, Naomi, do you? You don't.' So he didn't allow me to come back to him again. But I wouldn't have gone back. It wasn't the sort of relationship that I felt I deserved intellectually.

As we will see, being on the receiving end of a break-up in adolescence – to be loved by someone and then to experience their feelings change – can be devastating with significant long-term effects, but Naomi's story serves as a reminder that those who instigate the break-up can also find it desperately sad and be affected by it for a long time. This was the case for Naomi when she met Peter again, many years later:

> A few years ago, I saw him with his girlfriend, on a night out in Belfast. I'm not going to say it was easy. Because when you don't live in a place geographically, you're stuck in time. His life has completely transformed. Whereas I go back and, to me, he's still the nickname, you know, that we used. I still have that memory. For me, I'm always stuck in time in those relationships. I always expect to be special to him. But I would never ask him. I think if you do invite that kind of conversation, it's really dangerous. Because if I found out that he doesn't even think about it . . . It would be really painful for me. I don't want to know. I want to have the story that makes sense to me, my meaning-making. And he might remember me as someone who was really mean to him. I don't know. I suppose I'll never really know.

When it comes to understanding the events of our adolescence, we often land on the story that makes most sense to us, the one that is easiest to bear. The way we make peace with what happened to us is not by repeatedly recounting mere facts, but by creating a logical, often comforting narrative around those facts. A story. This is so helpful to us that, as Naomi shows, any opportunity to update the story with new information or perspectives is seen as unwelcome. When it comes to remembering significant romantic relationships, the end story usually involves painting your first boyfriend or girlfriend as someone who, on some level, must still care about you now, all these years later. This is inevitably important for those who have their heart broken, as we shall soon see with Tess. But for those who initiate the break-up, like Naomi, this narrative can be just as important. No one wants to believe they are lodged in someone else's mind for painful reasons, that they are written in someone else's story as a heartbreaker. Part of the solution is believing they still care about you, but another part might be telling yourself that, in the long run, they are better off without you. This was the case for Naomi, when she later saw Peter with his new partner:

When I saw him with his girlfriend, I could see that he loved her. I could see that they had what we had. She was a lot like I was in that dynamic, you know? I could see why he loved her. And they went on to get married. I think with her, he probably found a lot of those elements that we had in our relationship. But with someone who loved him for who he was. Someone who didn't want him to change.

When dating is harder – or impossible

Although the end of Naomi's relationship was full of sadness and continues to be a bittersweet memory, the relationship also left her with a profound and lifelong sense of self-worth. By the same token, adolescents whose opportunity for such experiences is restricted in some way may suffer from this lack intensely, not only at the time but over the long term. Some teenagers have no desire to date, but others very much want romantic and sexual experiences and are unable to find a reciprocal partner. Instead, they are left to witness these relationships happen to their friends and peers from the sidelines. To be in such a position as a teenager can be a profoundly lonely experience: when a young person is aching to be understood, to be loved, to be touched, they are instead left to wonder what might be wrong with them, why they might not be desired the way everyone else seems to be.[5, 6] To make matters even harder, for some teenagers, their peers will tell them explicitly why they are deemed undateable: usually some aspect of their personality or appearance that is considered unattractive. Understandably, this can have profound effects on a person's self-worth and confidence in relationships many years into adulthood.

There is another group for whom adolescent romantic and sexual exploration is often more complex, and sometimes entirely impossible: those who are lesbian, gay, bisexual or who belong to other sexual minority groups. This is partly because, in order for these teenagers to establish, understand and express their sexual orientation, they must first take on a formidable challenge, what sociologist Mary Robertson describes as 'violating compulsory heteronormativity';[7]

heteronormativity being the assumption embedded in society that there are only two 'opposite' genders – men and women (or boys and girls) – and that 'normal' romantic and sexual relationships ought only to exist between these two opposing genders. In recent years, this has started to change – and landmark marriage legislation for gay and lesbian couples has played an important role. But the implicit assumption still pervades: that because heterosexual relationships are the majority, anything else is somehow deviant or not worthy of representation. This is the case despite the fact that almost seven per cent of sixteen- to twenty-four-year-olds in England and Wales identify as gay, lesbian, bisexual or another minority sexual orientation, equating to 436,000 young people – not exactly a small group.[8] The hope is that adolescents growing up today will better see themselves reflected in the world around them, but this certainly hasn't been the case in the past, and progress is slow. As Robertson says, 'Society is bombarded with heteronormative images' – in advertising, in children's books, in the media – 'all of which suggests to queer youth day in and day out that their sexual desires and behaviours are wrong'.[9] While representation has improved, it hasn't solved the problem. In the words of psychologists Daniel Alonzo and Deborah Buttitta, 'We cannot assume that all is easy in a culture simply because there is an increase in the number of lesbian, gay and bisexual characters on television.'[10]

It's obvious but it's worth reminding ourselves: heterosexual adolescents don't need to go through the process of realising that they are straight because they are generally assumed to be straight by default. Sexual minority adolescents, on the other hand, must realise that they are different to the majority, different to what is expected of them, and that their desires and identity deviate from this strong cultural expectation and script. For many, this sense of being different first emerges in childhood and then solidifies in adolescence, when changes in the brain and body mean that romantic and sexual attraction begin to take centre stage in a person's mind.

This challenge can be immense, because one of the places where heteronormativity is most pervasive is secondary school. Among teenage boys in particular, where homophobic slurs can be used routinely, in the most casual way, there is a considerable personal risk involved in openly exploring gay relationships, both in terms of social ostracism and also physical harm. It is sadly very well established in the literature that lesbian, gay and bisexual adolescents, along with adolescents who are questioning their sexual orientation, are more likely to be bullied than their heterosexual peers,[11] which in turn can increase the risk of mental health problems and reduce school attendance, all of which can have significant long-term consequences.

'Coming out'

For some, especially those of older generations than today's adolescents or those who live, say, in ultra-conversative countries, being able to express one's true sexual identity may never be possible. Even in liberal societies today, gay, lesbian and bisexual teenagers will often date within the group that they are expected to date, at least initially, for example because they are actively attempting to disguise their sexual orientation from their peers. In time, however, most adolescents will reach a point where the need to express their sexual orientation and share it with others outweighs the potential barriers and disincentives they face. This is the process of 'coming out' – which, importantly, is not a single event. Coming out is a slow process in which an individual first understands themselves, and then gradually discloses their sexual orientation to others, multiple times in many different contexts. As Alonzo and Buttitta have written, 'It must be emphasized that coming out is not one identifiable event in time . . . It is a complex, nonlinear, and never-ending process.'[12]

As society becomes more progressive, the concept of coming out is starting to shift. For starters, the hope is that in a less heteronormative society, there might be less need for such disclosures: if we were all more tolerant of the many variations of human sexuality, there might be less demand for anyone to announce that they deviate from the supposed default. But the notion of coming out is also shifting because there is better recognition that sexual orientation for some people can be fluid, and thus the idea of making a repeated singular statement about one's identity doesn't make sense.[13] But we are still in the beginning stages of this shift, and there is a long way to go. For now at least, there is generally still the need for young people to announce that their sexual orientation is something other than heterosexual.

When they do this, some adolescents are met with support and acceptance; it may even be that their sexual orientation does not come as a surprise to the person they confide in. (It is a familiar anecdote: a teenager plucks up a great deal of courage to come out to their mum, only to have her respond, 'Oh yes, we've known that for years.') But for others, the stakes are exceptionally high: they may be met with shame and humiliation; some are disowned by their families entirely or thrown out of their homes. Studies show that individuals carefully weigh up the potential costs and benefits in advance, often for many years.[14] And yet, coming out is often a vital part of a person's development and self-understanding. In the words of psychologists Daye Son and Kimberly Updegraff, 'regardless of its positive or negative familial implications, sexual identity disclosure to family itself serves as an important breakthrough in identity development during adolescence', because it facilitates 'identity integration' – i.e. multiple aspects of the self can be brought together, and known to others – as well as 'self-acceptance and self-empowerment'.[15]

Scott is a bisexual man, now twenty-seven, who grew up in the north-east of England. He went to a mixed comprehensive secondary school, a place where homophobia was rife and normalised: 'The impression that I got from those boys was that any sexual activity with boys or men was just inherently, you know, kind of disgusting. They acted like it was an innate, reflexive sort of thing [to be disgusted],' he tells me. But he knew, quietly, that he didn't feel the same way. He was attracted to boys, and wondered for some time if he might be gay – but knew that wasn't quite right either. What followed was a common experience for bisexual adolescents: a period of trying to understand what exactly their sexuality is, in the face of considerable stigma and a lack of helpful role models:

> I'd gone through a phase where I thought maybe I'm just in denial about what's going on and I'm just gay. And I did go through a phase

of telling people that. But then I realised that just wasn't true. It was like, what am I suppressing here? Is it homosexuality or heterosexuality? You know, because no one ever talks about this. It's not something that's really explored in any meaningful way in popular culture or anything. There is a common trope that, if you say you are a bisexual man, you must just be pretending to like women. It's taken me years to accept that that's not what's going on and that actually I just don't have a major preference in that regard. I like both.

Scott had early sexual experiences with boys from school, but at the age of seventeen, he was in a long-term relationship with a girl. She had heard rumours about his previous relationships with boys, and asked him if they were true. 'My instinct at the time was that it was just too much hassle to try and navigate the situation,' he tells me. 'So I thought, I'll just deny it. I'll just say no, it's just a rumour. It wasn't going to change anything. I didn't want to leave her. And I thought she just wouldn't understand anyway.'

He decided not to tell her, and the relationship ran its course over the next few months and came to an end for other reasons. But he realised that his instinct – his reluctance about telling her the truth – was well founded, when a year later, aged eighteen, he was in a relationship with another girl. This new girlfriend had recently lost a close friend who had been gay and who had died by suicide. (In part because of stigma and prejudice, lesbian, gay and bisexual teenagers, as well as those who are transgender or non-binary, are at a heightened risk of suicidal behaviour.[16]) After her friend's death, Scott's girlfriend was very vocal about supporting gay rights, 'about how tragic [it is] that the treatment of gay people is so bad and all the rest of it', Scott tells me. 'And I thought, "Well, she's going to get it. Maybe this is going to be low-risk." But that was not the outcome I got.' On the contrary, when Scott told his girlfriend he was bisexual, her response was deeply upsetting:

I still remember vividly the look on her face when I told her and it was just absolute disgust. A real revulsion at what I'd said. And then it was just about firing off questions about, you know, 'Have you ever acted on that? Who have you done it with? How many? How many people?' It was almost like I'd just told her, 'You might have AIDS,' or something, you know. And I remember thinking, 'This is horrible. This relationship isn't going to last.' I didn't act on that immediately, but we broke up soon after. Because you can't move on from that.

An attempt to tell his parents soon after was also unsuccessful. His mum, he said, didn't seem bothered by it, but his dad didn't respond well: 'I have a good relationship with my dad, but it just seemed like he didn't want to acknowledge it, didn't want to think about [bisexuality] in the context of his own son. I remember at the time thinking, "I'm going to withdraw all this pretty quickly again. Because there's no getting around this. It's not something people are ever going to understand."'

Several years down the line, when Scott was about to move in with a long-term girlfriend, he again felt a reluctant obligation to tell her about his bisexuality. It was five years after they had started dating, and he had never mentioned it:

> I thought, she's going to have to know, because if this is going to be another case of, 'It's repulsive and I don't want anything to do with you,' we're going to have to know that because we're about to make a big financial commitment. So I thought she needs to know about it – if she finds out about it later down the line, that's really not okay. But I had to get really, really drunk to tell her because I really didn't want it to go down the route that it had gone with the other people. I didn't want that to happen at all.

This time, his admission wasn't met with disgust, but instead with a new challenge:

> And she was really upset when I told her. Really, really upset about it. It wasn't the same kind of upset I'd had with other people – ignoring it or thinking I'm lying about it or thinking it's repulsive. It was purely that she was worried that she wasn't going to be enough, that somehow I would have to have both men and women in my life.

Which isn't true. I have no intention of leaving her. But she was worried about me leaving her in the future for a man.

Considering these experiences, it is perhaps unsurprising that now,
as an adult, Scott almost never says anything about his sexual orientation. He tells people 'on a strictly need-to-know basis', and to his
mind, the majority of people simply never need to know. He balks at
the idea of telling colleagues, of joining LGBTQ+ societies at work,
even of admitting his sexuality on anonymous demographic monitoring forms. He has never spoken to his parents about it again. Of
course, most people prefer not to talk about their sexual preferences
and activities at work or among family, but people often disclose
their sexuality in other ways – for example by referring to their partner by name. And most people have not experienced what Scott has
during his adolescence: every attempt he's ever made at disclosing
who he is has had a painful or humiliating outcome. His reasons for
keeping quiet about this aspect of himself are of a different order
altogether.

He's not alone: it is well established in the research that bisexual
people continue to face challenges in having their identity accepted
and recognised.[17, 18] They often feel as though they fall between the
gaps, and experience scepticism and mistrust from all camps. However, the situation may be improving. This was indicated by one 2020
study that assessed 1,491 participants aged eighteen to sixty who identified as either gay, lesbian or bisexual. They were from three different
birth cohorts – i.e. three different generations – and researchers asked
them the age they were when they experienced five so-called 'sexual
identity development milestones':[19] when they first experienced
attraction to someone of their own sex (note that 'sex' and not 'gender'
was the researchers' original wording); when they first realised they
were gay, lesbian or bisexual; when they first had sex with someone
of their own sex; when they first disclosed their sexual orientation to
a straight friend; and when they disclosed this to a family member.
The researchers found that there were considerable differences across
the cohorts. For example, the oldest group – the fifty-two- to fifty-
nine-year-olds – reported realising their sexual orientation at an

average age of nineteen. For the middle group (thirty-four- to forty-one-year-olds), the average age was sixteen, and for the youngest group (the eighteen- to twenty-five-year-olds), the average age was fourteen. Now that there is reduced stigma towards – and better awareness of – sexual minorities, and more open discussion online, for example, it may be that adolescents can more readily find the words they need to describe and understand themselves.

The other finding in this study is that gay, lesbian and bisexual individuals are coming out at younger ages. The older cohort first disclosed their identity to a family member at age twenty-six on average; for the middle group this happened at twenty-two, and for the youngest group in the study this happened at seventeen. In other words, the youngest cohort better understood themselves at a younger age, and felt able to share that identity with their family sooner. Perhaps most poignantly, in the youngest cohort, the first sexual experience with someone of the same gender and the first disclosure of identity to a straight friend happened almost simultaneously: they had an important sexual experience, and were immediately able to discuss it with their friends – an experience that most straight teenagers take entirely for granted. The older two cohorts, by contrast, reported waiting years until they could tell their friend. This captures well the painful predicament that many gay, lesbian, bisexual and other sexual minority adolescents still find themselves in – discovering a key part of their identity but having to keep it a secret. This study, at least, gives some hope that things might be changing for the better.

Finally, while it is true in general that gay, lesbian and bisexual adolescents are more vulnerable than their peers to bullying and discrimination, there is also, as sociologist Eleanor Formby has argued, 'the need for caution about overstating these "risks" and portraying (young) LGBT people as inherent "victims"'.[20] She goes on to say: 'presenting LGBT youth as inherently in need of protection continues to mark them out as fundamentally different from their heterosexual and/or cisgendered peers, which may not be helpful in the long term.'[21] In the end, as for any adolescent, it is being made to feel different, an outsider, abnormal, unaccepted by the wider group – however that may occur – that causes the lasting hurt.

Breaking up

Even the most beautiful, powerful relationships in adolescence almost always end. Indeed, the majority of these relationships are brief – one study found that seventy-four per cent of teenage couples last less than a year.[22] And for every adolescent, like Naomi, who initiates the separation, there is a Peter, her boyfriend, for whom the end may come suddenly, unexpectedly. The memory of such an experience can remain painful forever. Tess, whom we met at the start of this chapter, was in Year 9 (age 13–14) when she began to fancy Rob, one of the boys in her year group:

> He was friends with some of the boys in my tutor group. But I didn't know him very well. He was sort of on the edges of the circle. He wasn't very sociable. From what I remember, he was a bit mysterious, I think. I remember that he was known to have a temper. And it was quite common for people to be going out with someone for a few weeks and then they were going out with someone else, and I was part of that. But he never went out with anyone else. I think I quite liked that, that he wasn't quite part of things. I thought he was impressive for being a bit distant. That was part of the appeal, sadly.
>
> There'd been other people in that same school year that I'd kind of had relationships with, but this for me was completely different. I completely fell for him. We were really well known for being together and we spent a lot of time together. We spent all of that summer together, and I do remember kind of relaxing into it. I know that sounds strange, but I just became really comfortable with him. It's hard to say if it was love. I've thought about that a lot. I've been with my husband for twenty-five years now and you know, that's love. And I can't see many parallels between the two things. But it definitely felt like love at the time. It was literally all-consuming.

They were very close for six months – 'which felt like a lifetime at that age' – but around Christmas in Year 10, cracks began to appear. First, Rob started acting more distant around her, and then suddenly he ended things with her, leaving her 'just completely broken'. About ten days later, she tells me, he asked her to go out again, and she said yes. But two weeks after that, he dumped her again:

Then things really, really changed. Rumours went round that he'd said I was fat. Boys started sniggering when I went past. I can't remember how it ramped up from there . . . maybe we had an argument about it. I know he called me a fat bitch. And from then on, so did all his friends. From that point on, for two years – until he left the school – he did not speak to me or look at me, and almost all of his friends did the same – except to call me the Fat Bitch. And it was a large group of people.

I still have no idea why he changed so suddenly. There were loads of theories at the time. I think going out with me probably brought him into the fold a bit, and so he became a bit more accessible to other girls and therefore they were also accessible to him. So there were probably other people he fancied and you know, he was now somebody who people might pick. So I think he needed to break from me. One of his friends remained relatively polite to me – and genuinely that was rare because almost none of them would even acknowledge my existence – but on a couple of occasions we spoke about the situation and his view was, you know, 'He really likes you, but he has to hide that.' Lots of people said that – that there's no real reason why he would go out of his way to be so evil if there wasn't still some emotional attachment there.

The ripples were huge. I naturally have a short temper and that became super-charged. I spent all day every day expecting, waiting for, looking for an attack. And I started to believe what I heard about myself. I could have been fitter but I was never overweight. But I bought clothes too big for me. I felt disgusting. I couldn't see myself clearly in a mirror, I saw myself as much larger than I was. I was treated as if I was gross. I was laughed at, called names. And maybe what was even worse was when I was treated as if I didn't exist. It made me believe I was repulsive. I know that's a strong word – I've just surprised myself a bit by saying that, where did that come from? – but that was literally how they made me feel.

There are a number of reasons why being dumped as an adolescent can be far more painful than it is as an adult. Obviously, when a long-term marriage ends, it can be utterly devastating. But as an adolescent, one's relationship takes place very much in public and with the involvement of peers, and that makes it uniquely hard. As often happens in teenage relationships, Tess had to continue going to school with her ex-boyfriend every day. Even adults who have children together generally don't have to see each other every day, unless they happen to work together. In adolescence, if your ex-boyfriend or girlfriend goes to the same school, you are trapped. Even if they don't, you are likely to have a shared peer group. There are none of the opportunities for privacy available to an adult, and the opportunity for and likelihood of cruelty and social ostracism by those peers is far higher. What Tess experienced was a vicious and explicit form of bullying that is simply far less likely to occur among adults in the aftermath of a break-up.

And of course, as an adolescent, such cruelty is far more likely to have a long-lasting impact. Comments about your appearance get written into your bones as a teenager, even when they aren't made by people that you love. This is the first time you really become aware of your appearance, the first time you recognise that other people can evaluate your attractiveness, and the first time such evaluation affects how much value you give yourself. In adolescence we form the bedrock of how we feel about ourselves, so even if people are kind about us later on, their comments can only be laid lightly over deep-rooted, entrenched foundations. For Tess, it wasn't just one person slinging a one-off insult: it was a whole group of peers, saying the same thing over and over again, and that group included the person she loved. As with so many other people, it doesn't matter how much validation she has received subsequently, or how much her later partners have tried to support her – her lasting feeling is that those teenagers were telling the truth, and she carries their evaluation of her to this day:

This feeling, that image of myself as overweight and gross, has stayed with me. The long-term relationship I'm in now, thirty years later, is still impacted by this internalised view of myself. My husband and I have a mainly happy life together – we have our children, objective successes in life, and a greater understanding of each other, all of that . . . but despite all that, I still feel – not *think*, but *feel* – that he would want to cuddle me if only I was 'more attractive'. I still feel crucifying shame if I am ever rejected, like part of me is stuck as a teenager.

What is so interesting about these feelings, which continue to affect Tess, is that they endure despite her story's unusual finale. Ten years after her GCSE year group had finished their exams, left school and gone their separate ways, Tess was invited by the school to a reunion. By that time, Tess was twenty-five. She had been working as a teacher for several years and was in a relationship with the man who would become her husband. She was at a point in her life, she tells me, where she felt more confident. When the invitation arrived, she thought immediately about whether Rob would be there – and in fact, hoped that he would be there. Because, she realised, she wanted to see him:

The thing is, I still really liked him. On some level there was still a part of me that just wanted to see him and wanted to find out if he would talk to me. Because although he was evil to begin with when we first broke up, over time, the evil was other people. They were the ones doing the direct, explicitly nasty way of talking to me. He just literally blanked me. Absolutely like I didn't exist. Wouldn't look at me. So I was kind of thinking to myself, 'Could he sustain that?'

The reunion was held at the school, and Tess remembers having butterflies on the way there. The main event was in one of the dining halls, and as she was standing around one of the tables with a few other people, she realised that Rob was nearby. She had anticipated the possibility of being in the same room as him, she tells me, but not necessarily that they would 'actually communicate'. What happened next was far more than she had hoped:

I remember he looked at me and sort of smiled, openly, and I remember thinking, 'Oh my God.' I was almost vibrating with nerves. And then he just turned to talk to me, as if it was perfectly normal. I nearly fell over. And then when we were not being heard by other people, he said to me, 'I really hoped I would see you. I really wanted to apologise.'

I really appreciated the apology. That can't have been easy for him to do. And it made me realise . . . it obviously meant something to him as well, what he had done. For it to have been retained for that length of time and to make the effort to raise it. Because I wouldn't have raised it. I'm sure I wouldn't have. I am not a shrinking violet, but if he'd just spoken to me normally like nothing ever happened, I probably would have gone along with that. That would have been enough. But him to apologise, that was just . . . wow.

For the rest of the night Tess and Rob didn't leave each other's sides. This meant they were still with each other once the party moved on to a nearby pub, by which point everyone had been drinking for hours. And they were still with each other as the night started to wrap up, when Tess told Rob that a friend's partner was coming to pick them up and drop her home. But Rob didn't want her to go. As everyone hugged goodbye, Rob 'hugged me for longer than probably was necessary', she says, and instead of kissing her on the cheek, he leaned in to kiss her on the lips. 'I remember him saying, "Don't go, don't go with them, come back to mine."' But her lift had arrived by then: her friends were leaving, and she went with them. Which, on reflection, was the right decision, she tells me:

And you know, if I hadn't been picked up . . . if I hadn't been ushered away by people who knew . . . I probably would have gone home with him. And it's a good thing I didn't, because I was with my partner, who I'm still with. But it wasn't my adult self who was responding to what was going on. That was me at fifteen. Absolutely.

I think the reunion brought Rob and I to an end, it brought that story to an end. It made me realise it was equally meaningful to him, probably. And it made me realise that, by the look of it, he still fancied me. There was closure in that respect. But it hasn't been a solution to my need to be validated. My focus on my appearance. It doesn't take away the two years of perceiving myself as repulsive and all the consequences of that. I still have a lot of vulnerability about my appearance, about being desired, needing to be validated for how I look. It really matters to me. And I say that and it's utterly ridiculous because I don't think like that, but clearly I *feel* like that. I really think that's two different things. Cognitively, I appreciate it's a nonsense, but emotionally there's a need in me . . . There's lots of shame associated with it all. And it's just so powerful.

Why adolescents break up

Without the trappings of a marriage or a mortgage or children, teenagers are freer than adults to press the eject button when a relationship isn't working for them. This is surely a good thing, given the experimental and exploratory nature of teenage romance, but it does result in a lot of heartbreak and lasting pain. Quite why Rob broke up with Tess and why he behaved as he did in the aftermath remains a mystery to her, but the reasons why adolescents in general tend to initiate break-ups has been well studied. This research shows, once again, that what may appear to be fickle or selfish behaviour is in fact a lot more complex than it seems. For people like Tess, understanding why they might have been rejected – and why it was not their fault – is often a crucial step towards making peace with their past.

In 2017, researcher Valeyira Bravo and colleagues asked 268 fifteen- to seventeen-year-olds who had experienced a relationship break-up in the past year to complete a questionnaire about why they felt the relationship had ended.[23] The reasons given tended to fall into one of five categories. First was what the researchers termed *romantic affiliation* – one or other of the partners was no longer in love or had lost interest in the relationship because the romantic attraction was no longer there. Second was *intimacy* – for example, people felt their partner wasn't communicating well, wasn't putting in enough effort, or was being dishonest. Sometimes, this dishonesty was more explicitly problematic: the third reason given for a break-up was *infidelity*.

Fourth, some participants gave explanations relating to *autonomy*: they felt their boyfriend/girlfriend expected too much commitment from them, or prevented them from spending time with their friends or on other activities. Finally, and perhaps most relevant of all to adolescence: some participants broke up with their partners for reasons of *status* – they felt their partner was not part of the right crowd, and that this was affecting their own popularity. This last one perhaps holds a clue to understanding what happened to Tess. When she and Rob started going out, there was a significant shift in Rob's social status – a shift that, ironically, she herself brought about.

In other words, adolescents end things when they feel the relationship is hindering or blocking certain fundamental needs. Yes, adolescents have a powerful need for romantic and sexual experiences, which drives them *towards* relationships, but this happens in parallel with everything else we know is happening at this time, particularly the need to be independent and explore one's identity, and to fit in and have fun with peers. A relationship represents an opportunity for all these things – novel experience, personal affirmation, social status, fun – but if it then traps them into a commitment it can quickly end up becoming precisely the opposite. In the words of psychologists Jennifer Connolly and Caroline McIsaac, 'the relationship problems that lead to a dissolution are the mirror image of the attributes that initially attract adolescents to a romantic relationship'.[24]

As we have seen many times, adolescents know their own minds and often actively shape the social world around them to fulfil their needs and seek out the experiences they want, far more than adults tend to do: they leave friendship groups, eject others from their own group, and seek out like-minded peers. They may be plagued by doubts and insecurities but they can also be hungry, ambitious and bold. It should be no surprise that they are also proactive in ending romantic relationships that no longer serve them – and that they might feel a strong sense of liberation or relief as a result. Unfortunately, though, there is always the other partner in the relationship, who may still be very much in love. Adolescent identity is fragile, and at this age we rely heavily on others' treatment and perception of us to build our self-worth. To lose a teenage relationship when you don't want it to end can be devastating and can have a profound impact on someone's sense of self for decades, and possibly forever.

Is it worth it?

There is an argument that adolescence is simpler and ultimately happier for those who don't fall in love at that age. Plenty of research shows that adolescent relationships can involve extreme feelings of anxiety, anger, jealousy and longing.[25] This is true for adult relationships as well, but the concern of some academics, and indeed parents, is that adolescents don't yet have the cognitive and emotional capacity to cope with these challenges without there being a great deal of distress and pain. According to this view, you're probably better off not falling in love as a teenager.

Teenagers who don't have relationships are certainly not odd or dysfunctional in any way. In a 2019 study carried out in the US, public health researchers Brooke Douglas and Pamela Orpinas assessed nearly 600 fifteen- to sixteen-year-olds and categorised them into one of four groups depending on how many relationships they had had.[26] The researchers found that the group of students with the least dating experience were rated by their teachers – independently – as having the best social skills, the best leadership skills and the fewest signs of depression. The group who dated most frequently, by contrast, fared worse than the least-dated group on all three measures. Participants also completed their own questionnaire about any depressive symptoms they might be experiencing, and the same result was found: those with minimal dating experience had the fewest number of symptoms; those with the most dating experience reported the highest. Of course, this study doesn't tell us that the dating was the cause of their depression; it might have been that teenagers who are particularly prone to depression are more drawn to dating, relative to their less-depressed peers. But the study does at least provide evidence that teenagers who don't date are certainly not social misfits. In the authors' words, 'our results refute the notion

that non-daters lack general social competence or are socially isolated, at least within this age group'.[27]

So should adolescents be discouraged from dating? Not necessarily. Romantic relationships can offer a teenager the opportunity to
discover and explore their nascent identity, to explore that with
someone who cares for them, who finds them attractive, and to have
that identity encouraged and validated. Stop a teenager from dating
and you reduce the heartache, but you also prevent a potentially life-
enriching and profoundly affirming experience. Even an adolescent
relationship that goes wrong or ends painfully can teach important
lessons – maybe even more than ones that run smoothly. For starters,
they teach the valuable lesson that all experiences, even the wonderful ones, have to end. Bad relationships can also teach us what we
don't want – the things we aren't willing to tolerate in a partner – as
well as the things that we really care about. They can teach us how
not to behave with future partners. Good or bad, romantic relationships can teach us, ultimately, how to better understand, respect and
love *ourselves* – and there are few more important outcomes from
adolescence than that.

We are going to return now to the topic that I sidelined at the start
of this chapter, the topic that is deeply intertwined with adolescent
romance and yet, just as in adulthood, can exist very separately from
it. It is the teenage behaviour that arguably causes the most problems
for teachers, lawmakers and health campaigners, and the behaviour
that makes even progressive parents want to bury their heads in the
sand. It is, in some respects, the most dangerous thing a teenager can
do, while simultaneously something that many teenagers do, all the
time, with no bad consequences at all. Dare I say it: it might even be
a source of pleasure. It's time to talk about adolescent sex.

6.   Sex education

I didn't like him at all. He was texting me and stuff after it happened
and I just never texted him back ever again. Because I felt so ashamed.
Like, 'What the hell have I done?' I knew straight away that it was just
a very bad idea. Why would I do that? It was stupid. I still can't say his
name out loud even now, and the thought of that night gives me the
shivers.

Keira, now thirty-four, is telling me about the first time she had sex.
She was fourteen, in Year 9 at a mixed comprehensive school in
Leicester ('Not a great school,' she tells me). Keira's best friend had a
nineteen-year-old boyfriend, and one night, Keira met one of his
friends, who was also nineteen. They were all sitting in a caravan that
was parked up in the boyfriend's back garden, hanging out and smoking weed. 'I guess I must have given the friend my number, and he
somehow ended up being my boyfriend, even though I didn't like
him at all. I'd never had those feelings [of attraction] before so didn't
know how it should feel,' she tells me.

After the night they first met, Kiera and her 'boyfriend' texted
each other for several weeks. He must have come to her house at one
point, she recalls, because her mum caught them kissing. Her mum
was concerned about how old he was, but for Keira herself, his age
wasn't particularly relevant to the story. In fact, she tells me, the
reason she ended up having sex with him had very little to do with
him at all:

After a few weeks I started putting pressure on myself to have sex
with this guy, even though I still didn't have any feelings for him.
Then, on a school night, I snuck out of my house and jumped over
the fence in my back garden. I remember not going out the front
because the driveway was pebbled and noisy. I walked miles to his

house and without saying much took off all my clothes and had sex with him. As you can imagine, it was painful and unpleasant. Afterwards, he called me a taxi and I went home, and I never saw or spoke to him again. I literally never spoke to this guy again. I ended up having my first good sexual experience at the age of sixteen, with someone I really liked, and it made me wish I had waited. I can't understand why I put so much pressure on myself to do something that I didn't even want to do.

This man was breaking the law, because Keira was underage when they had sex. The most common age of first sexual intercourse for heterosexual people in the UK is sixteen, but Keira's experience is far from unusual: around twenty-six per cent of women (and thirty per cent of men) have had penetrative sex before their sixteenth birthday.[1, 2] However, women are much more likely than men to report that they feel they were too young when they first had sex, and Keira is certainly not alone in regretting her first experience.[3] The evidence indicates that the younger a person is when they first have sex, the more likely they are to regret it; one study found that seventy per cent of women who had sex before the age of sixteen said they wished it had happened when they were older.[4] Plenty of research has shown that girls who first have sex with older boys or men, as Keira did, are particularly likely to have bad experiences: they are less likely to use contraception, and more likely to say they regretted the experience or felt pressured to do it.[5] For some girls, their first experience of sex is one of assault (and some boys too, although this is much more common for girls). What is somewhat unusual in Keira's case is that she wasn't pressured into having sex by her partner – the pressure came from herself, something that evidently still confuses her to this day. Why did she put this pressure on herself?

When I talk to Keira about her teenage years more generally, her behaviour that night starts to make more sense. For women especially, having sex involves risk, even more so when you're young and when it's with a new and relatively unknown partner. There is the risk of unwanted pregnancy or sexually transmitted infections, the risk of violence and coercion, and the social risk of being shamed or judged by family or peers. This is the key aspect of teenage sex that explains how it is viewed and dealt with by society – as something dangerous that should ideally be prevented – but it is also fundamental to understanding why teenagers do it anyway. Keira was, in general, a risk-taking teen. She tells me she was 'just particularly naughty', and I ask her to expand on what she means:

> I'm someone who doesn't like to stand out. I was probably trying to fit in a lot at the time. And I think I have a slightly rebellious nature. So yeah, my secondary school years were interesting. I was quite badly behaved, getting in trouble, but trying my best to hide it from teachers and parents. At school it would be just the typical stuff like not listening to teachers, not doing my uniform in the way they wanted me to, just in general being . . . not agreeable. And in with the wrong crowd. We started drinking very young. My friends were arrested for shoplifting. And I think my parents were very shocked by it. They kind of thought I was completely going off the rails. But it was reasonably normal amongst my friends.

On the face of it this is a classic description of adolescent risk-taking – a young teenager testing the boundaries, rebelling against rules, breaking the law. But it's the first thing that Keira says that gets to the heart of why she snuck out of her house that night to have sex: she wanted to fit in with her friends. We already know that teenagers are influenced by their friends to take risks, and that taking risks offers them social status and helps them fit in. It's no surprise, then, that having sex – the ultimate pseudomature behaviour – should fit squarely into this category of behaviours. It certainly did for Keira:

> I didn't really feel like I fitted in. But then I had my friends who I really liked and got on with, so I think being naughty and stuff bonded us together a bit. And I was probably looking for something, some kind of escape. Escape from feelings of not fitting in. I probably had some level of social anxiety, but then that was also coupled with being a person who liked being naughty and taking risks. And I think maybe that's quite a dangerous combination. It means you'll do

anything. In the early years it was smoking, then as we got older, it was drugs and alcohol. And then it was sex. By Year 9, when I was fourteen, a few of my friends were already having sex regularly, so it felt like the norm.

I also think having attention from boys was seen as . . . like some kind of validation thing. So my friends who had boyfriends or who were having sex, they seemed like they had some kind of elevated level of cool. Like, 'Ooh, boys like you.' So I think I was going for that really, wanting boys to like me too. But I was never pressured by [my friends]. It was definitely coming from me. It was me looking at other people and seeing what they were doing and wanting to do what they were doing.

In many ways, this single story is a culmination of everything we have learned so far about adolescence. The specific act of sex happens between two people but is embedded in a social context. What friends and peers are doing matters. It is well established in the literature that when an adolescent's peers are sexually active, that adolescent is more likely to have positive attitudes towards sex, to have their first experience of sex at an earlier age, to have more sexual activity in general, and to have a higher number of sexual partners.[6] Add to this what we have already seen about romantic and sexual desirability being a key indicator of social status, just as Keira said, and sex emerges as a key means for validating a nascent identity. Teenage sex, in other words, often isn't really about the sex itself.

Yet at other times, the cliché of the horny teenager is true: many teenagers have sex simply because it feels good, and it's a way of exploring and satisfying intense emerging feelings of desire. Most university ethics boards are reluctant for researchers to ask anyone under the age of sixteen about these feelings, but there has been some exploration via retrospective studies, where older teenagers and adults are asked to recall the experiences they had when they were younger. This research has shown that it is fairly common for even young adolescents to report experiences of sexual desire: i.e. to think about sex, to be attracted to other people, and to recognise that other people are attracted to them.[7] For example, one study found that, in a sample of eighteen-year-olds, 26.8 per cent of boys and 22.5 per cent of girls recalled thinking about sex regularly when they were eleven to twelve years old.[8] It is also common for adolescents to masturbate, as a means of exploring their developing interest in sexual pleasure. One study surveyed over 2,100 fourteen- to seventeen-year-olds in the US and found that, by age seventeen, eighty per cent of boys and fifty-eight per cent of girls report that they have masturbated (with boys reporting doing so more frequently).[9]

It is no surprise, then, that when relationships with peers begin to deepen and mature, this sexual interest starts to drive actual sexual behaviour. One study asked sexually-active fifteen- to twenty-one-year-olds to document each time they had sex over a one-week period and their primary reason for doing so, and in the majority of instances (seventy-one per cent), participants reported that their main motivation involved desire or intimacy – for example that they wanted to express being in love, or simply wanted the physical experience of sex.[10] This was the top reason given for both men and women. Other reasons given by participants included wanting to distract themselves or improve their mood, which are also arguably about the physical pleasure of sex. The simple fact of sexual desire, along with the potential social benefits, is key to understanding why adolescents continue to engage in this behaviour, sometimes recklessly. Even when – as we will see – they are repeatedly encouraged not to.

Why teenagers don't use contraception

Emma, now twenty-four, grew up in north-west England, where she went to a mixed state school and lived at home with her mum and younger brother. She spent a lot of time unsupervised, partly because her brother took part in competitive athletics, which meant their mum travelled with him to a lot of competitions across the country. By her own admission, she was badly behaved, and tended to do what she wanted, especially when her mum and brother were away. When she was thirteen, Emma started talking to a boy in her school, Luke, who was two years older than her:

He used to be in the class next to me during geography lessons. He would continually stare at me prior to going into lessons, and then he ended up messaging me on Facebook asking why it was always me that would stare at him. From there, we started talking all the time via text message. At first, we would never see each other and we would just text. He would disappear for a few days and then appear again, both in school and via text. It was more about when it was convenient on his behalf to speak to me. Then one day he asked me to come to his house, and we started seeing each other in person. He wasn't my boy-friend. We'd see each other all the time, but from his perspective it was, 'You're not my girlfriend, but I want all the added extras of you being my girlfriend.'

One of those extras was sex. Emma first had sex with Luke on her fourteenth birthday, and continued to see him sporadically after that. Five months later, in the January of Year 10, her friends started to notice that something was upsetting her. She tried telling them it was nothing: 'I think I knew before then, but I didn't want to entertain the idea. I don't think I wanted to tell my mum about it.' But her friends pushed the issue, and one of them offered to go to the doctor with her. By the time Emma had the appointment, she was five and a half months pregnant.

The nurse at the surgery was like, 'You need to speak to whoever you live with at home,' and I said, 'Yeah, yeah, I will,' but I had literally no intention of telling anyone. I just walked home and cried. But my friend spoke to the school the next day and obviously for safeguard-ing reasons, they had to report it. I was angry at my friend then, but actually I think it made it easier, for me at least. But not for my mum. I was taken into the office at school and they basically just point-blank asked me if I was pregnant, and I just broke down into tears. And then I remember they rang my mum, like, 'You need to come to school ASAP.'

She came to the school straight away and she was just . . . bouncing. I don't know whether she was so angry she was upset or so upset she was angry. She just kept saying, 'Why haven't you told me? Why have I heard it from someone else first?' And she was angry about me being pregnant as well, of course. I think it was just everything. It was sort of, 'How on earth has this kind of situation happened?' It wasn't her fault though. People are very fast to blame parents in this situation. But my mum had no idea what I was up to. She didn't. I didn't really ever bring trouble to the front door. So it was never as though my mum thought, 'Oh, she's up to that, she's up to that.' She didn't know.

By the time Emma went to the doctor, it was too late to consider an abortion. After an initial decision to have the baby adopted, she decided against this, and gave birth to her son towards the end of Year 10. Because she was young for her year group, she was still fourteen.

There is good reason why parents and policymakers are concerned about teenage pregnancies. To start, teenage mothers have increased risk of medical complications, including pre-eclampsia and anaemia in the mother, lower birth weight, infection and growth restriction in the baby, and preterm labour.[11] This is not about the biology of being a young mother per se: there is evidence that, provided there is good-quality, accessible healthcare (including adequate follow-up appointments), pregnant teenagers do not have worse medical outcomes than older pregnant women.[12] It's more that there are specific factors that increase a teenager's odds of becoming pregnant – for example, lower socioeconomic status, living in a deprived urban area, being an ethnic minority, having mental health problems – and it is these factors that affect the medical, material or social support a young mother will receive, thus increasing risk of bad outcomes from the pregnancy.[13, 14] But what is perhaps at the forefront of adults' worries are the social outcomes: relative to older mothers, teenage mothers are often heavily stigmatised, and they are also likely to go on to have poorer academic attainment, complete fewer years of education, be unemployed or have a low-paid job.[15, 16] Again, there is some difficulty with teasing apart how much the pregnancy itself leads to these outcomes, relative to pre-existing vulnerabilities or characteristics of young mothers – but it is inevitable that the massive physical, emotional and practical upheaval of having a baby will at least disrupt an adolescent's plans to set themselves up for adulthood.

Considering the stress and life-changing consequences of a pregnancy at this age, the question is why teenagers like Emma and Luke don't use contraception. When it comes to reluctance to take the contraceptive pill or have an intra-uterine device implanted, research has found that adolescents (fourteen- to nineteen-year-olds) express concerns about side-effects such as weight gain and irregular bleeding, mistrust the methods' effectiveness, have difficulties accessing the necessary medical appointments, or worry about their family finding out.[17] There is also some suggestion that, when adolescents take the pill, they are more likely to forget to take one every day, which reduces its effectiveness.[18] But the majority of the research exploring why adolescents use contraception – or rather, why they don't – focuses on condoms. Clearly, easy access to condoms is a prerequisite for their use – if they are hard to get hold of or expensive, then we shouldn't be surprised they don't get used. But access isn't the whole story. We know that many teenagers who have a condom in the drawer right next to them or in their wallet still have unprotected sex. What explains this?

I ask Emma why she and Luke didn't use contraception:

> I think there's a lot of stigma attached to young teenagers being on contraception. It makes them feel embarrassed to go to a clinic. I still wouldn't like going to a shop now and buying condoms! I'd feel really embarrassed, so I can't imagine what a young teenager would feel like. And having the conversation with parents is hard as well. Some people just don't have the relationship with their parents where they can go and say, 'Oh, I think I need to go on contraception.' And the morning-after pill too, there's a lot of stigma around that. I think that's why especially young girls don't want to go and get it. A lot of the time it's a male pharmacist. I wouldn't feel comfortable even now going to a male pharmacist and saying I need the morning-after pill.
>
> And in the moment . . . I just didn't want to ask him [about using a condom]. And I also think sometimes boys don't want to ask that

question either, they just think, 'Oh, it'll be fine,' and just assume that girls are on contraception. And if neither partner wants to ask, then the conversation just doesn't happen. And some people think, 'Oh, it's the first time, nothing will happen.' I mean, I thought that too. That was probably the scariest part.

It is important to remember that having unprotected sex is not an exclusively adolescent behaviour. Adults do it all the time, knowing the risks involved full well. Just like teenagers, adults often have sex when they're drunk, when risks seem more distant and less real (psychologists refer to this as 'alcohol myopia'). Research shows that drinking is especially likely to lead to unprotected sex among individuals who are already ambivalent about using condoms, which may be one of the least surprising results of a psychological study.[19] But even sober, many people (of all ages) choose not to use condoms. So what is crucial to understand is that ambivalence.

The fact is that sex with a condom is different from sex without one, and plenty of people prefer it without. When people (of any age) are asked to articulate why they don't like condoms, their justifications generally fall into three camps: condoms reduce the physical pleasurable sensation of sex, they reduce the sense of intimacy or emotional connection, and they 'kill the mood', disrupting what participants say should be a spontaneous, smooth trajectory towards penetrative sex.[20] So even in the cold light of day, many people aren't keen – and decisions about condoms are made in the heat of the moment, when the psychological and physiological fog of sexual arousal clouds people's thinking and amplifies their goal of sexual pleasure.[21] In the moment, this state of arousal can easily override any distant concerns about risk. On top of this, condoms are a sensible safety precaution, so to suggest wearing one not only cuts directly against the prevailing mood – like halting an action sequence in a film to insist that the protagonist don the appropriate safety equipment before saving the world – but also means they are simply uncool. As we already know, the idea of safety behaviours (such as wearing a cycling helmet or using kneepads when skateboarding) can be mortifying for teenagers, who get social kudos for taking risks and disregarding sensible advice from adults. All these factors conspire together to make condom use, for some teenagers, a very unappealing prospect.

Yet teenagers today are bombarded with the message that they should use condoms, and many of them are justifiably worried about the risks of not doing so. Thus what often takes place just before the deed is a process psychologists call 'condom negotiation': a discussion about whether or not to use a condom during sex.[22] It involves both verbal and non-verbal communication – it is a 'set of behaviours, not a singular act'. Research has shown that, when an adolescent (or adult) wants their partner to use a condom, they engage in at least one of a multitude of negotiation strategies. They might try *emotional coercion* (e.g. saying they will be angry or upset if their partner doesn't comply); *presenting risk information* (e.g. reminding their partner about the risk of pregnancy or STIs); *deception* (such as citing pregnancy prevention concerns when the primary concern is STI prevention); *seduction* (using sexual arousal to encourage condom use); *promising rewards* if a partner complies; and *withholding sex* if they don't.[23] As you might imagine, employing any of these as a teenager, especially in the face of a reluctant partner, will require considerable levels of self-confidence and assertion.

Even more so because there are just as many negotiation strategies to *avoid* condom use. To push back against a request to use condoms, some adolescents (usually boys) may attempt to *reduce the perceived risk* (e.g. by telling the partner they have been recently tested and don't have an STI), which may or may not involve lying. They might use *seduction* (this time to distract their partner from the negotiation); draw on arguments relating to the *quality of the relationship* ('Don't you trust me?'); cite a *lack of physical sensation* when using a condom, or *withhold sex* altogether. Note here that some adolescents (usually girls) will threaten to withhold sex if the couple *doesn't* use protection; others (usually boys) will withhold sex if they are asked to use protection. In the worst-case scenarios, some teenagers – almost always boys – will use *threats and physical force* to resolve the negotiation, forcing their partner to have unprotected sex.[24]

In other words, the apparent simplicity of the instruction 'use a condom' belies an often very complex social interaction. To quote psychologist Lynne Hillier and colleagues, condom promotion strategies aimed at young people are 'based on an assumption of rational decision-making in sexual encounters and obscure the non-rational nature of arousal and desire, and the unequal power relations that exist between young men and women engaging in sex'.[25] In short, we should probably be more surprised that so many adolescents *do* use condoms rather than surprised that so many do not. Unfortunately for this age group, the costs are so much higher than they are for adults.

Which brings us back to Emma. Unsurprisingly, becoming a mother when she was fourteen had a significant impact on her school work and social life. She tells me that before becoming pregnant, she had opted to take some of her GCSEs a year early – something offered to her because she was in the top sets for Maths and English. But this meant revising during a prolonged hospital stay with a new baby, because her son was unwell when he was first born. Her routine in the early weeks, she tells me, was 'sleeping in a hospital bed, getting up, revising, going to school, going back to the hospital'. She tells me about the challenges with her friends too, and the clash between her new-found adult responsibilities and her friends' adolescent priorities:

> When he was born, it was all glorified [by my friends]. It was all great at the start when he was born. And then later it was like, 'We're going out,' and I would have to say, 'Well, I can't come.' And they'd say, 'We're going out' again and I'd say, 'I can't come' again. And I'd understand that I couldn't do everything they could do. I did get it. And I think if it was the other way round, I don't think I'd stop what I was doing just because someone couldn't come. I get that. But I didn't get that at the time. I was like, 'Why don't my friends want to see me?' But I do understand now. They were children themselves.

This fits with what we know so far about teenage motherhood: it's a lonely path, and it makes everything from succeeding at school to fitting in with friends much harder, constraining a young person's future prospects. For Emma, however, the story turned out very differently. At one point in our interview, I ask about her son now. She is twenty-four, so I know he will be around ten years old, on the cusp of adolescence himself. I am utterly unprepared for her reply: she tells me that her son died when he was ten months old. He had a genetic disorder, passed down through her side of the family; the same disorder that led him to have a prolonged stay in hospital when he was first born. Not only did she navigate the exceptional challenge of having a baby as a teenager – she navigated the exceptional challenge of losing him, too.

Emma tells me that, soon after her son died, she was offered specialist counselling designed to support parents who have lost a baby, but because she was so young a lot of the guidance and advice didn't apply to her. She felt like she fell through the cracks and wasn't listened to, so she stopped attending the sessions and was left to cope on her own. The initial aftermath was incredibly difficult:

> I just wanted to keep my head down [at school]. Because I was still dealing with everything. I was kind of like, 'Just leave me alone.' And I would have really angry outbursts. If people said the wrong thing, or derogatory comments, it would be like . . . bang. It was never constant anger, just outbursts at certain things. For about a year after he died, I would drink a lot with my friends, just staying out till whatever time I felt like. I was doing whatever I wanted. My mum would ring the police because I'd basically go missing, I'd just disappear. Because I didn't know what to do. I didn't know how to cope. I wasn't coping but I also knew my mum wasn't coping because it was all in the house, you know. It was like she was the dad to him. So I was like, 'Well, I can't speak to my mum, because she's going through it as well.'

This situation went on for the rest of Year 11, until she had finished her GCSEs. At that point, she moved to a new school for sixth form, and told herself that something had to change.

'I thought, "This can't carry on. It's not going to get me very far." And I'd always wanted to do something with my life,' she tells me. Because few people at the new school knew what had happened to her, it was easier to start a new chapter. She got her head down, worked hard for her A-levels and got into university. At university, she watched as people around her 'went wild', but she just didn't want to behave like that anymore. It was around that time, she says, that people started saying she seemed much older than she actually was. That's no surprise: she'd had a life's-worth of challenges before she'd even hit sixteen. Importantly, though, Emma did indeed do something with her life: when I speak to her, she is studying for a PhD and working part-time in a boys' secondary school. She tells me that she's built up a good rapport with the students. In particular, she always encourages them to be open with her about sex:

> Now I've formed a really good relationship with the boys, they will openly ask me about sex and stuff. And they laugh and giggle but I say, 'No, I'd rather you came and spoke to me about it and about what you're doing. Better to do that than you telling me three months down the line, "I got a girl pregnant."'

Sex education

Emma's story illustrates quite how high the stakes are when it comes to adolescent sex, and this is why many parents, teachers, health professionals and lawmakers view adolescent sex almost exclusively as a 'risk behaviour'. In some societies, such as the US, it is often stigmatised as immoral, as inherently deviant, a 'sickness best prevented', in the words of sociologist Amy Schalet. In such places, the primary approach of sex education is typically 'abstinence-only'. This can be summed up thus: until you're married, kids, just do not, ever, have sex.

For many adults today, this will have been the only message they received at school about sex. Consider the 1991 sex education documentary *No Second Chance*, which promoted abstinence before marriage and particularly focused on the risk of contracting HIV. At one point in the documentary, a teacher is seen explaining this approach to her class:

> You can think of it in terms of Russian Roulette. What is it, [a] one in six chance that you're going to die? When you use a condom, it's like you're playing Russian Roulette. There's less chance that when you pull the trigger you're going to get a bullet in your head, but who wants to play Russian Roulette with a condom?
>
> So the next time someone wants to go to bed with you, with or without a condom, then just picture that you're actually going to bed with – it's not just you and him, or you and her – it's that you're packing along a loaded revolver with you when you go. And not only that: when you go to bed with that person, you're not just going to bed with them, you're going to bed with every other person that person has gone to bed with before in their life. So just picture it's as if you're all crawling into bed together.

At this point the teacher starts to look more cheerful, and she tells the group of teenagers that she has a solution. If everyone stops having sex, she says, there wouldn't be any fun – but there's an alternative. She asks the class what the answer to the dilemma might be, and one of the students puts her hand up. 'Monogamy,' the student says, and the teacher agrees: 'Only having sex with one person, in marriage, in a monogamous relationship, for life. That's the answer to the problem. You don't have to worry about disease at all when you do that.' Most of the class seem satisfied with this. But then one brave soul puts his hand up and asks what happens if you want to have sex *before* marriage. The teacher doesn't skip a beat. 'Well, I guess you just have to be prepared to die.'

The problem with abstinence-only education is that it doesn't work. In the three decades since this video was released we have learned that teenagers who are taught about sex in this way are no less likely to end up pregnant or with an STI than teenagers who receive no sex education at all.[26] In fact, teenagers who receive abstinence-only sex education are significantly more likely to become pregnant than their counterparts who have comprehensive sex education programmes, where they are taught to have sex safely rather than not have sex at all. The USA, which still favours abstinence-only sex education in many regions, ends up with more teenage pregnancies and STIs than developed countries that are more progressive and accepting of teenage sexuality such as Denmark and the Netherlands.[27, 28] The reason is pretty simple: whatever you tell them, some teenagers are going to have sex anyway. You might succeed in terrifying some of them out of having sex but beyond that you cannot win against a biological imperative. As the psychologist Kathryn Paige Harden says, 'From an evolutionary perspective, sex is the point of adolescence. The overarching function of the biological, intrapersonal, and interpersonal changes of adolescence (pubertal maturation, increased novelty seeking, and social reorientation away from parents and toward peers) is to facilitate reproduction.'[29] An abstinence-only approach is counterproductive because it denies adolescents the information about contraception and healthy sex practices that would actually reduce the risk of bad outcomes when they inevitably end up having sex.

Can teenagers have good sex?

There is a better way, and it goes further than just teaching adolescents about how to have sex safely. The *sex-positive movement* is now well established in some European countries such as the Netherlands and has a small but growing number of advocates in the UK and USA. Harden sums it up as follows:

> Supporters of the sex-positive perspective regard consensual sexual activities, for teenagers and adults, as potentially positive and healthy. Thus, sex-positivity encompasses a variety of sexual behaviours, sexual identities, and gender identities that are traditionally viewed as deviant, including not only sex that has been deemed deviant on the basis of age or marital status (such as teenage sex) but also lesbian, gay, and bisexual sexual orientations and experiences.[30]

Supporting a sex-positive approach doesn't mean thinking that all teenage sex is a good thing. Indeed, in this framework, it may still be that abstinence is the preferred and best choice for an individual adolescent at any one time (or indeed for all their adolescent years). In fact, for asexual teenagers (who do not experience sexual attraction to anyone), abstinence is entirely appropriate, and usually the most desired option. There are plenty of teenagers who, for myriad reasons, do not want to have sex. All this is captured within a sex-positive framework, because a fundamental part of it is about respecting what an individual needs and wants.

The sex-positive movement is also not about trivialising risk. Promoting safe sex is integral to the whole approach. It's more that, while supporters of the movement view risk management as an essential foundation for adolescent sex, they also believe that healthy sexuality is about more than avoiding unwanted consequences, and we should teach that as well. This approach recognises sex as a normal and healthy part of adolescent development and its three key priorities are pleasure, consent and agency.

These messages are especially important for girls and women, who are not only at more risk of harm from sex but whose sexual pleasure is often undervalued or ignored. As we've seen, social norms influence all aspects of adolescents' lives, and sex is no exception. 'Sexual scripts', according to psychologists, are the cultural norms and expectations that people learn about sex – which, like actors following a film script, powerfully dictate their actual sexual attitudes and behaviour.[31] Repeatedly, research has shown that these scripts are gendered and heteronormative in a way that is unhelpful for girls and women (and probably ultimately for boys and men too).[32] According to the dominant sexual script in Western societies, straight men actively pursue sex, prioritise it over emotional connection, and objectify women. Straight women are expected to be passive, use their appearance to attract men, prioritise men's needs and pleasure, and limit their own number of sexual partners. This isn't just a theory: research has analysed how sex is portrayed and discussed in popular TV and film and found that these scripts appear frequently.[33] In the words of psychologist Janna Kim and colleagues, this messaging 'compels girls/women to deny or devalue their own sexual desire, to seek to please boys/men, to "wish and wait" to be chosen, and to trade their own sexuality as a commodity'.[34] The upshot of all this is that teenage girls receive a great deal of risk-orientated, judgement-laden information about sex, but very little guidance about how to actually explore or advocate for their own often intense sexual wants and needs – a problem that psychologist Deborah Tolman has described as adolescent girls' 'dilemmas of desire'.[35] This dilemma persists even when girls have solo sex: when asked about their attitude towards masturbation, it is much more common for girls than boys to report feelings of shame, disgust or inner conflict about this behaviour.[36]

A 2017 study recruited women, transgender and non-binary participants aged eighteen to sixty, and asked them what message they would have liked to receive about sex when they were younger, but did not, 'from both their family system and from society as a whole'.[37] One of the most common answers was about pleasure. One twenty-year-old woman summed it up simply: 'I wish I was told it's normal to want to have sex.' The impact of this lack of messaging can linger for years, with many of the participants continuing to feel shame or uncertainty around their own sexual desire. The trouble is that even advocates of strict abstinence-only education accept that most people will end up having sex as adults, which means that in order to have a fulfilling sex life, the messages about danger and immorality promoted so exhaustively in adolescence must somehow be *unlearned*, and that's not easy. Entirely new understandings must be built on non-existent foundations. As the authors Valerie Rubinsky and Angela Cooke-Jackson conclude, 'For parents and educators especially, what they do not say about sexual health may be as impactful as what they do say.'[38]

This is a key problem that the sex-positive framework seeks to solve. The ultimate ambition of this framework is to help teenagers (of all genders) develop a sense of what psychologists call *sexual well-being*, which encompasses four components, all of which are relevant in adulthood too.[39] The first is *sexual self-esteem*, which includes an overall sense of self-worth about yourself as a sexual person, a sense that you are sexually attractive, and a sense of pride about how you express your sexual behaviour and desires. The second is *sexual self-efficacy* or *sexual agency*. This refers to a person's belief in their ability to assert their sexual preferences and desires with a partner (in terms of what they want but also what they don't want) and a belief that they can take steps to prevent unwanted outcomes. The third component of sexual wellbeing is *experiencing positive aspects of sex*, including arousal, pleasure and satisfaction – and recognising that one is entitled to these experiences. Finally, sexual wellbeing involves *freedom from negative experiences of sex*, such as pain, anxiety or other negative feelings relating to one's sexuality. According to a sex-positive framework, all of these components can and should be developed gradually across adolescence.

Sex education begins at home

Some parents will be unable or unwilling to discuss sex with their teenage children because the taboos associated with sex are so deeply rooted and long-standing in so many cultures. But in recent years psychological research has shown that there *is* a good way to discuss sex at home – and this was highlighted in a 2004 study run by sociologist Amy Schalet.[40] She conducted 130 interviews with parents of teenagers aged fifteen to seventeen. Among many topics she discussed with her interviewees was the question: 'Would you permit [your teenager] to spend the night with a girlfriend or boyfriend in his or her room at home?' Half of the parents were from the USA, where attitudes towards teenage sex are generally conservative, and half were from the Netherlands, where the public health approach is that adolescent sex is inevitable and normal, and that safe sex should be promoted. These national attitudes were reflected in the interviews: ninety per cent of the American parents said they would not allow the sleepover in their house – whereas ninety per cent of the Dutch parents said they would.

When asked to explain their answer, the American parents commonly said that adolescent sexuality was an overpowering force driven by raging hormones that teenagers couldn't control. There was a sense that teenagers hadn't yet developed the cognitive or emotional capacity to manage these feelings. They felt that boys are so driven to have sex that they wouldn't stop to think about the importance of safe sex, and that girls fall in love too easily, have sex to impress and hold on to their boyfriends, and end up heartbroken (and possibly pregnant) after the relationship inevitably deteriorates. In Schalet's words: 'It strikes [American parents] as self-evident that parents must be vigilant to make sure their children do not fall prey to dangerous and premature relational entanglement. Permitting a sleepover at home would thus mean sanctioning relationships they believe their teenage children are not yet equipped to successfully negotiate.'[41] Some of the parents accepted that their teenager might have sex anyway, and some of them said they would be willing to help them access contraceptives if needed, but what was nearly universal was that they felt that, by actively allowing it to happen within the home, they would effectively be endorsing or encouraging the behaviour. As one American parent said, 'It's like giving them a license to do as they please, and I am not ready to do that.'

The Dutch parents, by contrast, were confident that their teenagers would know for themselves when they were ready to have sex, and trusted them to make that decision on their own. These parents considered sexual development to be a gradual thing that happens in stages, and believed that their teens could pace their own development as they became ready for each stage. Crucially, the Dutch parents trusted that, when their child did feel ready for penetrative sex, they would arrange and use contraception. In contrast to the American parents, the Dutch parents rarely talked about gender differences, instead seeing both boys and girls as sexual agents who could fall in love and would gradually want to explore their sexuality. Lastly, the Dutch parents frequently emphasised that adolescent sexuality is normal and natural – a part of healthy development. It need not be emotionally disruptive or cause conflict between teenagers and parents. As a result, it need not be a secret – and that means it can be permitted to happen within the home.

Both groups of parents felt uncomfortable to some degree about their teenage children having sex – the crucial difference is what they did with those feelings. As Schalet says:

> At least some Dutch parents, like their American counterparts, experience discomfort at the thought of their children becoming sexually involved. But while American parents take this discomfort and dramatize it – that is, make it a basis for action and see it as indicative of the need for radical separation between the sphere of teen sexuality and the sphere of the parental home – Dutch parents do something different with this discomfort. They normalize it. That is, they seek to remove the emotionally and relationally disruptive components of teenage sexuality by talking about it as something that is normal and everyday and that can be easily integrated into the domestic sphere of the parental home.

Rates of teenage pregnancy and STIs are far lower in the Netherlands than the USA, suggesting that the Dutch may be taking the better approach.[42] This tells us that it is possible to raise teenagers who can navigate sex safely and responsibly. But more than that, and in line with the sex-positivity framework, it's also possible for teenagers to have sexual relationships that are not only safe but also a profound source of meaning and intimacy.

Pornography

Arguably, sex education – at home and at school – is more important now than ever before. This is because, today, adults trying to teach teenagers about healthy sex are up against an opponent that has unleashed a tidal wave of sexual content among this age group: online porn. Considering its ubiquity, and the fact that these videos can be accessed on personal smartphones via a few taps, it is no surprise that adolescents curious about sex will sometimes view this content, either intentionally or unintentionally (for example by clicking a wrong link online, or being sent something by a friend).[43]

While there are many moral and legal concerns about the industry, particularly around the girls and women involved – their age, whether they are being exploited, whether they have consented to the video appearing online – the primary concern with teenage viewers is the type of sex that is depicted, and what it might be teaching them. Sex in pornography is often violent, even if it appears to be consensual; it rarely involves condoms; and it tends to prioritise and focus on men's sexual gratification rather than women's. The concern is that these videos teach teenagers that this version of sex is the norm, with obvious possible implications for how they then behave when they have sex in the real world.

It's difficult to establish from the research how justified these worries are. Some studies have found that adolescents who watch porn are more likely to have unprotected sex and more likely to have problematic, gender-stereotypical attitudes towards sex (for example that women should be objectified).[44] But other studies have found mixed results, and most of the studies that find a relationship between porn use and these bad outcomes are cross-sectional (i.e. measuring everything at a single point in time), making it difficult to ascertain whether the pornography is actively contributing to problem behaviours and attitudes or whether the teenagers who were prone to these things anyway are the ones who tend to be interested in watching porn.[45] Even when longitudinal research has been conducted – for example, one study found a positive statistical relationship between intentional viewing of violent pornography in ten- to fifteen-year-olds and later sexually aggressive, coercive behaviour – it remains unclear whether the adolescents who seek out this violent material were different to begin with or whether the material is triggering behaviour that otherwise would never have happened.[46]

The justified concern around the negative implications of porn also tends to drown out the more nuanced truth, backed up by the evidence, which is that teenagers vary enormously in terms of whether they watch porn, why they watch it, and what they're doing in the real world. The impact porn has will thus inevitably depend on the teenager.[47] There is also the reality, which many are reluctant to acknowledge, that porn might be helpful for some teenagers, particularly those who are not yet free or able to have sex in the real world. Referring to gay, lesbian and bisexual adolescents, psychologists Josh Grubbs and Shane Kraus write that some teenagers 'may find pornography use to be one of the few activities that is available to them to explore their sexuality in private and non-judgmental settings'.[48] For these teenagers, it is often the only place they have to learn about how to have sex – although this is really an argument for better avenues for sex education for these groups, rather than a justification for the use of porn.[49]

All this presents a considerable dilemma to educators. Many sex education programmes now teach young people about porn – for example, that the sex portrayed usually involves actors and is not realistic, or that it can be exploitative or illegal. But the trouble is that by the time adolescents are officially taught all this in school, many of them have seen these videos already, meaning the harm has perhaps already been done. The alternative, though, is to teach young people about porn before they've seen it or even heard of it – which realistically could mean teaching children about it in primary schools. There are no easy answers here, but the fact of the matter, as with all aspects of sex, is that teenagers are going to see porn eventually anyway, whether they are taught about it or not. Thus the onus is on adults to be pragmatic about how to guide young people through this inevitable new aspect of sex education. Through a realistic, sex-positive framework, the hope is that teenagers are capable of learning about pornography, while maintaining healthy attitudes and behaviours about sex in the real world.

An example of good teenage sex

Teenagers today are learning about sex in a far more complicated landscape, but ultimately their task in this domain is the same as it has always been. And it *is* possible to gradually explore sexual behaviour in adolescence in a healthy, satisfying way. Neil is now fifty-three, married with two teenage sons of his own. In his teenage years, he went to an all-boys secondary school. Conveniently, there was an adjacent all-girls school – 'literally right next door' – and it was through that school that he met his girlfriend, Sam, when he was fifteen:

> I remember the party where we first had a snog and I just remember what a lovely feeling it was. We were sitting on the floor at a party. And we snogged and then held hands. And there was something kind of – hey, look, all these years on, maybe I'm romanticising it a bit – but I do remember it being something very special from early on and having a recognition of that. The party when we kissed was on a Saturday, and I was working on the Sunday. I had a job in a shop. And Sam came to the shop on the Sunday, just to say hi to me, I remember that. Then a month or so later, it was her sixteenth birthday, and I remember being outside her house and the words 'I'm falling in love with you' tumbling out of my mouth. She didn't say it immediately, but that was reciprocated not long after that. And there was a very tender, special, loving relationship that was born.

Neil's mother was seriously unwell throughout his teenage years with what he calls a 'mystery illness' – which was only diagnosed and managed many years later. She was often unable to speak, and would communicate with her family by writing notes. There were many misdiagnoses, each worrying in its own way. All the while, there was no discussion between Neil, his older sister and his dad about how the illness was impacting them as a family. 'It was talked about, but not in a kind of open way,' he tells me. 'Emotions weren't talked about. And yet [her illness] touched everything.' Unsurprisingly, he remembers periods of being very upset – and the loneliness and difficulty of managing what was happening at home made his relationship with Sam all the more powerful:

> I think against that backdrop, being in a loving relationship – being part of a unit, a loving unit, and having a sense of belonging and being part of a relationship that surprised me – was very important. I think I had quite low self-esteem before I met Sam, and then when she fell in love with me, I felt like it was almost like a gift. I think on

one level, I did kind of think, 'Why do I deserve this?' Before her, I questioned my own self-worth. So it was incredible to be part of something like that. She was like a life raft. If I hadn't been in a relationship that was so loving, that gave me such a sense of belonging, that felt so meant to be . . . I don't know how I might have survived some of those years.

It was in the context of this loving relationship, which provided Neil with confidence, comfort and self-discovery at such a crucial time, that he and Sam began to have sex, but not right away:

Before Sam, I had a thing going on for a few months with another girl, and that was kind of a first girlfriend. That first brief relationship was quite passionate, sexual, experimental, playful. I had an initial attempt at having [penetrative] sex with her. My parents went away for a few days with my sister, leaving me alone in the house. So my girlfriend and I thought we'd have a bottle of wine each, that would be a good way to do it. But then obviously we were just too pissed. Difficulties getting the condom on, maybe not the best sexual position for losing your virginity . . . you know, that sort of thing. It was surprising, in a way, that I went from that to waiting with Sam. With Sam, we waited maybe a year and a bit to have sex.

We had an initial sexual relationship for a while before we did it. We had a sex life, but it was built on this idea that we waited for a while before we had [penetrative] sex. And you know, I didn't have much experience with women or women's bodies, so it was kind of a learning thing for me. We were being horny with each other and figuring out how to pleasure each other, all those kind of things, we were having good sexual experiences.

I don't remember ever feeling like, you know, 'God, when can I go inside you?' That was her. I remember her just saying, 'I'm going to go to the doctors.' We were sixteen. She just went and got an appointment at the GP by herself and went on the pill. I hadn't even thought all that through. I wasn't naive, I was just a young boy, really. And then she said, you know, 'I've been taking the pill for enough time now, we can have sex.' So we lost our virginity to each other in my very small childhood bedroom above where my parents were sitting downstairs. They had some friends round for dinner, I remember.

Researchers refer to adolescents who are ready to have sex as being 'sexually competent'. This generally means that, when they first have sex, the young person meets four criteria: they use contraception; there is equal willingness from both individuals to have sex (i.e. they both consent equally and without coercion); they feel subjectively that it is the right time; and they have sex because they intrinsically want to rather than for external reasons such as peer pressure.[50] If any of these criteria are not met, the teenager is likely not ready. According to this definition, it is clear that when Neil and Sam first had sex, both of them were ready. In the eyes of the law, of course, all teenagers are able to consent to sex on their sixteenth birthday and not a day before, but research suggests that people arrive at sexual competence at different ages. For some adolescents, it will be many months or years beyond that date before they are sexually competent; equally, some teenagers may be ready to have sex when they are fifteen.[51] However, it is universally agreed among academics and policymakers that, globally, adolescents aged fourteen or younger are always too young to safely have sex.[52] As said by the sociologist Ruth Dixon-Mueller, this is because adolescents this age 'lack the physiological and cognitive maturity and the information, skills, and agency to protect their health and rights'.[53] The threshold of sixteen as the age of consent is thus a pragmatic judgement, rather than a hard-and-fast rule – an imperfect estimation of the age when someone is likely to be capable of having consensual, safe sexual relationships.

Interestingly, Neil had this positive sexual experience despite receiving almost no information about sex from the adults in his life. He tells me that his parents never spoke to him about sex or contraception – 'which I suppose is not surprising, considering what was going on with my mum' – but he also learned nothing about it at school, beyond being sold a porn magazine by one of the other pupils. He regrets this lack of formal sex education, but in practice he received the best education possible: he learned about sex gradually in the context of a loving relationship. Ultimately, schools and parents can teach teenagers important principles about consent, respect, contraception and feeling ready, but beyond that it's out of their hands: the rest of the education must happen behind closed doors. Much as parents might dislike the idea of their teenager having an exciting, explorative sexual relationship, as Neil and Sam did, really it is one of the best adolescent experiences possible, as it is likely to set them up for having pleasurable, respectful sexual relationships for life.

Older guys

What may also have contributed to Neil's positive experience is that he and Sam were the same age. Plenty of teenagers have bad sexual experiences with same-age partners, but as we saw with Keira, teenage girls who have sex with older men are especially likely to have first experiences of sex that they regret. Compared to peers who have sexual partners their own age, they are also more likely to get an STI, likely because they are encouraged or coerced to have unprotected sex.[54, 55] If the girl is fifteen or younger, the man is breaking the law, but even if she is sixteen or older, the inherent power imbalance between an adult man and a teenage girl means there is the potential for manipulation. And yet this phenomenon is pervasive, so why do teenage girls want to date older men, and why do older men want to date teenage girls?

For teenage girls, older boys and men offer a number of benefits relative to boys their age. They will have more independence: they might drive or have their own place. They might have more money, which means more gifts or more opportunities to do interesting things. They might have more sexual experience. They might have more life experience and seem more mature, making them more interesting and fun to be with. On top of that, they will have moved beyond the often-awkward phase of puberty: they're taller, they have more facial hair, more muscle mass. Because of all this, dating older boys and men is often perceived by teenage girls and their friends to be cool.

Recall in Chapter 5 how Lauren was ostracised by her friendship group when she kissed two boys at her new school. Later, however, she started dating an older man – she was fifteen and he was twenty-three – and this had the opposite effect:

> This was somebody that I had liked for a very long time. He was in a youth group that I used to go to, so I kind of knew him through that. I'd always liked him and I just could not quite believe my luck when he showed an interest in me. And then I think the status of being able to go back to my boarding school and go, 'You'll never guess what, I'm going out with this bloke,' you know. It was seen as being very cool. And then the fact that we started having a sexual relationship a little bit later on, again I was able to go back to the girls and say, 'We had sex,' and they would all say, 'Oh my God.' They totally couldn't get over me doing that, you know? They weren't doing that yet, and it was seen as being so exciting.

As Keira showed us at the start of this chapter, having sex has cachet because it is one of the key pseudomature behaviours. By this same logic, the most adult thing of all is not only to have sex but to have sex *with an adult*. For girls who are drawn to risk-taking, the fact that parents and teachers are likely to disapprove only adds to the attraction.

The reasons why some men date and have sex with teenage girls should be obvious. Teenage girls may have the bodies of adult women but they don't yet have adult minds. For adult men who are unable or unwilling to navigate relationships with women their own age, teenage girls are an opportunity: to appear mature, to have more authority and to be adulated. Considering the perceived benefits for both parties, it should come as no surprise that teenage girls and adult men end up in sexual relationships with each other. But there are good reasons why relationships such as these are and should be strongly discouraged even if they are technically legal (which many are not).

Fay, now thirty-four, grew up in a village in south-west England and went to a state secondary school. She lived at home with her parents and older sister, and had good friends at school. She was also interested in playing the guitar, as was her dad. When she was twelve, she started having lessons with her dad's guitar teacher Olly, who at that time was twenty-two.

> He was originally my guitar teacher, and I would go to his house for the lessons. The beginning of it, I think, is quite textbook. He was an older and attractive guy that I kind of had a crush on. I think the allure was maybe just the romanticised idea of it. It felt like a classic romance novel or scenario about the kind of guy you shouldn't go after. 'It seems so wrong but it's so right,' you know. The drama of it. It wasn't like I was doing it to screw my parents. I think it was just trying to get some excitement – like, 'Everyone else talks about it, but I'm actually going to do it.' Like I'm actually living that life. And I remember thinking that was brilliant. I really heatedly pursued the whole relationship, I thought it was like the sexiest thing ever. Like I was living in a drama.

The relationship 'gradually crossed a line', Fay says, when she was fifteen and Olly was twenty-five. At first, she would sneak out of her house and meet him in his car, usually between midnight and 4 a.m. Later, she would go to his house, where he lived with his brother. They didn't have penetrative sex until she was sixteen: she remembers him saying that he would only feel 'comfortable' doing that once she was sixteen. The relationship and the sneaking around continued for another year or so – until Fay's mum read her diary and found out everything.

They were strict parents, and Fay expected them to ground her and forbid the relationship. But they did quite the opposite: they stepped back and allowed the relationship to happen. 'Speaking to my mum about it since, she said that their logic was, "If we had tried to sanction it or step in, it would have made it more exciting and you would have wanted it more. And at least we knew about it. Like, if you wanted to do it, you were going to do it."' This might sound like a very controversial approach, negligent even, but it worked. Part of the appeal of dating older men is the forbidden nature of it – so once Fay's parents had accepted it, it lost its appeal:

From that point onwards, it went from being really exciting to suddenly being a bit like . . . it was weird that it had been legitimised, you know? And then I just wasn't as interested in it anymore. And I had just started sixth form college, and there were all the college boys, and I was more interested in them. And my parents sensed that. There was this awful moment where my dad says to me, 'Well, you're going to have to break up with him, then. You have to do it right now.' And he gives me the phone. That was really horrible. I just had to call him and break up with him, in front of my dad. That was so weird. But that was it. I never saw him again after that.

What is most interesting about Fay's relationship, though, is how she reflects on it now. At the time, this was not a relationship where she was obviously coerced or manipulated, but she sees that differently now, particularly regarding their sexual relationship:

I did feel very in control of the relationship. He was more into me than I was into him and that meant – I thought – that I was in the position of power. I felt like, 'Oh, these are all my decisions.' But now I think, well, I thought that then, but I was still fifteen. I felt like I was very empowered, like I was making these choices myself. But now I think there was loads of sexual stuff that I wouldn't have done otherwise. And I think I was . . . I don't think 'betrayed' is the right word . . . I was conned, maybe. The bit I struggled with was realising, 'Oh, that's exactly what he'd want you to think.' He'd want you to think, 'Oh, this is all your choice, and that means I'm not a bad guy in any way.'

This gets to the heart of why these age-gap relationships are so problematic. Even when teenage girls are not being pressured or forced to engage in sexual activities against their will, a subtler form of exploitation is still at play. Girls like Fay believe that they have sexual agency with men like Olly – they sexually desire these men, and they consent to having sex with them (and technically Fay was above the legal age of consent when they had sex and thus able to give that consent) – so they may indeed be sexually competent, but they are ultimately still adolescent and do not yet have adult brains or minds. Invariably what they are living out is an adolescent fantasy – an experience propelled by their adolescent desires for romance, sensation seeking and pseudomature behaviour – and it is only once they have grown up that they are able to see the reality:

> I've thought about it a lot over the years. And I've felt very differently about it at different stages. At some points, I've felt like it was a very positive thing. Like, 'Oh, I was so liberal, I was so free.' Other times, I felt really damaged by it, thinking it was terrible, like, 'How could that ever happen to me?' Especially when I was twenty-five – it really bothered me when I was the age he had been when the relationship started. I worked in a cinema [when I was twenty-five], and there were often kids who would come in and try to see an 18-rating film and I'd think, 'I reckon you're about fifteen, sixteen.' And I would have this real intense feeling of disgust because they would seem so young to me. And I would think, 'Oh, but he was my age right now. This was the exact age gap.' And there was this real shock. I think for me, that was the most difficult time of it. It really hit it home for me, seeing it from the other side of things and just thinking, 'Oh no, I really was young, I was too young.' And it suddenly felt very gross to me.

Fay's relationship with Olly had wide-reaching and long-lasting effects following this realisation. It changed the way she saw men and relationships in general. It had a 'really damaging effect' on her relationship with her dad because he hadn't stopped it sooner. Unsurprisingly, it had a considerable impact on her experience of sex:

> I think I was very unrealistic with subsequent boyfriends. This makes me sound horrible, but I'm just trying to be candid. I think it made me almost belittle them, because I'd be like, 'Oh, well, why wouldn't you have sex this way?' or 'That's so immature,' or whatever. And actually, they were being very age-appropriate. I had just been accelerated. So there was this fallout, not just that it impacted me, but it had this ripple effect on other people. Even with my friends I'd be

like, 'Oh, you guys have had a snog and that's it, is it? He hasn't asked you to move in?' And of course he hadn't, he was seventeen or eighteen.

There was lots of very inappropriate experimenting for me for a while, after the relationship ended. Because I think once I'd had that excitement and that high and buzz so early, everything that my friends were doing seemed so pedestrian. I still wanted to be involved in those things, but I already felt like I'd kind of done it. When it came to sexual development and how I connected romantically to people, I think things just got so out of whack because of what had happened. It really negatively impacted pretty much all of my twenties because any relationship I had, anything that was to do with sex, was so off-kilter. It took a long time to recalibrate to finding someone my age who I felt was on the same page as me.

By having a sexual relationship with an older man, Fay had been put on an accelerated path that totally disconnected her from her peers, and it took years to gradually fall back in line with them. For a teenage girl this is often the cost of having sex with an older man: when the relationship ends, as it invariably does, it becomes apparent to her that she has been taken advantage of by someone who was far more aware of her vulnerability than she was, and a painful process of realisation and readjustment must take place. Fortunately for Fay, this did eventually happen:

I'm very pleased to say that I'm there now, that I'm back on the same page with someone. I've been with my current partner for seven years. I think if I wasn't in the stable relationship I am now with him, I would probably still be on that journey. It took being in the right relationship to kind of make peace with stuff. Now I'm in my early thirties, I still feel very shaped by that relationship, but finally I feel a bit more on the other side of it. I feel more at peace with it. Maybe not ambivalent, as such, but just more at peace with it.

In this book we have seen many common threads of adolescence, the patterns that help us understand typical adolescent behaviours. But of course every adolescence is unique, and that is perhaps more true when it comes to sex than with any other topic in this book. Some young people go through their teenage years without having sex at all (for example, one US study found that twenty-six per cent of both men and women have not had sex by their twentieth birthday).[56] This bothers some of them deeply, while others are unfazed (indeed, for the one to two per cent of people who identify as asexual, not having sex will be preferred).[57] Some adolescents have exceptionally negative experiences of sex, experiences that can affect them for a lifetime – especially when they have sex before they are ready, when the sex is coerced, or when that sex results in pregnancy or disease. Not all will come to terms with difficult experiences as Fay has done. But while sex *can be* one of the worst experiences a teenager can have, it can also be one of the best: an expression of love, a profound learning experience, and an essential source of meaning and pleasure. In the next chapter, we will come up against a similar contradiction. All of the adults we will meet have endured an experience in adolescence that you wouldn't wish on anyone, and yet the ways in which they ultimately find meaning and even benefit from that experience offers lessons for us all.

7. Loss

Grace is telling me about the day, ten years ago, that she realised her mother was going to die. Grace had just turned fifteen, and five months earlier, her mum had been diagnosed with glioblastoma, a particularly aggressive form of brain cancer. The first few months were full of hope, she says, with her mum determined to ignore the statistics – that only fifteen per cent of people diagnosed with glioblastoma survive for two or more years. In those early months, she remembers her mum planning a holiday, planning a future that would never come. 'She wasn't able to talk to me about her dying. I think it was too painful for her to have to say goodbye to three children, to me and my sisters,' she tells me. But on the day Grace is describing to me, she says they could no longer deny the facts. 'I will never forget my dad in the kitchen that December, crying and telling me the tumour was back and even bigger than before,' she tells me. 'That really, everybody knew she wasn't going to recover. Looking back, I think that's the day my childhood ended.'

Grace's mum died five months later, in their living room, surrounded by people who loved her: Grace's dad holding her mum close, Grace's aunt and grandmother beside the bed, a close neighbour holding Grace. It was late at night, and Grace's two younger sisters were asleep beside her on the couch. She tells me she is grateful she was awake when it happened, grateful to be there to witness her mum taking her last breaths. 'I remember the silence after her last breath. I remember the taste of chicken curry we ate the next day. And I remember the grief in the months after, which was suffocating.'

Many adolescent experiences involve loss: the end of a friendship, a romantic break-up, parental divorce. In some respects, adolescence is a continual process of loss, of repeatedly shedding the layers of innocence and naivety that protect our childhood selves. But in this chapter, we're going to focus on one form of loss in particular: what happens when an adolescent experiences the death of someone they love. This is because, perhaps surprisingly, experiencing bereavement at this age is fairly common. If you include second-degree relatives (such as grandparents), the majority of young people will have lost someone by the age of sixteen.[1] (Even losing a parent, as Grace did, is not quite as rare as you might expect: around four per cent of all children experience the death of a parent before their eighteenth birthday.)[2] As well as being important on its own terms, bereavement is also a useful way to examine what happens when the typical course of adolescent development is disrupted or, in some cases, entirely derailed. It is also a way of bringing into view quite how impressive and resilient adolescents can be.

What is grief?

For many decades now, psychologists have studied how people tend to think, feel and behave in the aftermath of a bereavement, with the goal of understanding how best to support people through what can be an awful experience. In particular, there have been attempts to understand what exactly leads to the extreme distress that is a common feature of grief. One useful model is 'multidimensional grief theory', proposed by psychologist Julie Kaplow and colleagues, which identifies three primary aspects of distress.[3] The first is *separation distress*: the intense heartache associated with the finality of death, the yearning and longing to be reunited with the person you have lost. The second component is *existential/identity distress*, which centres on the challenge of understanding who you are, and the purpose of your existence, once this person is no longer in your life. As well as these bigger philosophical questions, it also involves coping with daily disruptions – the changes in routine and life plans, dealing with financial changes and hardship, and taking on new roles and responsibilities, especially those previously carried out by the deceased. Finally, there is *circumstance-related distress*: distress that centres around *how* the person died, rather than the fact *that* they died. As you might

imagine, this component of distress is particularly potent and difficult when there were traumatic aspects of the death – for example, if
they were murdered or died by suicide or in an accident. But there
are deeply distressing circumstances even in the most common forms
of death: the pain of seeing someone experience the prolonged suffering that comes with illness, the shock of losing someone suddenly
to a heart attack.

These three forms of distress are common to grief in general, but
how they collide with adolescence is distinct. For starters, cognitively and emotionally, adolescents are not yet fully mature, especially
those in the early years of puberty. This means that they are less well
equipped to navigate any of the forms of distress described above, all
of which are exceptionally demanding even for adults. In addition, as
adolescents grow up, they will progressively develop more cognitive
and emotional resources, which means that as they return to the
death in their mind, they will repeatedly understand and interpret it
in a new way.[4] Young people are also more likely than adults to experience extremes of mood anyway, both highs and lows, and this could
easily exacerbate the distress they feel.[5] And then there is the fact that
the key tasks of growing up that we've been examining in this book –
namely understanding yourself and fitting in with your friends – must
continue to happen.

Adolescence happening in parallel

A teenager's biological development doesn't stop when someone
dies, and nor do the lives of their friends around them. Alongside
their grief, many adolescents continue to feel the entirely normal
teenage urges to explore, socialise and have fun. In the weeks and
months following her mother's death, Grace describes how she continued to participate in many social activities with her friends and the
internal conflict this caused:

> I was going out drinking alcohol for the first time, going to parties,
> talking about boys and people we had a crush on, talking about

fashion, everything. And sports – I was always in a sports club and all those things. I would say I was still able to participate in normal teenage things. But that was something that I struggled with. Immediately after my mum died, I remember it was hard for me to go on with life and I was like, 'How can I go to this party when my mum just died two or three weeks ago?' It was hard, it was difficult. It was a struggle and it felt weird at times. But also I definitely had a fear of missing out, of not wanting to miss out and wanting to still be a part of everything. So they were happening together, the grief and then still not wanting to miss out.

What Grace describes is actually a very common (and important) aspect of grief at all ages. Grieving people typically fluctuate between focusing on their loss – being desperately distressed, dwelling on what happened, yearning for the person they have lost – and focusing on what are called 'restoration' activities: planning and doing things that help them come to terms with what happened and move into a new future. This is at the heart of the *Dual Process Model*, first devised by psychologists Margaret Stroebe and Henk Schut in 1999,[6] which lays out how people ultimately cope with bereavement. As the authors say, this oscillation between the positive and negative is 'an integral part of the coping process'. In Grace's case, it was actually a good thing that the age-old adolescent fear of missing out could still punctuate her grief: it drove her to turn up to parties, to meet up with her friends, even with her grief by her side. Many people (of all ages) who have been bereaved feel conflicted and guilty about engaging in anything restorative, like attending to life changes, doing new things or distracting themselves from their grief – when actually, this is entirely healthy, common and indeed necessary for them to adapt to their new life.

What is most touching and enlightening about Grace's story is not simply that there were typical adolescent experiences to be had, but how her friends behaved in the face of her grief. When I ask her about how her peers responded to what happened, she prefaces her response by telling me that this is where she tends to get emotional, and I can hear it in her voice. First she tells me about the classmates who didn't know what to do: 'I remember coming back to school and just the tension in the classroom, like people just looking at me, looking away and not knowing how to deal with it. And it's understandable. A lot of people didn't know how to deal with the grief,' she says. But then she tells me about the ones who did help:

Other people at school who had also lost a parent reached out to me. Even if they didn't dare to reach out to me in person, they sent me some lovely messages. There was a guy who contacted me and said, 'Hey,' you know, 'I lost my dad years ago, and Grace, I just want you to know that I'm thinking of you all the time.' That meant a lot. And in the early weeks, I remember there was a party and I didn't want to go. But one of my friends had also lost his mum two years before, and he said, 'Grace, come on, you need to cry, but you can't always be crying, so come on, come to the party.' And so I went. So I had people around me who were encouraging me to just still participate.

I remember being at a party and having had a beer or two and just crying in the toilet and having my friends just hugging me and patting my back. It definitely was important that I knew I could cry with them. We also went on a class trip, only about a month after she died, we were away for a week in Berlin. And one night I just started crying, and then I had three or four girls just sitting beside me and they were keeping everybody else out of the room. In the first weeks and months, it really was just knowing that [my friends] were there and they weren't going away. In the first months, I don't even remember talking that much about it with them because it was so hard to. I didn't have any words. I mean, I always journaled before she died. I didn't journal in the first three months. I just couldn't. I was just crying all the time. So I think it was really about having [my friends] there and just knowing they were there. But also knowing I could do things with them that helped me not think about it all the time.

Grace and her friends were fifteen years old. This is the age at which teenagers bitch and gossip about each other, make judgements about each other's sexual promiscuity, and bully and exclude each other. Teenagers this age create social rules and hierarchies and police them viciously; they are self-involved, moody, reckless. And yet what Grace's story tells us is that when it matters, teenagers can step up. People not much out of childhood themselves, often with little or no personal experience of grief, know how to be a good friend. By encouraging Grace to go to parties, by letting her feel safe enough to cry, by protecting her from those who might not understand, these impressive teenagers helped her get through the most difficult months of her life.

Adolescence on pause

For some adolescents, the devastation caused by the death of a loved one is so significant that their adolescent development is entirely derailed, with lifelong effects. Sometimes, the death triggers serious mental health problems such as depression, post-traumatic stress disorder and suicidality. Some bereaved teenagers end up engaging in risk-taking behaviours, as Emma did when her baby son died: drinking, taking drugs, truanting and engaging in criminal activity. Since adolescents are already inclined towards risk-taking, bereavement can add fuel to the fire.[7] Researchers have suggested many possible explanations for this: sensation seeking may offer grieving adolescents temporary distraction or comfort; they might be acting out retaliatory fantasies; the cognitive demands of grief might be interfering with their ability to regulate their emotions and control their behaviour; or they might have a sense of nihilism as a result of the loss – an attitude of 'I don't care if I live or die' once something so important has been taken from them.[8] All of this might be happening in parallel.

Whether or not they 'act out' like this, there is evidence that teenagers who experience bereavement are more likely to have lower academic achievement.[9] This is to be expected: grief takes up huge amounts of cognitive and emotional resources, which will make it harder to concentrate at school. There may also be new practical responsibilities to contend with, such as helping to look after younger siblings after a parent has died. And as psychologist Christopher

Layne and colleagues have written, 'the loss of a loved one may evoke existential or identity-related challenges that undermine a youth's future outlook, life ambitions, and motivation for school'.[10] In other words, when your world has been turned upside down and the future looks utterly bleak, it may be hard to see the point of doing something as banal as homework. Since the education system runs to such a fast-moving and unforgiving timetable, all this can add up to scuppered academic results and shattered ambitions.

Not every bereaved teenager follows this path. In some cases, bereavement does not impact a teenager's school performance at all; in others, there might be a temporary dip in grades that then bounces back in subsequent years.[11] There is also huge variability in terms of the psychological impact of the death, with some bereaved teenagers experiencing long-term mental health difficulties as a result of the loss and others proving to be highly resilient.[12] So what is it that allows some adolescents to cope and continue, while others suffer life-changing consequences?

The importance of social support

What seems to be particularly important in determining whether teenagers experience these difficult long-term outcomes is what kind of social support they receive in the aftermath of the death – whether or not they are guided and comforted through their pain by their family, friends or a professional, whether they have the opportunity to explore and discuss their feelings, and whether they receive practical help and loving distractions. Indeed, social support is a key factor that predicts whether a person will experience what is known as 'complicated' or 'maladaptive' grief.[13] This term refers to the minority of cases of bereavement that continue to cause enormous levels of distress and disruption many months or years after the death. Some academics have argued that this type of bereavement should be considered a form of mental illness or disorder because of the degree to which it interferes with a person's life and how much they would benefit from outside help, but this continues to be a complicated debate.[14] What is clear, though, is that the minority of individuals who do have this very prolonged form of grief tend to be the people who lacked social support after the death.

Typically, adolescents will want to turn to their friends for support, but not all will react as Grace's friends did. Most will have no experience of bereavement and many won't have the cognitive and emotional maturity needed to be a supportive friend. In normal circumstances, parents are of course a key source of emotional and practical support, but when it comes to grief, this often breaks down. It may be that the supportive parent, the very person an adolescent would normally turn to for help, is the person who has died. The remaining parent, meanwhile, may be preoccupied with their own grief, while adjusting to becoming a single parent, often with considerable financial changes, and so have fewer emotional resources available to support their children. Research with adolescents who were bereaved between the ages of twelve and eighteen found that many of them were reluctant to share their distress with remaining family members because those relatives were already struggling; many of the participants reported a sense of needing to be self-reliant rather than expecting support from their family.[15]

This situation only becomes more acute when the person who has died is the adolescent's sibling. Indeed, losing a sibling in childhood or adolescence is often referred to as a 'double loss', since the grieving individual loses their brother or sister but also their parents' capacity to fully support and care for them in the aftermath.[16] Isabel, now forty-six, grew up in Devon. By her own admission, she grew up in a family that was already dysfunctional. She had a challenging relationship with her mother – 'She was difficult and was very self-absorbed . . . There was a lot of emotional neglect and I was often in the carer role,' she tells me. Her father moved out when she was fifteen and her sister was ten. It was against this already difficult backdrop that, two years later, doctors found a well-advanced tumour in her sister's kidney. Her illness made the two of them inseparable, Isabel tells me, and she shared the caring duties with both of her parents, travelling to her sister's medical appointments and treatments. When her sister became an inpatient at the hospital, Isabel often stayed there overnight with her. This lasted for eleven months. 'Initially the chemotherapy and surgery seemed successful, but further tumours developed in her neck, leaving her paralysed for the last three months of her life,' she tells me. 'After unsuccessful radiotherapy, she died just before Christmas, aged thirteen, when I was eighteen.'

In contrast to Grace, Isabel had very little social support during or after this harrowing experience, and she could not return to any semblance of a normal life. Her family unit, already fractious before her sister's illness, fell apart. She understandably struggled to keep up with her school work while caring for her sister, and once she had died, the grief prevented her from picking it back up again. She tells me she had dreamed of being a doctor, but that became impossible because of the effect her sister's death had on her studies. She had once been part of a strong friendship group, but her friends had no idea how to support her, and she found herself alone:

> The loss separated me from peers in an indescribable way. I felt so different to them after [the death]. People my age didn't know about people dying. I mean, obviously they did, but in an abstract way. I knew very, very few people of my age who could relate to what I'd been through in any way. Most others my age had no reference point for what had happened and few wanted to talk about it or recognise it. I think it made me grow up in the sense that I knew things about life that people my age didn't know. It made me quite serious, I think. It made me quite serious for a very long time. I had to start life again from scratch, in many ways.

At a time when shared experiences and similar interests are an essential means of fostering a sense of belonging and of fitting in with your peers, Isabel conveys how isolating and alienating teenage bereavement can be. Typically, people who experience a significant death in their teenage years have to wait until they are much older, in their forties or fifties, for their friends to experience equivalent bereavements themselves, by which time of course the opportunity to help them through their grief has long passed.

For Isabel, there was a flicker of light at that time: she met her boyfriend. There was an age gap – she was seventeen and he was twenty-three when they first starting dating – but occasionally such relationships work out and this was one of them: ultimately, they got married. In fact, she tells me, his additional life experience and maturity proved vital. 'I don't think a seventeen-year-old boy would have been any good with it [her grief] at all,' she tells me. She does recognise how vulnerable she was and concedes that it was 'just dumb luck' that he turned out to be a good man. But he was indeed a good man, helping her navigate a devastating experience when she had almost no other support – just as Neil's girlfriend in the previous chapter was a 'life raft' to him during his mother's chronic illness. In fact, the same is true for teenagers the world over and across history: romantic partners are an invaluable source of support, whatever the severity of the problem, which is one of the many reasons we should take these relationships so seriously, especially when they end.

But while social support mitigates the suffering, the effects of grief cannot be avoided altogether. For the first few years of her relationship with her boyfriend, Isabel was extremely anxious about death, wondering every day if her boyfriend would die on the way home. This heightened sense of vulnerability is common in teenagers who experience grief.[17] In Isabel's mind, she says, 'Death was a constant possibility.' When she went on to have three children, who are now all in their teens themselves, her parenting was affected too. This was partly because of her own experience of neglectful parents, which meant she needed to learn, in her own words, 'how to parent in a better way'. To do this she went on parenting courses and read parenting books, gradually learning how to relate to her children in a way her parents had never related to her. But her sister's death loomed large, again and again, as her children hit different milestones:

[Parenting] has been particularly hard when they were the ages that relate to things that happened to me. And quite a lot of that is around my sister. Like when my oldest was the age that my sister was when she got ill, and then when my oldest got to the age where I would have been caring for my sister. That was hard. I was just exhausted all the time. I feel like there was a chronic tiredness that came from that year of caring for my sister and I just didn't recover from all of that for a very long time. Some sort of chronic fatigue and a sort of freeze response, shutting down because I feel too much too easily. But I do feel like I'm coming out the other side of it now. Now my children have got past those trigger points of age, it's easier. We're all on good terms, and they're mostly doing okay. And we all survived.

Importantly, Isabel was eventually able to return to some aspects of her adolescence that had long been put on pause.

I did have times of fun [in those early years]. But I was more happy sort of snuggling up at home and doing gentle things. I had come to the point of thinking that I was basically an introvert, and I didn't need those things – socialising, parties, group activities. I think I was quite dissociated from my body as well, I wasn't that physical, wasn't into sports or anything. And I think I slowly realised that actually I do enjoy those things and do need them. I've been doing lots of sport. I'm doing tennis and netball, and I'm really enjoying them. I've had the time to reclaim some of those things. It's taken me over twenty years and lots of therapy to be able to try and reclaim some of the fun and freedom that was lost when I was younger.

Positive outcomes from grief

Isabel's experience, and a huge body of psychological research, demonstrate how the negative effects of adolescent bereavement can linger for decades. But it's also true that grief can sometimes have ultimately positive outcomes, even when the bereavement occurs at a young age. Time and again, in fact, researchers have encountered adolescents who take positive lessons from losing someone they love. In a study published in 1991, psychologist and educationalist Kevin Oltjenbruns recruited ninety-three adolescents (sixteen- to twenty-two-year-olds) who had experienced a bereavement of a close family member or friend in the last two years.[18] Participants were asked: 'What positive outcomes, if any, do you feel were the result of your grief experience(s)?' They were given a list of seven different possible positive outcomes, as well as the option to say that there had been no positive outcomes at all.

Ninety-six per cent of Oltjenbruns' participants said they'd experienced at least one positive outcome as a result of the death. Most commonly they reported a deeper appreciation of life, followed by greater caring for loved ones and strengthened emotional bonds. They also reported increased empathy, better communication skills, and enhanced problem-solving skills. When given a blank space to describe any other potential positive outcomes, the participants reported, among a variety of answers, a reduced fear of death, a clearer sense of their priorities, and feeling more independent. Oltjenbruns argues that it might actually be useful to teach adolescents, including those who haven't yet experienced bereavement, about these possible positive outcomes to help them understand 'that life-enhancing outcomes might ultimately be part of their bereavement experience'.

Ben, who is now thirty-five, grew up in rural Scotland with his parents and older sister. When he was eleven, late one night, his dad had a heart attack. Ben didn't wake up even when the paramedics arrived and took his dad to hospital, and so only found out when he came down in the morning and his mum told him what had happened. His dad was in hospital on life support for several days. 'At first, she [Ben's mother] came home from the visits quite positively, saying, like, "He's going to be okay," ' Ben tells me. 'But I think she knew he was not going to survive this. And if he was going to survive, there would be extensive brain damage.' A week after the heart attack, a friend of Ben's mum came over to look after him and his sister, while his mum went to the hospital alone. She had made the decision to turn off her husband's life support machine, before coming home to tell Ben and his sister that their dad had died:

It hit us almost immediately. You know some people say they feel grief later on . . . for my sister and me, I would say it hit both of us pretty immediately. Like: it's happened, and we need to get on with that. I never remember having a dip later. I had two weeks, three weeks of just crying constantly. We as a family would sit down and just cry together. And I do remember being very tearful in lessons at school, and having these moments where I would just cry. But then we just . . . we just cracked on. We just got on with it.

Ben's mum's approach was to maintain a sense of normality as much as possible. Ben went to school the day after the heart attack and didn't take time off after his dad died. He played a cricket match that had been planned for that weekend. Soon after, his mum returned to work full-time, and brought up Ben and his sister on her own. 'She was just an absolute hero, just the most amazing person for doing that,' he tells me. The early days and months after his father's death were 'horrific', but he then goes on to say something unexpected. 'I really would say, thinking about the way I am now, that despite losing my dad . . . I would say it was overall a positive experience. It's quite a weird thing to say. But I'm so much stronger as a result of it.'

Ben's dad had been suffering from mental health problems and alcohol abuse. His drinking never led him to be violent or abusive – 'He just kept himself to himself,' Ben says – but it took an enormous toll on the family. His death, despite being deeply painful, actually offered them some sense of relief.

When he was alive, my mum was effectively looking after another person, so his death was just . . . it was freedom. We felt free again, to be a family, to go to all these events. There were so many things we had to turn down because he'd drunk that day and we couldn't go. We couldn't plan things, ever. When we were on holiday once, he left without telling anyone. I just remember that he went off and didn't come back for two days. And mum was like, 'Oh, it's fine,' we just normalised it. But looking back at it now I think, wow, that was quite weird – to go to France and your dad just going off and then coming back a few days later. So, yeah, I think a few years after he died . . . there was a little bit of relief as a family.

Ben's particular sense of relief stemmed from the specific context of their family and his dad's alcohol problem, although relief is a common aspect of bereavement when a preceding illness or the death itself has been prolonged or when the person who has died was challenging to care for.[19] For Ben, as an adolescent, there were other benefits too, he tells me. First, he says it helped him grow up, be more independent. Every day after school, he had a bit of time to himself: his mum was out at work, and his sister was at a school in a different town, meaning she always got home later than him. Knowing his mum had a lot on her plate, Ben started helping out around the house. Those solitary hours taught him to be comfortable in his own company, he said. For some adolescents this would all be too much – too much adult responsibility, too many overwhelming demands when they are barely out of childhood and still processing their loss. But Ben found he enjoyed it. When the time came for him to move to university, he says, he was excited about living away from home, whereas other people seemed to be dreading it, not ready to live independently. But more important than any of this, Ben's experience of bereavement taught him an incredibly valuable life lesson: that he could cope.

> At that time, it was the worst thing that could happen. Losing an immediate family member is the worst thing that can happen. But from then on, I look at everything in proportion to that. If I've been in [. . .] a challenging situation or something, I kind of reflect on [my dad dying] and think, 'Gosh, if you got through that, you can honestly . . . you can tackle things.' Yeah, I guess that's it. It's been a good thing to reflect on in life.

Psychologists sometimes refer to this phenomenon as *stress inoculation*: when future stressful events rear their head, people who have experienced stress already – and in Ben's case, at a formative age – are better able to navigate it.[20] There is some evidence for this theory, but with a crucial caveat: it only applies to moderate amounts of stress.[21] When stress levels become very high, especially when that stress is impossible to control and is repeated over a prolonged period, this almost always has terrible long-term consequences for a person's physical and mental health. It is also not the case that everyone benefits from moderately stressful experiences in adolescence: some will experience *stress sensitisation* rather than inoculation – i.e. difficult events will make them hypersensitive, not desensitised, to the effects of any later stress.[22] Some events are just too damaging to teach anything useful about coping, and some individuals who experience adolescent bereavement learn only that they can't cope, not that they can. But with these important caveats, it is undeniably true that difficult events in adolescence can serve a useful function for some people, and Ben is clearly one of them. Losing his dad became the yardstick against which all future emotional challenges were measured, and since he had managed to get through that, he was confident he could handle most other things that would come his way.

This was put to the test only a few years later when Ben experienced a second sudden death of someone close to him. ('It sounds like I've had really bad luck,' he says, which strikes me as a considerable understatement.) When he was nineteen, he was home for the weekend from university and went to the pub with some old school friends, including his best friend, Jamie. Most of them weren't drinking, which was often the case when they were back home: living in rural Scotland meant needing to drive to meet up, which ruled out having a drink. At the end of the evening, they went their separate ways in different cars. Ben went home and went to bed, but was woken by the house phone ringing in the early hours of the morning. It was the police, telling him that Jamie had died in a car crash as he drove home. In the aftermath, Ben tells me how important it was that he had existing experience of loss:

> It was worse, at the time, than my dad dying. But the way I responded to Jamie's death . . . all my friends, I could see around me, were absolutely devastated. Of course, I was absolutely devastated too. But it was like . . . I felt I could look after them. I felt like, 'I've been through this. I know what it's like.' I knew you just needed to get through the first few weeks and it starts to get better. And it was as though my role wasn't to be sad myself. It was to help my friends. And I could see it

just didn't affect me as much as many other people. And I think it's because I had experienced it already and I knew you need to keep moving forward in life. And obviously remember people as well, of course. But I think it made me realise how strong I was.

In some respects, according to Ben, the loss of his father on the cusp of adolescence had been the making of him. Not only did he know he would find a way to cope, he showed others that they, too, would find a way through the immediate and overwhelming pain. This is the very essence of *resilience*: the ability to maintain or regain mental health or wellbeing despite experiencing adversity or trauma. As you might expect, this is a subject of great interest to psychologists, with researchers trying to understand why some people are more likely to be resilient in the face of hardship, and how we can use that information to increase resilience in everyone. While we don't have any answers yet, we do have certain clues.

What we know so far is that, to an extent, this is about biology: in part due to genetics, some people are just physiologically very reactive to difficult events and others far less so (which helps explain the diverging pathways of stress sensitisation and stress innoculation). As we have seen, the social environment is also important: whether the adolescent has a supportive family and friends around them. But what also really matters – and this is linked to both the biological and social factors – is individual differences in psychology. When faced with the loss of someone they love, young people vary considerably in how they think and feel about the death. As the years go by, they make sense of it in very different ways in their minds. In other words, part of what predicts the long-term outcomes of bereavement is the story that adolescents tell themselves about it.

It has long been recognised that, in the months and years after losing someone they love, people who are grieving use storytelling to make sense of what happened to them.[23] When remembering the person they loved and their death, people do not merely recount facts, they imbue those facts with meaning. Indeed, the story a person tells about their bereavement *is* their bereavement: as psychologists James Gillies and Robert Neimeyer have written, 'the process by which bereaved persons question, find, and make sense of their bereavement is central to the experience of grief'.[24] Critically, for some, the story they tell themselves is a negative one: what they take from the loss, often very understandably, is that life is unfair or the world is unsafe. The resounding message may be that they won't find happiness again, or that relationships with others are not worth it, because they can disappear at any moment. When death is apparently so random and unjust, a person's own life – and life in general – may suddenly seem meaningless or fragile in a horrible, frightening way. When the bereavement happens during adolescence, when a person is forming their foundational understanding of the world, that story can stay with them for life.

By the same token, adolescents who tell at least a partly positive story about their bereavement can find this brings some benefit to their adult life. For some, the positive element is about a change in their own identity. Over many years, their stories gradually feature themes of themselves as more resilient, more confident and wiser, just as we saw with Ben.[25] This can be an exceptionally useful way for a young person to see themselves as they grow up and navigate the challenges of the adult world. For others, the positive theme is about life itself. Perhaps counterintuitively, their experience of death enriches their attitude towards life. This was the case for Grace, who lost her mother to cancer at fifteen and whom we met at the beginning of this chapter:

> I often say we don't know if we'll be alive tomorrow because that's something that I see as helpful. It reminds us of our vulnerability. I just find it very helpful to be aware of that and to bring to mind often that we're all going to die someday. And we don't know when. It might be tomorrow. I think I'm very aware of how precious life is. For me, it makes every day that I have and every moment and time that I can spend with loved ones very precious. Of course, I forget that sometimes. I'm human and I forget that in everyday life and with the hustle and my hectic lifestyle. But I see people around me acting like they're going to live forever and they focus on things that I don't think will matter at the end of life. What makes life meaningful, at least for me, is feeling connected to people and to the world. Being

aware of my own vulnerability and of the world's vulnerability makes me feel more grateful for the people I have who are here.

I say that without wanting to go into any toxic positivity stuff, or sugar-coating any of the pain and the loss of how shitty it is to get cancer and how shitty it is to lose somebody. Nothing can make that easier. It's awful and it's really hard to live on with that. But at the same time, it can make you feel more grateful and see more meaning in the people and the relationships that you have. I am so grateful for the life I have now, and especially for my husband. We often say to each other, you know, we don't know how long we have, we never know how much time we have with each other. Every day is a gift. And that helps.

The start and middle of Grace's story was full of sadness, but the note she chooses to end on is one of gratitude. An exceptionally painful experience at a fragile age taught her that relationships are wonderful and deserve her attention, and this shapes the way she lives her life every day. It is this process – this capacity to know how to end our self-defining stories, and how to end them well – that holds the secret to understanding adolescence, for everyone.

8. The end of the story

I was a really good distance runner, and I knew it. In fact, almost everyone around me knew it too. For my first two years in high school, I excelled in athletics. I climbed my way up the all-time lists and won race after race. I loved every bit of it. Everyone told me, and my parents, that I could go to college on this. Not only that, but that elite universities would want me – they would actually pay for me. That is, as long as I kept running fast and winning. I drank the Kool-Aid and kept going, kept running. My entire identity was being a runner. I barely knew myself outside of it, but that was okay because I thought it was going to lead me to success. Success was climbing this ladder of being extraordinary at my sport, going to an elite university, and that was it. I was defined by my accolades, which sounds terrible, but it was all I knew.

Nicholas, now twenty-one, spent his adolescence in the beautiful San Francisco Bay Area of California: he lived with his parents and sister in what he describes as a 'privileged upbringing', and had good friends at school. At a time when most adolescents explore their multifaceted identities – their personalities, their music choices, their clothes, their love interests – Nicholas' was defined by how fast he could run. Running dictated not only his day-to-day life but also his future. Which seemed to work out okay, until his mental health began to deteriorate, and everything started to collapse. In his words, 'my world came crashing down'.

The enormous pressure – to be an exceptional athlete, to excel academically at the same time, and to sacrifice everything else – was making Nicholas crack. He began to feel extremely anxious in social situations, and he developed an eating disorder, obsessively thinking about what he ate and how he looked. Running, which had once been a source of joy, became a way to meticulously manage his weight – a tool, in other words, to enable his eating disorder. In his junior year of high school, when he was sixteen, he attempted suicide for the first time. Two other attempts followed soon after. Because he was in and out of hospital, and because of the effects of the disorder on his body, he was forced to give up athletics. The defining feature of his life disappeared, and the hope of going to an elite institution on an athletic scholarship crumbled to dust.

When one aspect of someone's nascent identity swells to become its entirety, as it did with Nicholas, it's devastating when the bubble bursts. This often happens with junior athletes and sports players: many teenagers show exceptional talent, but inevitably only a very small handful make it to the top, leaving a trail of disappointed hopefuls in their wake. In the UK, for example, around 3,500 boys are currently signed to Premier League football academies.[1] Most have been scouted by the professional clubs while playing for smaller, local teams. At this point, many of them begin to dream – as do their parents, their teachers and their friends. An identity comes into view: a sporting superstar. But over ninety-nine per cent of those signed to an academy aged nine will never go on to have a footballing career. Thousands of young people will have to rethink their identities: from potential global superstars – and millionaires – to something else entirely, sometimes to seemingly nothing at all.

Nicholas had all of this to contend with when he became unwell, but for him, there was something else bubbling up from beneath the surface. When he could no longer run, Nicholas began to realise that pinning his identity on being an athlete had been masking something else, something very important. In his high school years, when he was excelling academically and breaking athletic records, Nicholas was a girl. But deep down, he knew that wasn't right. In fact, he remembers first questioning his gender identity when he was about ten or eleven. In his running years, he says, he tried to convince himself that he was the skinny, straight girl that he was supposed to be, and that everyone else expected him to be: 'I held on to her for a long time because I idolised what she represented, but it would never work. I could never be her because it wasn't me.'

In the early years of high school, the girls around him started to talk about liking boys, but he could never join in, because he realised he wasn't attracted to boys. The logical explanation, he thought then, was that he was a lesbian. When he was fifteen, he told his counsellor – who he was seeing because of his mental health difficulties – that he was gay. He then told his parents and his friends, all of whom were supportive. He had a relationship with a girl, partly conducted in secret, because the girl's parents 'were not accepting' of her sexual orientation. To Nicholas, this 'felt better than being a straight girl. But it still wasn't exactly right. And so my identity was always something that I struggled with, but I didn't know the answer for a long time until after high school.'

The answer – that he was transgender – first occurred to him in eleventh grade, when he was sixteen. He went back and forth, over and over it in his mind: questioning whether he was in fact a boy, then denying it. Denying it felt easier, because of the pressure to perform academically and athletically, and because of his poor mental health. There was, he says, just too much else going on at that time. But then he graduated from high school, and despite his mental health difficulties, secured a place at a good college – albeit without the athletic scholarship. Some of the huge pressures on him that had existed at school started to lift, and there was more headspace to focus on understanding who he really was.

His first step, in the summer before college, was to start socially transitioning, which began with a shift to using they/them pronouns (he now uses he/him). He told his parents – his dad first, then his mum. They were supportive, he tells me, although his mum was very hurt he hadn't told her sooner, and said she wished he'd felt able to come to her earlier. His sister also struggled to make sense of the news at first: she was upset and in shock, he says, telling him she felt like she didn't have a sister anymore, that she was losing him. 'But I said to her, no, you aren't losing me. Actually, if anything, it's the opposite.' He was finally showing her – and everyone – his true self.

Nicholas then began to medically transition to being a man and started using his new name. Because there were so many people to tell, he decided to make an announcement on social media, which, he says, was 'amazing and liberating and also very scary'. The order in which he disclosed his gender identity is typical: research shows that transgender and non-binary people typically first tell a healthcare professional (making their response of vital importance), followed by their friends, then their close family, then extended family, until finally they make a mass disclosure, commonly on social media.[2] The whole process can take several years. When Nicholas wrote his post and pressed send, he then turned off his phone and waited, too scared to see the reaction. But when people started getting in touch, they were supportive and kind.

For transgender and non-binary teenagers, the key task of adolescence – working out who you are – can be so much harder. It involves facing the fact that they will need to undertake a major social and in some cases medical transformation, all in the knowledge that they may be targeted or shunned for doing so. For some people, like Nicholas, coming out is met with understanding and support, but for others, disclosing their gender identity is met with violence, harassment, rejection or ostracism.[3,4] In addition, coming out as transgender or non-binary involves using a new name and pronouns, and sometimes other people can simply refuse to go along with this request. As academic Breanne Fahs writes, for transgender and non-binary people, 'the "coming out" process feels less declarative and is instead more of a negotiation in order to gain approval of their identities and their transitional processes'.[5] But research shows that the alternative – the process of repeatedly trying to hide or deny your own gender identity – is at best stressful and exhausting, and at worst significantly damaging to a person's mental health.[6,7] Often, transgender and non-binary adolescents end up being both open and closeted in parallel, making strategic decisions to be open about their gender identity only in the contexts they feel safe to do so.[8] In adolescence, when everyone just wants to be understood and have a cohesive identity that is recognised by others, this inevitably takes a considerable psychological toll.

Nicholas, however, is now able to live fully as a man. When he moved to the UK to study for a year, he was finally able to introduce himself this way:

It's not quite a happy ending just yet, I still struggle with my mental health a lot. But it's a hell of a lot better than it used to be. For the first time in my life, I am excited to meet new people. Because the person that I am introducing them to, myself, is someone that I feel more connected and aligned to than I ever have in my life before.

He has also started running again:

I originally started running because I enjoyed it. In the periods in high school when I couldn't run because of the mental health problems, I was always very determined to get that joy back one day. Because I love it, regardless. So now, for the first time, after several years, I am trying to get back into competitive running. I've been running on my own, but there are aspects of competition that I enjoy and the team camaraderie and things like that. Hopefully I can keep doing it, as long as I'm doing it for the right reasons. Because running will always bring me joy.

Closure

The transition that transgender and non-binary adolescents like Nicholas face is a particularly monumental one. It is a process that takes many years and involves a transformation not only in how a person understands themselves, but how they are understood by other people in their life and in society more broadly. To upend or renegotiate gendered expectations in this way, in the context of considerable prejudice and stigma, is arguably the biggest and most difficult transition that any adolescent has to make and one that, by definition, only a small number of young people will go through. But Nicholas' story can offer us clues about what is happening in adolescence for everyone else. On a smaller scale, the fact is that all adolescents are making some form of transition all the time.

In a sense, adolescence itself is just one big period of change, as a person gradually transforms from a vulnerable child into a capable, independent adult. Then within this overarching change there are many other important shifts: a young person might change friendship groups, become sexually active, or change their appearance; they might go through a romantic break-up, give up a sporting dream or lose a family member they love. All adolescents will start secondary school and go through different stages of education, and then either go to university or enter the world of work. With each shift, the young person changes: they learn new things, take on new roles, see the world in a different way. Sometimes these shifts happen without much impact on a person's sense of self, but sometimes – as with most of the stories we've seen in this book – adolescent transitions involve a fundamental reckoning with who we are.

In these cases, each juncture presents a challenge: in order to move on to the next chapter, we must make sense of our former self. We must figure out why we felt or behaved the way we did, why other people treated us a certain way, and why circumstances played out the way they did. Many people cannot simply choose to forget that they were the person who was bullied throughout school, or the girl who was dumped, or the teenager who lost their mum. They need to form a logical narrative around it before they can put it to bed, or else they end up being haunted by their former self; the only way to comfortably inhabit a new version of ourselves is to fully bring the previous one to a close. This usually explicitly requires a person to be removed in time or place from the circumstances that once defined them: we can only understand our teenage years with the benefit of time, once we know all the facts, once we know what we later experienced or understood about ourselves. This is, of course, about telling ourselves stories, but it's about a specific part of the story – the end. What everyone needs, when they reflect back on difficult adolescent memories, is *closure*.

We know from the experience of reading literature or listening to music how rewarding and satisfying it is when something ends in a way that feels right and makes sense. As the philosopher Noël Carroll writes:

> The notion of closure refers to the sense of finality with which a piece
> of music, a poem, or a story concludes. It is the impression that

exactly the point where the work does end is just the right point. To have gone beyond that point would have been an error . . . But to have stopped before that point would also be to have committed a mistake. It would be too abrupt. Closure is a matter of concluding rather than merely stopping or ceasing or coming to a halt or crashing. When an artist effects closure, then we feel that there is nothing remaining for her to do. There is nothing left to be done that hasn't already been discharged. Closure yields a feeling of completeness. When the storyteller closes her book, there is nothing left to say, nor has anything that needed to be said been left unsaid.[9]

Fiction writers play upon our desire for the sense of relief and completion that accompanies a satisfactory ending. In the stories we tell about our own lives, we have the same need for resolution. That might come from the outside world: we might finally receive an online message from the boy who bullied us, for example, or see an ex-boyfriend at a school reunion. Or it might come from reworking the story in our own minds, as we will see. Either way, when we have achieved closure on a certain story, it is less likely to arouse strong, difficult emotions in us.

Psychologists Denise Beike and Erin Wirth-Beaumont examined this in a study in 2005.[10] They brought undergraduate students into the lab where they asked them to choose an event from their past and write about it. Half were asked to recall a positive event and half to recall a negative one. Having done so, they were then asked to rate their agreement with statements like, 'The event is a "closed book" to me' and 'I have put the event behind me completely.' The researchers then compared how much the participants' written descriptions contained mention of their emotions (for example, 'I felt very scared when it happened'). They found that the participants who described memories using a greater number of emotions and a greater intensity of emotions were less likely to report that they felt a sense of closure about the event.

The temporal relationship here between closure and lack of emotions is unclear: it might be that once we achieve closure, we feel less strong emotions – or it might be that once we reach a point of feeling less strong emotions about an event, we can move on to achieving closure. Either way, this tells us something rather important about what it feels like to find a conclusion to a story: when you find some sort of meaning in the events and you understand why it all happened, it no longer elicits the difficult feelings it once did. In your mind, the story's end has been written, the final full stop has been typed.

Redemption

Often, closure comes when we feel (or can persuade ourselves to feel) that some good has finally come from a difficult event. Psychologists refer to this as *redemption*. Very simply, redemptive personal stories are those in which 'the bad is redeemed, salvaged, mitigated, or made better in light of the ensuing good', according to Dan McAdams and colleagues.[11] Some researchers have argued that the habit of telling redemptive stories about ourselves is so common that it is essentially a *master narrative* in contemporary Western society. This doesn't mean we are especially likely to have rags-to-riches experiences compared to other cultures; it just means we are encouraged to interpret our experience through this lens, to construe whatever has happened to us in this particular way. Importantly, for a story to be redemptive, the good outcome need not necessarily outweigh the bad nor even result in a straightforwardly happy ending. For it to be a redemptive story, there need only be *some* positive outcome or consequence, whatever its scale, allowing us to choose *this* as the note on which to end the story.

We've seen redemptive stories being told many times throughout this book. Georgia made the difficult decision to walk away from her friendship group, in which she had been unhappy, and subsequently spent six months alone and being bullied by them, but ultimately she found a new group of friends, and now reflects on that decision to leave as the best she ever made. Likewise, Vicky left a friendship group that was wrong for her and found a new, far more suitable group, calling it a 'pivotal' moment in her life. Beth spent her adolescence desperately trying to change her hair but describes now how through that experience she came to realise that she and her children are beautiful just as they are. Freddie might wish he had never experienced bullying but he describes turning this experience into a meaningful ability to help other people. Emma had the harrowing experience of losing her son as a teenager but talks about how she now uses this experience and knowledge to support teenagers in her own work. Ben and Grace, who both lost a parent, were able to share hard-earned, life-affirming lessons that they had learned from their bereavements.

To be clear, this is not to say that all adolescent experiences can or should be seen through a redemptive lens. Some sad and traumatic events never lead to anything good or meaningful. And finding redemption is not as straightforward as simply *choosing* to see your past differently. Personality traits, thinking habits, mental health problems, past experiences and levels of social support – not to mention the specific nature of the event itself – will all dictate whether we are able to view episodes from our past through a redemptive lens. McAdams and colleagues (2022) acknowledge this carefully:

> In some cases it may be naïve, or even foolish, to expect that suffering will lead to growth, happiness, or any other positive outcome. Suffering may simply lead to more suffering . . . Some things that happen in life are too bad to be redeemed. And some narrators cannot find it in themselves to derive redemptive meanings from the suffering they have experienced, no matter how much they are urged to do so by their family and friends, and by the cultural narratives that they know.[12]

It is important to be realistic, then, and recognise that there is another theme that crops up in the stories we tell about ourselves: *contamination*. The sinister mirror of redemption, contamination stories are those which begin with positive events or feelings and end negatively, sometimes very negatively indeed. What was initially good is undermined or even ruined by what follows. Perhaps the best example of such a story from this book is Isabel's. Her sister's death aged thirteen not only meant she lost a very important relationship and was confronted with the harrowing reality of severe illness at a young age, it also left her family unit shattered. She ultimately received a lot of support in order to process this experience, but for Isabel and so many others, the suggestion that all suffering and hardship is worthwhile because it ultimately leads to some greater good would be disrespectful and insulting.

Acceptance

There is a middle ground, a compromise between finding a positive conclusion to a negative event and being entirely resigned to the sadness or horror of it. Here we arrive at a third common theme in life stories, and a common form of closure: *acceptance*. Much of the research on this theme has focused on older adults around sixty-five years and above: acceptance tends to crop up when this age group are asked to tell stories about their lives, possibly because people this age have the wisdom and life experience to recognise that acceptance is a kinder, more helpful and more realistic evaluation of events than the alternatives.[13] But adults of any age can foster a sense of acceptance, and they certainly can when they're remembering events from their adolescent years. Importantly, finding a story of acceptance is not about surrendering oneself to life's misery but more about a graceful recognition of its imperfections and even cruelty. It involves recognising the constraints that life places on us and the role that luck and randomness play in shaping our experience, and it takes a willingness to change one's perspective when the facts themselves remain painfully steadfast. It involves finding an ending that may not be happy but at least makes sense.

We saw this theme with Josie, now a mother-of-two, who reflects clear-sightedly and frankly on her drug-taking days with no desire to be that person again. We saw it with Tess: while her cruel teenage relationship continues to cast some long shadows, a school reunion allowed her at least to see what happened in a new light, to experience some version of a truce with the man who once broke her heart. And we see it with Chloe, who took many risks with her friend Natalie as a teenager. When Natalie was twenty-seven, she took her own life – a final, sudden ending to their shared story – and this caused a lot of soul-searching for Chloe:

> It's been three years now since Nat died. And I think now we've got the three-year anniversary behind us, I'm able to reflect on things much more positively now, now that more time has passed. I reflected on [our risk-taking] a lot in the earlier days, when she first died. I did have a lot of regrets and a lot of things that I wish I hadn't done, and I definitely know now that there's a lot of things that I shouldn't have done, and if I was to do it all again, I might not do it again. Things that I think were gateways to later bad decisions that she made.
>
> I sometimes wonder whether . . . when we were younger, if I hadn't been like, 'Let's take all the drugs and have sex with all of the boys,' and instead had said, 'Well why don't we try and do something a little bit more positive?', then something might be different. I wasn't always helpful in stopping things from spiralling. But I don't have the regrets in the same way now that I've processed the pain associated with them. I try not to harbour it as a regret as an adult because I see myself as a young person then and not as the adult that I am now.
>
> And I do love some of those memories. They definitely weren't the best years of our lives. They were hard, they were difficult times. But they were fun. We did so much fun shit. And I won't take her out of any of the memories, you know? And I wouldn't take away the pain that I've experienced. Some of the most traumatic experiences of my life happened directly or indirectly because of Nat. But I still wouldn't take her out of it. I wouldn't get rid of the pain to get rid of the good times. Definitely not.

Chloe is demonstrating something very important here. The clue is in this sentence of hers: 'I try not to harbour it as a regret as an adult because I see myself as a young person then and not as the adult that I am now.' This is something we can all do to come to terms with our own adolescent experiences, and it's why I wrote this book: if we can better recognise the psychological change that is taking place during those formative years, we can use this to understand who we used to be. If this research was more widely known, if there was a greater appreciation of the fundamental differences between adolescents and adults, we could all be kinder towards, and more accepting of, our former selves.

The power of understanding adolescence

No two adolescents are exactly the same, but as we have seen throughout this book, there are general developmental processes that drive a great deal of teenage behaviour. As adolescents we care desperately about developing an independent identity and about fitting in with our peers, and this affects almost everything we do, driving us to all sorts of self-destructive and sometimes cruel behaviour. When grappling with the consequences of those behaviours, an understanding of the general psychology of adolescence can help explain *why* we and others behaved as we did, even if that doesn't excuse those actions. It can still hurt. It can still be immoral and unfair. You can be embarrassed or angry or regretful about what you did, or how others treated you, and carry those feelings with you forever. But if you recognise *why* things happened, if you find a way for it to make *sense*, then you are on the way to an interpretation that will bring you peace.

Crucially, while our pasts cannot change, our stories can. They are based on real events, of course, but events seen through the broken mirrors of your memory, rehashed in your mind again and again over years and decades. For almost any event, there will be multiple potential effects and consequences, some good and some bad, and therefore multiple different aspects of the event we might focus on. Likewise, people's motivations and intentions are subjective and ambiguous and can be interpreted in all sorts of different ways. This is a good thing. You are not what happened to you. You are your mangled, half-true *interpretation* of what happened to you – and within that interpretation, there is always room for movement. In other words, whatever you've experienced, there might be some room to frame it in a different way. This is what makes it possible to rewrite the book of our own adolescence, or parts of it at least.

How memory works

In fact, most memories are not static but by their very nature are subject to a gradual, long-term process of change. The exception to this are some memories that derive from traumatic experience – in fact, their fixedness, along with how all-encompassing they are, is part of what makes them so distressing. But in general, memory can be surprisingly fluid. When you have an experience that you go on to remember many years later, three processes take place in your brain. First, in the moment of the experience itself, the memory is *encoded* – like being written down on a piece of paper. It's then *stored* in your brain over time – like putting the piece of paper in a filing cabinet. Finally, you *retrieve* it later on – you locate the filing cabinet, flick through related memories, and find and read the one you were after. Except it's not much like this at all because each of these three processes is fluid and subject to change, allowing some aspects of the experience to be forgotten entirely while others are embellished or reinterpreted. When you encode an event – even as it's happening – what you 'write down' are not the objective facts of what occurred but your subjective interpretation of it; as researchers have shown, our brain does not simply receive and transcribe information but is continually interpreting and constructing our experience based on its own assumptions and predictions, which are themselves derived from one's particular biology, personality, mood, biases and other factors.[14] In the words of psychologist Robyn Fivush and colleagues, what gets written into your memory is 'never pure'.[15]

Then, during storage, parts of the memory weaken or disappear. Let's say the filing cabinet gets left open, and the notes fade in the sunlight from a nearby window. Some of the detail gets lost altogether. Then, when you come to retrieve the memory, you recast it once again through the lens of your present self, with all of your new preoccupations, experiences and biases. The person who opens the filing cabinet is never the same person who wrote the note, nor the same person who opened it last time, and that affects how they interpret the fading words on the page. But more than this, the new interpretation of the note is what then gets filed away again, as if it's been written over with fresh ink. Every time you retrieve a memory, you re-encode it slightly, and the thing gets distorted further. As Fivush and colleagues say, the process of remembering is better conceptualised as *ongoing remembering*, because each time you recount something, it 'changes the system such that future retrievals will reconstruct somewhat different products'.

All this should give us hope. From the very moment they are encoded, our memories are not recordings of experience but interpretations of them: stories that will change, whether we like it or not, in the retelling. What matters isn't necessarily what happened in your adolescent years, but what you *think* happened in your adolescent years, and how you reflect on it now – in other words, how you retell the story.

Many people gradually rewrite their teenage stories on their own, after many years of processing and reflecting on their experiences. Often, these rewritten stories have themes of redemption or acceptance, and give people a peaceful sense of closure. But for others, navigating the rewriting process on their own is just too hard. In such cases, help is available in the form of therapy. A therapist can enable a person to reinterpret past events, to see things from different perspectives, and to question unhelpful assumptions about themselves. Psychologist Maya Benish-Weisman summed it up when she wrote that the goal of therapy was to 'compose new endings to unhappy stories'.[16]

To do this, a good therapist must do one thing above all others: truly *listen* to the person telling their story. Time and again, research has shown that a key factor that predicts good outcomes from therapy, perhaps more so than the type of therapy, is the so-called 'therapeutic alliance' between the client and the therapist, and fundamental to this is whether the client believes the therapist is listening.[17] This means the therapist doing some non-verbal basics – looking at the person, nodding – but also showing they have understood with 'verbal expressions of listening': reflecting the person's experience back to them in the therapist's own words, asking detailed questions. In fact, there is evidence that people are particularly likely to trust these verbal signs that they are being listened to, probably because they are much harder to fake.[18] Some academics have reflected on how good therapists not only do this but actually engage in 'double listening': they listen to the explicit story that the client is telling, but in parallel, they listen to the subtext, to alternative ways of understanding the events, mentally constructing an alternative, more helpful story to share.[19]

Many people in this book have had therapy relating to their adolescent years – indeed, I'd argue that many of them felt able to get in contact with me to share their experiences *because* they'd had therapy relating to those events. Certainly, many of the stories related in the interviews in this book are the end product of many years of reflection, often with the help of a therapist. Or at least, that's what I thought. Then, as I was coming to the end of writing the book, something unexpected happened.

Before finalising the manuscript, I contacted each of my interviewees to show them what I'd written about them, to ensure it was accurate and that they felt comfortable with the portrayal. What they wrote back surprised and moved me a great deal. Again and again, they said that reading their story reflected back to them, particularly in the context of the psychological research, had helped them understand what had happened to them – and thus who they are today – in a new way. One said that, twenty years on, they felt like their shoulders had finally dropped. Another said that, for the first time, they felt able to talk to other people about what had happened to them. Several had been moved to tears. Each interviewee had told me their story in their own words, which I had faithfully transcribed. But in telling their story back to them, in framing it and contextualising it and reinterpreting it, I had arrived at conclusions, found new endings, that they might not otherwise have seen themselves – and it helped.

Inspired by my interviewees, I have a confession to make. In the early stages of writing this book, I had imagined I might share some of my own adolescent stories. I decided not to because the stories I encountered through my interviews seemed in the end more interesting and more powerful than my own. Of course, that's part of the truth of adolescence: though everyone's is unique, our every heartbreak, our every bad decision, our every embarrassment has happened in some form to someone else, too. But through interviewing other people about their adolescent years and reading a great deal of research on this topic, something inside me began to shift.

As an academic psychologist I have studied adolescence for more than a decade, and yet it was only through writing this book that I really began to understand what had happened in my own. Half-written chapters in my life finally found endings; books that lay open in the back offices of my mind could finally be closed. There are certain memories that I feel at peace with for the first time in twenty years. In other words, I wrote this book to show how knowledge of adolescent development can help people better understand themselves, and in the process I ended up better understanding myself.

The whole of adult society is built on millions of adolescent stories. Each of us is standing on the shoulders of our fragile teenage selves. In childhood we established the basics – who we can trust, what actions lead to good and bad outcomes, how we're supposed to behave. But it is in adolescence that we truly come alive, that our experiences really start to shape the person we become. Knowing this has changed how I see everyone.

When I see groups of teenagers trudging home in their school uniforms, my heart aches for them. I notice when they all have matching bags or shoes or hairstyles. I notice whoever is standing at the side of the group, hovering on the edge of true belonging, and I wonder how hard they are finding it. I notice the solitary figures walking alone, headphones in, and I wonder what music they're listening to and what is on their mind. Perhaps more importantly, I see adults differently now too. When I see people going about their lives, I find myself wondering who is carrying around a lingering memory of their first love, who remembers something they were told about their appearance that still affects them today, and who is living with the lifetime consequences of teenage grief. I see that we were all adolescents once, every one of us, and we all have a story to tell.

Acknowledgements

First and foremost, thank you so much to the twenty-three people whose interviews gave this book its heart. You each shared your personal, often difficult memories with me with honesty and patience, and I am so grateful for your time. Writing is a lonely process, but my conversations with you all were welcome moments of intimacy and connection. Most importantly, your stories – along with the many other stories I gratefully received online – reminded me why this might be an important book to write.

Thank you to Will Francis at Janklow & Nesbit, for getting this idea off the ground in early 2021 and for providing excellent support ever since. I am also so grateful to Will Hammond at The Bodley Head, for being an exceptionally skilled and thoughtful editor. From big-picture discussions about key messages, down to conversations via Word comments about specific sentences and words, I'm not sure all authors get quite this lucky, so thank you. I know this is officially my book, but I see it as your book, too.

Thank you to my six sensitivity readers, who read over various sections of this book and who helped me think through some complex decisions about how to discuss particular topics. I am incredibly grateful for your consideration and help, and for your willingness to share your lived experience or professional expertise.

I also want to acknowledge my academic colleagues who work in the field of adolescent development and who continue to teach me a great deal about this formative period of life. Particular thanks to Prof Sarah-Jayne Blakemore, who was one of the first to promote how adolescence should be studied in its own right, and who helped usher me down this pathway when I was a postdoctoral researcher at UCL. I am also grateful to Dr Jack Andrews, for discussions about our work in this area on a near-daily basis, and to Dr Ola Demkowicz, for our fruitful conversations about adolescent girlhood and research more generally.

Lastly, thank you to my lovely and ever-changing research group at the University of Oxford, who continue to inspire and educate me as I move further and further away from my target demographic . . .

At home, I'm so grateful to Mark, who knew to stay away whenever I shut the door to write, but listened with convincing interest every lunchtime and evening when I was ready to talk. Thank you for giving an early version of the book an unbiased 10 out of 10. To my family and friends, to whom I am bound by my own adolescent stories: thank you for remembering to ask about how this was going. Last of all, I want to thank my mini dachshund, Michael, who sat on my lap for many hours while I wrote: you have absolutely no idea what's going on, but offer excellent emotional support nonetheless.

References

Introduction: The power of adolescence

1 Munawar K., Kuhn S. K., Haque S. 'Understanding the reminiscence bump: A systematic review'. *PLOS ONE*. 2018; 13(12):e0208595.

2 Coleman J. *The adolescent society: The social life of the teenager and its impact on education.* New York: Free Press of Glencoe; 1961.

3 Erikson E. H. *Identity, youth and crisis.* New York: W. W. Norton; 1968.

4 McAdams D. P., Josselson R., Lieblich A., editors. *Identity and story: Creating self in narrative.* Washington, DC: American Psychological Association; 2006.

5 McAdams D. P. 'Narrative identity: What is it? What does it do? How do you measure it?' *Imagin Cogn Pers*. 2018; 37(3):359–72.

6 Pinyerd B., Zipf W. B. 'Puberty – timing is everything!' *J Pediat Nurs*. 2005; 20(2):75–82.

7 Lucien J. N., Ortega M. T., Shaw N. D. 'Sleep and puberty'. *Curr Opin Endocr Metab Res*. 2021; 17:1–7.

8 Louzada F. 'Adolescent sleep: A major public health issue'. *Sleep Sci*. 2019; 12(1):1–7.

9 Blakemore S., Burnett S., Dahl R. E. 'The role of puberty in the developing adolescent brain'. *Hum Brain Mapp*. 2010; 31(6):926–33.

10 Larson R., Wilson S. 'Adolescence across place and time: Globalisation and the changing pathways to adulthood'. In: Lerner R. M., Steinberg L., editors. *Handbook of adolescent psychology.* Hoboken: Wiley; 2004; pp. 297–330.

11 Duell N., Steinberg L., Icenogle G., Chein J., Chaudhary N., Di Giunta L., et al. 'Age patterns in risk taking across the world'. *J Youth Adolesc*. 2018; 47(5):1052–72.

12 Conway M. A., Wang Q., Hanyu K., Haque S. 'A cross-cultural investigation of autobiographical memory: On the universality and cultural

variation of the reminiscence bump'. *J Cross-Cult Psychol.* 2005; 36(6): 739–49.

1. The paradox of popularity

1 Youniss J., McLellan J. A., Strouse D. ' "We're popular, but we're not snobs": Adolescents describe their crowds'. In: Montemayor R., Adams G. R., Gullotta T. P., editors. *Personal relationships during adolescence.* Beverly Hills: Sage Publications; 1994; pp. 101–22.

2 Brown B. B., Klute C. 'Friendships, cliques, and crowds'. In: Adams G. R., Berzonsky M. D., editors. *Blackwell Handbook of Adolescence.* Malden: Blackwell Publishing; 2003; pp. 330–48.

3 Ibid.

4 Laursen B., Veenstra R. 'Toward understanding the functions of peer influence: A summary and synthesis of recent empirical research'. *J Res Adolesc.* 2021; 31(4):889–907.

5 Mayeux L., Kleiser M. 'A gender prototypicality theory of adolescent peer popularity'. *Adolesc Res Rev.* 2020; 5(3):295–306.

6 Ibid.

7 Chu J. Y. 'Adolescent boys' friendships and peer group culture'. *New Dir Child Adolesc Dev.* 2005; (107):7–22.

8 Horn S. S. 'Adolescents' acceptance of same-sex peers based on sexual orientation and gender expression'. *J Youth Adolesc.* 2007; 36(3): 363–71.

9 Demkowicz O., Jefferson R., Nanda P., Foulkes L., Lam J., Pryjmachuk S., et al. 'Adolescent girls' explanations of high rates of low mood and anxiety in their population: A co-produced qualitative study'. https://doi.org/10.21203/rs.3.rs-3780794/v1

10 Hartl A. C., Laursen B., Cantin S., Vitaro F. 'A test of the bistrategic control hypothesis of adolescent popularity'. *Child Dev.* 2020; 91(3).

11 Mayeux and Kleiser, op. cit.

12 Rosen N. E., Lord C., Volkmar F. R. 'The diagnosis of autism: From Kanner to DSM-III to DSM-5 and beyond'. *J Autism Dev Disord.* 2021; 51(12):4253–70.

13 Deckers A., Muris P., Roelofs J. 'Being on your own or feeling lonely? Loneliness and other social variables in youths with autism spectrum disorders'. *Child Psychiatry Hum Dev*. 2017; 48(5):828–39.

14 Adreon D., Stella J. 'Transition to middle and high school: Increasing the success of students with Asperger Syndrome'. *Interv Sch Clin*. 2001; 36(5):266–71.

15 Cook J., Hull L., Crane L., Mandy W. 'Camouflaging in autism: A systematic review'. *Clin Psychol Rev*. 2021; 89:102080.

16 Wood-Downie H., Wong B., Kovshoff H., Mandy W., Hull L., Hadwin J. A. 'Sex/gender differences in camouflaging in children and adolescents with autism'. *J Autism Dev Disord*. 2021; 51(4):1353–64.

17 Bargiela S., Steward R., Mandy W. 'The experiences of late-diagnosed women with autism spectrum conditions: An investigation of the female autism phenotype'. *J Autism Dev Disord*. 2016; 46(10):3281–94.

18 Humphrey N., Hebron J. 'Bullying of children and adolescents with autism spectrum conditions: A "state of the field" review'. *Int J Incl Educ*. 2015; 19(8):845–62.

19 Fisher M. H., Taylor J. L. 'Let's talk about it: Peer victimization experiences as reported by adolescents with autism spectrum disorder'. *Autism*. 2016; 20(4):402–11.

20 Sosnowy C., Silverman C., Shattuck P., Garfield T. 'Setbacks and successes: How young adults on the autism spectrum seek friendship'. *Autism Adulthood*. 2019; 1(1):44–51.

21 Cooper R., Cooper K., Russell A. J., Smith L. G. E. ' "I'm proud to be a little bit different": The effects of autistic individuals' perceptions of autism and autism social identity on their collective self-esteem'. *J Autism Dev Disord*. 2021; 51(2):704–14.

22 Pellicano E., Houting J. 'Annual Research Review: Shifting from "normal science" to neurodiversity in autism science'. *J Child Psychol Psychiatry*. 2022; 63(4):381–96.

23 Rose A. J., Swenson L. P. , Waller E. M. 'Overt and relational aggression and perceived popularity: Developmental differences in concurrent and prospective relations'. *Dev Psychol*. 2004; 40(3):378–87.

24 Cillessen A. H. N., Rose A. J. 'Understanding popularity in the peer system'. *Curr Dir Psychol Sci*. 2005; 14(2):102–5.

25 Hartl, Laursen, Cantin and Vitaro, op. cit.

26 Eder D. 'The cycle of popularity: Interpersonal relations among female adolescents'. *Sociol of Educ.* 1985; 58(3):154–65.

27 Ibid.

28 Almquist Y. B., Brännström L. 'Childhood peer status and the clustering of social, economic, and health-related circumstances in adulthood'. *Soc Sci Med.* 2014; 105:67–75.

29 Ibid.

30 Arseneault L. 'The long-term impact of bullying victimization on mental health'. *World Psychiatry.* 2017; 16(1):27–8.

31 Mayeux L., Sandstrom M. J., Cillessen A. H. N. 'Is being popular a risky proposition?' *J Res Adolesc.* 2008; 18(1):49–74.

32 Allen J. P., Schad M. M., Oudekerk B., Chango J. 'What ever happened to the "cool" kids? Long-term sequelae of early adolescent pseudomature behavior'. *Child Dev.* 2014; 85(5):1866–80.

2. *Image is everything*

1 Ortmeyer D. H. 'The we-self of identical twins'. *Contemp Psychoanal.* 1970; 6(2):125–42.

2 Twins Trust. 'Multiple birth statistics' [internet]. Aldershot, UK; 2019. Available from: https://twinstrust.org/static/89af4d2a-49fe-4d23-bbcf 8475f099762f/5cdfb852-318c-4eb8-955ef8f6b8f5d6c0/Key-stats-and-facts.pdf

3 Jones D. C., Crawford J. K. 'The peer appearance culture during adolescence: Gender and body mass variations'. *J Youth Adolesc.* 2006; 35(2): 243–55.

4 Lowy A. S., Rodgers R. F., Franko D. L., Pluhar E., Webb J. B. 'Body image and internalization of appearance ideals in Black women: An update and call for culturally-sensitive research'. *Body Image.* 2021; 39: 313–27.

5 Van Geel M., Vedder P., Tanilon J. 'Are overweight and obese youths more often bullied by their peers? A meta-analysis on the relation between weight status and bullying'. *Int J Obes.* 2014 Oct; 38(10): 1263–7.

6 Kearney-Cooke A., Tieger D. 'Body image disturbance and the development of eating disorders'. In: Smolak L., Levine M. P., editors. *The Wiley handbook of eating disorders.* Hoboken: Wiley; 2015; pp. 283–96.

7 Ahrberg M., Trojca D., Nasrawi N., Vocks S. 'Body image disturbance in binge eating disorder: A review'. *Eur Eat Disorders Rev.* 2011; 19(5): 375–81.

8 Favaro A., Busetto P., Collantoni E., Santonastaso P. 'The age of onset of eating disorders'. In: De Girolamo G., McGorry P. D., Sartorius N., editors. *Age of onset of mental disorders: Etiopathogenetic and treatment implications.* Cham: Springer; 2019; pp. 203–16.

9 Zipfel S., Giel K. E., Bulik C. M., Hay P., Schmidt U. 'Anorexia nervosa: Aetiology, assessment, and treatment'. *Lancet Psychiatry.* 2015; 2(12):1099–1111.

10 McGrath J. J., Al-Hamzawi A., Alonso J., Altwaijri Y., Andrade L. H., Bromet E. J., et al. 'Age of onset and cumulative risk of mental disorders: A cross-national analysis of population surveys from 29 countries'. *Lancet Psychiatry.* 2023; 10(9):668–81.

11 Giedd J. N., Keshavan M., Paus T. 'Why do many psychiatric disorders emerge during adolescence?' *Nat Rev Neurosci.* 2008; 9(12):947–57.

12 Rapee R. M., Oar E. L., Johnco C. J., Forbes M. K., Fardouly J., Magson N. R., et al. 'Adolescent development and risk for the onset of social-emotional disorders: A review and conceptual model'. *Behav Res Ther.* 2019; 123:103501.

13 Brook C. A., Schmidt L. 'Social anxiety disorder: A review of environmental risk factors'. *Neuropsychiatr Dis Treat.* 2008; 123–43.

14 Piacentini M., Mailer G. 'Symbolic consumption in teenagers' clothing choices'. *J Consum Behav.* 2004; 3(3):251–62.

15 Isaksen K. J., Roper S. 'The impact of branding on low-income adolescents: A vicious cycle?' *Psychol Mark.* 2008; 25(11):1063–87.

16 Piacentini and Mailer, op. cit.

17 Isaksen and Roper, op. cit.

18 Piacentini and Mailer, op. cit.

19 Isaksen and Roper, op. cit.

20 Gal D. 'Identity-Signaling Behavior'. In: Norton M. I., Rucker D. D., Lamberton C., editors. *The Cambridge handbook of consumer psychology.* Cambridge: Cambridge University Press; 2015; pp. 257–81.

21 Rowe P. 'Becoming metal: Narrative reflections on the early formation and embodiment of heavy metal identities'. *J Youth Stud.* 2017; 20(6): 713–31.

22 McDermott M., Samson F. 'White racial and ethnic identity in the United States'. *Annu Rev Sociol.* 2005; 31(1):245–61.

3. In defence of risk-taking

1   Martin L. 'Ten years have passed – yet I'm still haunted by Leah's death'. *The Observer* [internet]. 2005; 30 October; available from: https://www.theguardian.com/society/2005/oct/30/drugsandalcohol. drugs

2   Duell, Steinberg, Icenogle, Chein, Chaudhary, Di Giunta, et al., op. cit.

3   Ibid.

4   Millstein S. G., Halpern-Felsher B. L. 'Judgments about risk and perceived invulnerability in adolescents and young adults'. *J Res Adolesc.* 2002; 12(4):399–422.

5   Ibid.

6   Ibid.

7   Steinberg L., Albert D., Cauffman E., Banich M., Graham S., Woolard J. 'Age differences in sensation seeking and impulsivity as indexed by behavior and self-report: Evidence for a dual systems model'. *Dev Psychol.* 2008; 44(6):1764–78.

8   Steinberg L. 'A dual systems model of adolescent risk-taking'. *Dev Psychobiol.* 2010; 216–24.

9   Pfeifer J. H., Allen N. B. 'Arrested development? Reconsidering dual-systems models of brain function in adolescence and disorders'. *Trends Cogn Sci.* 2012; 16(6):322–9.

10 Maslowsky J., Owotomo O., Huntley E. D., Keating D. 'Adolescent risk behavior: Differentiating reasoned and reactive risk-taking'. *J Youth Adolesc.* 2019; 48(2):243–55.

11 Ibid.

12 Gardner M., Steinberg L. 'Peer influence on risk taking, risk preference, and risky decision making in adolescence and adulthood: An experimental study'. *Dev Psychol.* 2005; 41(4):625–35.

13 Johnson S. B., Dariotis J. K., Wang C. 'Adolescent risk taking under stressed and nonstressed conditions: Conservative, calculating, and impulsive types'. *J Adolesc Health*. 2012; 51(2):S34–40.

14 Blakemore S. J. 'Avoiding social risk in adolescence'. *Curr Dir Psychol Sci*. 2018; 27(2):116–22.

15 Ibid.

16 Andrews J. L., Foulkes L. E., Bone J. K., Blakemore S. J. 'Amplified concern for social risk in adolescence: Development and validation of a new measure'. *Brain Sci*. 2020; 10(6):397–411.

17 Ungar M. T. 'The myth of peer pressure'. *Adolescence*. 2000; 35(137): 167–80.

18 Michell L., West P. 'Peer pressure to smoke: The meaning depends on the method'. *Health Educ Res*. 1996; (1):39–49.

19 Patrick M. E., Schulenberg J. E., Maggs J. L., Maslowsky J. 'Substance use and peers during adolescence and the transition to adulthood: Selection, socialization, and development'. In: Sher K. J., editor. *The Oxford handbook of substance use and substance use disorders*. Oxford: Oxford University Press; 2016; pp. 526–48.

20 Henry D. B., Schoeny M. E., Deptula D. P., Slavick J. T. 'Peer selection and socialization effects on adolescent intercourse without a condom and attitudes about the costs of sex'. *Child Dev*. 2007; 78(3):825–38.

21 Fortuin J., Van Geel M., Vedder P. 'Peer influences on internalizing and externalizing problems among adolescents: A longitudinal social network analysis'. *J Youth Adolesc*. 2015; 44(4):887–97.

22 Goodwin N. P., Mrug S., Borch C., Cillessen A. H. N. 'Peer selection and socialization in adolescent depression: The role of school transitions'. *J Youth Adolesc*. 2012; 41(3):320–32.

23 Bentley K. H., Nock M. K., Barlow D. H. 'The four-function model of nonsuicidal self-injury: Key directions for future research'. *Clin Psychol Sci*. 2014; 2(5):638–56.

24 Gillies D., Christou M. A., Dixon A. C., Featherston O. J., Rapti I., Garcia-Anguita A., et al. 'Prevalence and characteristics of self-harm in adolescents: Meta-analyses of community-based studies 1990–2015'. *J Am Acad Child Adolesc Psychiatry*. 2018; 57(10):733–41.

25 Mars B., Heron J., Klonsky E. D., Moran P., O'Connor R. C., Tilling K., et al. 'Predictors of future suicide attempt among adolescents with

suicidal thoughts or non-suicidal self-harm: a population-based birth cohort study'. *Lancet Psychiatry.* 2019; 6(4):327–37.

26 Crudgington H., Wilson E., Copeland M., Morgan C., Knowles G. 'Peer-friendship networks and self-injurious thoughts and behaviors in adolescence: A systematic review of sociometric school-based studies that use social network analysis'. *Adolesc Res Rev.* 2023; 8(1):21–43.

27 Ibid.

28 Bernasco E. L., Van Der Graaff J., Nelemans S. A., Kaufman T. M. L., Branje S. 'Depression socialization in early adolescent friendships: The role of baseline depressive symptoms and autonomous functioning'. *J Youth Adolesc.* 2023; 52(7):1417–32.

29 Ibbetson C. 'How many children have their own tech?' [internet]. London: YouGov UK; March 2020. Available from: https://yougov.co.uk/topics/society/articles-reports/2020/03/13/what-age-do-kids-get-phones-tablet-laptops-

30 Available from: bark.us

31 Lejuez C. W., Aklin W. M., Zvolensky M. J., Pedulla C. M. 'Evaluation of the Balloon Analogue Risk Task (BART) as a predictor of adolescent real-world risk-taking behaviours'. *J Adolesc.* 2003; 26(4): 475–9.

32 Maner J. K., Richey J. A., Cromer K., Mallott M., Lejuez C. W., Joiner T. E., et al. 'Dispositional anxiety and risk-avoidant decision-making'. *Pers Individ Diff.* 2007; 42(4):665–75.

33 Blumenthal H., Leen-Feldner E. W., Badour C. L., Babson K. A. 'Anxiety psychopathology and alcohol use among adolescents: A critical review of the empirical literature and recommendations for future research'. *J of Exp Psychopathol.* 2011; 2(3):318–53.

34 Kaczkurkin A. N., Foa E. B. 'Cognitive-behavioral therapy for anxiety disorders: An update on the empirical evidence'. *Dialogues Clin Neurosci.* 2015; 17(3):337–46.

35 Borkovec T. D., Hazlett-Stevens H., Diaz M. L. 'The role of positive beliefs about worry in generalized anxiety disorder and its treatment'. *Clin Psychol Psychother.* May 1999; 6(2):126–38.

36 Berenbaum H., Thompson R. J., Bredemeier K. 'Perceived threat: Exploring its association with worry and its hypothesized antecedents'. *Behaviour Research and Therapy.* October 2007; 45(10):2473–82.

37 Foulkes L., Andrews J. L. 'Are mental health awareness efforts contributing to the rise in reported mental health problems? A call to test the prevalence inflation hypothesis'. *New Ideas Psychol.* 2023; 69:101010.

4. The psychology of bullying

1 Wójcik M., Flak W. 'Frenemy: A New Addition to the Bullying Circle'. *J Interpers Violence.* 2021; 36(19–20):NP11131–54.

2 Pan B., Zhang L., Ji L., Garandeau C. F., Salmivalli C., Zhang W. 'Classroom status hierarchy moderates the association between social dominance goals and bullying behavior in middle childhood and early adolescence'. *J Youth Adolesc.* 2020; 49(11):2285–97.

3 Hawkins D. L., Pepler D. J., Craig W. M. 'Naturalistic observations of peer interventions in bullying'. *Soc Dev.* 2001; 10(4):512–27.

4 Thomas H. J., Connor J. P., Scott J. G. 'Why do children and adolescents bully their peers? A critical review of key theoretical frameworks'. *Soc Psychiatry Psychiatr Epidemiol.* 2018; 53(5):437–51.

5 Bowen M. 'The use of family theory in clinical practice'. *Compr Psychiatry.* 1966; 7(5):345–74.

6 Zych I., Ttofi M. M., Llorent V. J., Farrington D. P., Ribeaud D., Eisner M. P. 'A longitudinal study on stability and transitions among bullying roles'. *Child Dev.* 2020; 91(2):527–45.

7 Zych I., Ttofi M. M., Farrington D. P. 'Empathy and callous–unemotional traits in different bullying roles: A systematic review and meta-analysis'. *Trauma Violence Abuse.* 2019; 20(1):3–21.

8 Ibid.

9 Waller R., Hyde L. W., Baskin-Sommers A. R., Olson S. L. 'Interactions between callous unemotional behaviors and executive function in early childhood predict later aggression and lower peer-liking in late-childhood'. *J Abnorm Child Psychol.* 2017; 45(3):597–609.

10 Hyde L. W., Dotterer H. L. 'The nature and nurture of callous–unemotional traits'. *Curr Dir Psychol Sci.* 2022; 31(6):546–55.

11 Salmivalli C., Lagerspetz K., Björkqvist K., Österman K., Kaukiainen A. 'Bullying as a group process: Participant roles and their relations to social status within the group'. *Aggr Behav.* 1998; 22(1):1–15.

12 Salmivalli C. 'Bullying and the peer group: A review'. *Aggress Violent Behavior*. 2010; 15(2):112–20.

13 Ibid.

14 Thornberg R., Delby H. 'How do secondary school students explain bullying?' *Educ Res*. 2019; 61(2):142–60.

15 Gaffney H., Ttofi M. M., Farrington D. P. 'What works in anti-bullying programs? Analysis of effective intervention components'. *J Sch Psychol*. 2021; 85:37–56.

16 Pöyhönen V., Juvonen J., Salmivalli C. 'What does it take to stand up for the victim of bullying? The interplay between personal and social factors'. *Merrill-Palmer Q*. 2010; 56(2):143–63.

17 Foulkes L., Leung J. T., Fuhrmann D., Knoll L. J., Blakemore S. J. 'Age differences in the prosocial influence effect'. *Dev Sci*. 2018; 21(6):e12666.

18 Chierchia G., Piera Pi-Sunyer B., Blakemore S. J. 'Prosocial influence and opportunistic conformity in adolescents and young adults'. *Psychol Sci*. 2020; 31(12):1585–1601.

19 Busching R., Krahé B. 'With a little help from their peers: The impact of classmates on adolescents' development of prosocial behavior'. *J Youth Adolesc*. 2020; 49(9):1849–63.

20 Brechwald W. A., Prinstein M. J. 'Beyond homophily: A decade of advances in understanding peer influence processes'. *J Res Adolesc*. 2011; 21(1):166–79.

21 Ibid.

22 Perkins H. W., Craig D. W., Perkins J. M. 'Using social norms to reduce bullying: A research intervention among adolescents in five middle schools'. *Group Process Intergroup Relat*. 2011; 14(5):703–22.

23 Paluck E. L., Shepherd H., Aronow P. M. 'Changing climates of conflict: A social network experiment in 56 schools'. *Proc Natl Acad Sci USA*. 2016; 113(3):566–71.

24 Gaffney H., Farrington D. P., Ttofi M. M. 'Examining the effectiveness of school-bullying intervention programs globally: A meta-analysis'. *Int J Bullying Prev*. 2019; 1(1):14–31.

25 Koyanagi A., Oh H., Carvalho A. F., Smith L., Haro J. M., Vancampfort D., et al. 'Bullying victimization and suicide attempt among

adolescents aged 12–15 years from 48 countries'. *J Am Acad Child Adolesc Psychiatry*. 2019; 58(9):907–918.e4.

26 Arseneault L. 'Annual Research Review: The persistent and pervasive impact of being bullied in childhood and adolescence: Implications for policy and practice'. *J Child Psychol Psychiatry*. 2018; 59(4):405–21.

5. First love

1 Rubin D. C., Berntsen D. 'Life scripts help to maintain autobiographical memories of highly positive, but not highly negative, events'. *Mem Cogn*. 2003; 31(1):1–14.

2 Brown B. B. ' "You're going out with who?": Peer group influences on adolescent romantic relationships'. In: Furman W., Brown B. B., Feiring C., editors. *The development of romantic relationships in adolescence*. Cambridge: Cambridge University Press; 1999; pp. 291–329.

3 Ibid.

4 Erikson, op. cit.

5 Stijelja S., Mishara B. L. 'Psychosocial characteristics of involuntary celibates (incels): A review of empirical research and assessment of the potential implications of research on adult virginity and late sexual onset'. *Sex Cult*. 2023; 27(2):715–34.

6 Donnelly D., Burgess E., Anderson S., Davis R., Dillard J. 'Involuntary celibacy: A life course analysis'. *J Sex Res*. 2001; 38(2):159–69.

7 Robertson M. A. ' "How do I know I am gay?": Understanding sexual orientation, identity and behavior among adolescents in an LGBT youth center'. *Sex Cult*. 2014; 18(2):385–404.

8 Office for National Statistics. 'Sexual orientation by age and sex, England and Wales: Census 2021' [internet]. January 2023. (Census 2021). Available from: https://www.ons.gov.uk/peoplepopulationandcommunity/culturalidentity/sexuality/articles/sexualorientationageandsexenglandandwales/census2021

9 Robertson, op. cit.

10 Alonzo D. J., Buttitta D. J. 'Is "coming out" still relevant? Social justice implications for LGB-membered families'. *J Fam Theory Rev*. 2019; 11(3): 354–66.

11 Kahle L. 'Are Sexual Minorities More at Risk? Bullying Victimization Among Lesbian, Gay, Bisexual, and Questioning Youth'. *J Interpers Violence*. November 2020; 35(21–22):4960–78.

12 Alonzo and Buttitta, op. cit.

13 Epstein R., McKinney P., Fox S., Garcia C. 'Support for a fluid-continuum model of sexual orientation: A large-scale internet study'. *J Homosex*. 2012; 59(10):1356–81.

14 Grafsky E. L. 'Deciding to come out to parents: Toward a model of sexual orientation disclosure decisions'. *Fam Process*. 2018; 57(3): 783–99.

15 Son D., Updegraff K. A. 'Sexual minority adolescents' disclosure of sexual identity to family: A systematic review and conceptual framework'. *Adolescent Res Rev*. 2023; 8:75–95.

16 Di Giacomo E., Krausz M., Colmegna F., Aspesi F., Clerici M. 'Estimating the risk of attempted suicide among sexual minority youths: A systematic review and meta-analysis'. *JAMA Pediatr*. 2018; 172(12):1145.

17 McCormack M. 'Issues in bisexual men's lives: Identity, health and relationships'. *Curr Opin Psychol*. 2023; 49:101501.

18 Borver J., Gurevich M., Mathieson C. '(Con)tested identities: Bisexual women reorient sexuality'. *J Bisex*. 17 October 2001; 2(2–3):23–52.

19 Bishop M. D., Fish J. N., Hammack P. L., Russell S. T. 'Sexual identity development milestones in three generations of sexual minority people: A national probability sample'. *Dev Psychol*. 2020; 56(11):2177–93.

20 Formby E. 'Limitations of focussing on homophobic, biphobic and transphobic "bullying" to understand and address LGBT young people's experiences within and beyond school'. *Sex Educ*. 2015; 15(6): 626–40.

21 Ibid.

22 Connolly J., McIsaac C. 'Adolescents' explanations for romantic dissolutions: A developmental perspective'. *J Adolesc*. 2009; 32(5): 1209–23.

23 Bravo V., Connolly J., McIsaac C. 'Why did it end? Breakup reasons of youth of different gender, dating stages, and ages'. *Emerg Adulthood*. 2017; 5(4):230–40.

24 Connolly and McIsaac, op. cit.

25 Larson R. W., Clore G. L., Wood G. A. 'The emotions of romantic relationships: Do they wreak havoc on adolescents?' In: *The development of romantic relationships in adolescence*. Cambridge: Cambridge University Press; 1999.

26 Douglas B., Orpinas P. 'Social misfit or normal development? Students who do not date'. *J Sch Health*. 2019; 89(10):783–90.

27 Ibid.

6. Sex education

1 Wellings K., Nanchahal K., Macdowall W., McManus S., Erens B., Mercer C. H., et al. 'Sexual behaviour in Britain: Early heterosexual experience'. *Lancet*. 2001; 358(9296):1843–50.

2 Hawes Z. C., Wellings K., Stephenson J. 'First heterosexual intercourse in the United Kingdom: A review of the literature'. *J Sex Res*. 2010; 47(2–3):137–52.

3 Sprecher S., O'Sullivan L. F., Drouin M., Verette-Lindenbaum J., Willetts M. C. 'Perhaps it was too soon: College students' reflections on the timing of their sexual debut'. *J Sex Res*. 2022; 59(1):39–52.

4 Dickson N., Paul C., Herbison P., Silva P. 'First sexual intercourse: Age, coercion, and later regrets reported by a birth cohort'. *BMJ*. 1998; 316(7124):29–33.

5 Sprecher S., O'Sullivan L. F., Drouin M., Verette-Lindenbaum J., Willetts M. C. 'The significance of sexual debut in women's lives'. *Curr Sex Health Rep*. 2019; 11(4):265–73.

6 Suleiman A. B., Deardorff J. 'Multiple dimensions of peer influence in adolescent romantic and sexual relationships: A descriptive, qualitative perspective'. *Arch Sex Behav*. 2015; 44(3):765–75.

7 Fortenberry J. D. 'Puberty and adolescent sexuality'. *Horm Behav*. 2013; 64(2):280–87.

8 Larsson I., Svedin C. G. 'Sexual experiences in childhood: Young adults' recollections'. *Arch Sex Behav*. 2002; 31(3):263–73.

9 Robbins C. L. 'Prevalence, frequency, and associations of masturbation with partnered sexual behaviors among US adolescents'. *Arch Pediatr Adolesc Med*. 2011; 165(12):1087.

10 Dawson L. H., Shih M. C., De Moor C., Shrier L. 'Reasons why adolescents and young adults have sex: Associations with psychological characteristics and sexual behavior'. *J Sex Res.* 2008; 45(3):225–32.

11 McCarthy F. P., O'Brien U., Kenny L. C. 'The management of teenage pregnancy'. *BMJ.* 2014; 349:g5887.

12 Raatikainen K., Heiskanen N., Verkasalo P. K., Heinonen S. 'Good outcome of teenage pregnancies in high-quality maternity care'. *Eur J Public Health.* 2006; 16(2):157–61.

13 McCarthy, O'Brien and Kenny, op. cit.

14 Amjad S., MacDonald I., Chambers T., Osornio-Vargas A., Chandra S., Voaklander D., et al. 'Social determinants of health and adverse maternal and birth outcomes in adolescent pregnancies: A systematic review and meta-analysis'. *Paediatric Perinatal Epid.* 2019; 33(1):88–99.

15 Hofferth S. L., Reid L., Mott F. L. 'The effects of early childbearing on schooling over time'. *Fam Plann Perspect.* 2001; 33(6):259–67.

16 Corcoran J. 'Consequences of adolescent pregnancy/parenting: A review of the literature'. *Soc Work Health Care.* 1998; 27(2):49–67.

17 Chernick L. S., Schnall R., Higgins T., Stockwell M. S., Castaño P. M., Santelli J., et al. 'Barriers to and enablers of contraceptive use among adolescent females and their interest in an emergency department based intervention'. *Contraception.* 2015; 91(3):217–25.

18 Chabbert-Buffet N., Jamin C., Lete I., Lobo P., Nappi R. E., Pintiaux A., et al. 'Missed pills: Frequency, reasons, consequences and solutions'. *Eur J Contracept Reprod Health Care.* 2017; 22(3):165–9.

19 Dermen K. H., Cooper M. L. 'Inhibition conflict and alcohol expectancy as moderators of alcohol's relationship to condom use'. *Exp and Clin Psychopharmacol.* 2000; 8(2):198–206.

20 Braun V. ' "Proper sex without annoying things": Anti-condom discourse and the "nature" of (hetero)sex'. *Sexualities.* 2013; 16(3–4): 361–82.

21 Ariely D., Loewenstein G. 'The heat of the moment: The effect of sexual arousal on sexual decision making'. *J Behav Decis Mak.* 2006; 19(2):87–98.

22 Peasant C., Parra G. R., Okwumabua T. M. 'Condom negotiation: findings and future directions'. *J Sex Res.* 2015; 52(4):470–83.

23 Ibid.

24 Ibid.

25 Hillier L., Harrison L., Warr D. ' "When you carry condoms all the boys think you want it": Negotiating competing discourses about safe sex'. *J Adolesc.* 1998; 21(1):15–29.

26 Kohler P. K., Manhart L. E., Lafferty W. E. 'Abstinence-only and comprehensive sex education and the initiation of sexual activity and teen pregnancy'. *J Adolesc Health.* 2008; 42(4):344–51.

27 Sedgh G., Finer L. B., Bankole A., Eilers M. A., Singh S. 'Adolescent pregnancy, birth, and abortion rates across countries: Levels and recent trends'. *J Adolesc Health.* 2015; 56(2):223–30.

28 Panchaud C., Singh S., Feivelson D., Darroch J. E. 'Sexually transmitted diseases among adolescents in developed countries'. *Fam Plann Perspect.* 2000; 32(1):24–32, 45.

29 Harden K. P. 'A sex-positive framework for research on adolescent sexuality'. *Perspect Psychol Sci.* 2014; 9(5):455–69.

30 Ibid.

31 Wiederman M. W. 'The gendered nature of sexual scripts'. *Fam J.* 2005; 13(4):496–502.

32 Ibid.

33 Kim J. L., Lynn Sorsoli C., Collins K., Zylbergold B. A., Schooler D., Tolman D. L. 'From Sex to sexuality: Exposing the heterosexual script on primetime network television'. *J Sex Res.* 2007; 44(2):145–57.

34 Ibid.

35 Tolman D. L. 'Dilemmas of desire: Teenage girls talk sexuality'. Cambridge, MA: Harvard University Press; 2005.

36 Kaestle C. E., Allen K. R. 'The role of masturbation in healthy sexual development: Perceptions of young adults'. *Arch Sex Behav.* 2011; 40(5): 983–94.

37 Rubinsky V., Cooke-Jackson A. ' "Tell me something other than to use a condom and sex is scary": Memorable messages women and gender minorities wish for and recall about sexual health'. *Women's Stud Commun.* 2017; 40(4):379–400.

38 Ibid.

39 Harden, op. cit.

40 Schalet A. 'Must we fear adolescent sexuality?' *Med Gen Med.* 2004; 6(4):44.

41 Ibid.

42 Weaver H., Smith G., Kippax S. 'School-based sex education policies and indicators of sexual health among young people: A comparison of the Netherlands, France, Australia and the United States'. *Sex Educ.* 2005; 5(2):171–88.

43 Peter J., Valkenburg P. M. 'Adolescents and pornography: A review of 20 years of research'. *J Sex Res.* 2016; 53(4–5):509–31.

44 Ibid.

45 Pathmendra P., Raggatt M., Lim M. S., Marino J. L., Skinner S. R. 'Exposure to pornography and adolescent sexual behavior: Systematic review'. *J Med Internet Res.* 2023; 25:e43116.

46 Ybarra M. L., Mitchell K. J., Hamburger M., Diener-West M., Leaf P. J. 'X-rated material and perpetration of sexually aggressive behavior among children and adolescents: Is there a link?' *Aggr Behav.* 2011; 37(1): 1–18.

47 Farré J. M., Montejo A. L., Agulló M., Granero R., Chiclana Actis C., Villena A., et al. 'Pornography use in adolescents and its clinical implications'. *J Clin Med.* 2020; 9(11):3625.

48 Grubbs J. B., Kraus S. W. 'Pornography use and psychological science: A call for consideration'. *Curr Dir Psychol Sci.* February 2021; 30(1): 68–75.

49 Litsou K., Byron P., McKee A., Ingham R. 'Learning from pornography: Results of a mixed methods systematic review'. *Sex Educ.* 2021; 21(2):236–52.

50 Palmer M. J., Clarke L., Ploubidis G. B., Mercer C. H., Gibson L. J., Johnson A. M., et al. 'Is "sexual competence" at first heterosexual intercourse associated with subsequent sexual health status?' *J Sex Res.* 2017; 54(1):91–104.

51 Ibid.

52 Dixon-Mueller R. 'How young is "too young"? Comparative perspectives on adolescent sexual, marital, and reproductive transitions'. *Stud Fam Plan.* 2008; 39(4):247–62.

53 Ibid.

54 Mercer J. 'Evidence of potentially harmful psychological treatments for children and adolescents'. *Child Adolesc Soc Work J.* 2017; 34(2):107–25.

55 Staras S. A. S., Cook R. L., Clark D. B. 'Sexual partner characteristics and sexually transmitted diseases among adolescents and young adults'. *Sexually Transmitted Diseases.* 2009; 36(4):232–8.

56 Finer L. B., Philbin J. M. 'Sexual initiation, contraceptive use, and pregnancy among young adolescents'. *Pediatrics.* 2013; 131(5):886–91.

57 Rothblum E. D., Krueger E. A., Kittle K. R., Meyer I. H. 'Asexual and non-asexual respondents from a U.S. population-based study of sexual minorities'. *Arch Sex Behav.* 2020; 49(2):757–67.

7. Loss

1 Harrison L., Harrington R. 'Adolescents' bereavement experiences: Prevalence, association with depressive symptoms, and use of services'. *J Adolesc.* 2001; 24(2):159–69.

2 Berg L., Rostila M., Hjern A. 'Parental death during childhood and depression in young adults – a national cohort study'. *J Child Psychol Psychiatr.* 2016; 57(9):1092–8.

3 Kaplow J. B., Layne C. M., Saltzman W. R., Cozza S. J., Pynoos R. S. 'Using multidimensional grief theory to explore the effects of deployment, reintegration, and death on military youth and families'. *Clin Child Fam Psychol Rev.* 2013; 16(3):322–40.

4 Robin L., Omar H. A. 'Adolescent bereavement'. In: Merrick J., Tenenbaum A., Omar H. A., editors. *School, adolescence, and health issues.* Hauppauge: Nova Science Publishers; 2014; pp. 97–108.

5 Larson R., Csikszentmihalyi M., Graef R. 'Mood variability and the psychosocial adjustment of adolescents'. *J Youth Adolesc.* 1980; 9(6): 469–90.

6 Stroebe M., Schut H. 'The dual process model of coping with bereavement: A decade on'. *Omega* (Westport). 2010; 61(4):273–89.

7 Layne C. M., Greeson J. K. P., Ostrowski S. A., Kim S., Reading S., Vivrette R. L., et al. 'Cumulative trauma exposure and high risk behavior in adolescence: Findings from the National Child Traumatic Stress Network Core Data Set'. *Psychol Trauma.* 2014; 6(Suppl 1):S40–49.

8 Ibid.

9 Elsner T. L., Krysinska K., Andriessen K. 'Bereavement and educational outcomes in children and young people: A systematic review'. *Sch Psychol Int*. 2022; 43(1):55–70.

10 Layne C. M., Kaplow J. B., Oosterhoff B., Hill R. M., Pynoos R. S. 'The interplay between post-traumatic stress and grief reactions in traumatically bereaved adolescents: When trauma, bereavement, and adolescence converge'. *Adolesc Psychiatry*. 2018; 7(4):266–85.

11 Elsner, Krysinska and Andriessen, op. cit.

12 Lin K. K., Sandler I. N., Ayers T. S., Wolchik S. A., Luecken L. J. 'Resilience in parentally bereaved children and adolescents seeking preventive services'. *J Clin Child Adolesc Psychol*. 2004; 33(4):673–83.

13 Lobb E. A., Kristjanson L. J., Aoun S. M., Monterosso L., Halkett G. K. B., Davies A. 'Predictors of complicated grief: A systematic review of empirical studies'. *Death Studies*. 2010; 34(8):673–98.

14 Shear M. K., Simon N., Wall M., Zisook S., Neimeyer R., Duan N., et al. 'Complicated grief and related bereavement issues for DSM-5'. *Depress Anxiety*. 2011; 28(2):103–17.

15 Andriessen K., Mowll J., Lobb E., Draper B., Dudley M., Mitchell P. B. '"Don't bother about me." The grief and mental health of bereaved adolescents'. *Death Studies*. 2018; 42(10):607–15.

16 Rosen H., Cohen H. I. 'Children's reaction to sibling loss'. *Clin Soc Work J*. 1981; 9(3):211–19.

17 Rask K., Kaunonen M., Paunonen-Ilmonen M. 'Adolescent coping with grief after the death of a loved one'. *Int J Nurs Pract*. 2002; 8(3):137–42.

18 Oltjenbruns K. A. 'Positive outcomes of adolescents' experience with grief'. *J Adolesc Res*. 1991; 6(1):43–53.

19 Keene J. R., Prokos A. H. 'Widowhood and the end of spousal caregiving: Relief or wear and tear?' *Ageing and Society*. 2008; 28(4):551–70.

20 Romeo R. D. 'Perspectives on stress resilience and adolescent neurobehavioral function'. *Neurobiol Stress*. 2015; 1:128–33.

21 Seery M. D., Holman E. A., Silver R. C. 'Whatever does not kill us: Cumulative lifetime adversity, vulnerability, and resilience'. *J Pers Soc Psychol*. 2010; 99(6):1025–41.

22 McLaughlin K. A., Koenen K. C., Bromet E. J., Karam E. G., Liu H., Petukhova M., et al. 'Childhood adversities and post-traumatic stress

disorder: Evidence for stress sensitisation in the World Mental Health Surveys'. *Br J Psychiatry*. 2017; 211(5):280–88.

23 Gillies J., Neimeyer R. A. 'Loss, grief, and the search for significance: Toward a model of meaning reconstruction in bereavement'. *J Constr Psychol*. 2006; 19(1):31–65.

24 Ibid.

25 Ibid.

8. *The end of the story*

1 Segalov M. ' "What if you don't make it?": Trent Alexander-Arnold on football's brutal talent machine'. *The Guardian* [internet]; 30 April 2023; available from: https://www.theguardian.com/football/2023/apr/30/liverpool-trent-alexander-arnold-on-football-academies-and-the-games-brutal-talent-machine

2 Haimson O. L., Veinot T. C. 'Coming out to doctors, coming out to "everyone": Understanding the average sequence of transgender identity disclosures using social media data'. *Transgender Health*. 2020; 5(3): 158–65.

3 Brumbaugh-Johnson S. M., Hull K. E. 'Coming out as transgender: Navigating the social implications of a transgender identity'. *J Homosex*. 2019; 66(8):1148–77.

4 Galupo M. P., Krum T. E., Hagen D. B., Gonzalez K. A., Bauerband L. A. 'Disclosure of transgender identity and status in the context of friendship'. *J LGBT Issues Couns*. 2014; 8(1):25–42.

5 Fahs B. 'The coming out process for assigned-female-at-birth transgender and non-binary teenagers: Negotiating multiple identities, parental responses, and early transitions in three case studies'. *J LGBT Issues Couns*. 2021; 15(2):146–67.

6 Rood B. A., Maroney M. R., Puckett J. A., Berman A. K., Reisner S. L., Pantalone D. W. 'Identity concealment in transgender adults: A qualitative assessment of minority stress and gender affirmation'. *American Journal of Orthopsychiatry*. 2017; 87(6):704–13.

7 Testa R. J., Michaels M. S., Bliss W., Rogers M. L., Balsam K. F., Joiner T. 'Suicidal ideation in transgender people: Gender minority stress and interpersonal theory factors'. *J Abnorm Psychol.* 2017; 126(1):125–36.

8 Brumbaugh-Johnson and Hull, op. cit.

9 Carroll N. 'Narrative closure'. *Philos Stud.* 2007; 135(1):1–15.

10 Beike D., Wirth-Beaumont E. 'Psychological closure as a memory phenomenon'. *Memory.* 2005; 13(6):574–93.

11 McAdams D. P., Reynolds J., Lewis M., Patten A. H., Bowman P. J. 'When bad things turn good and good things turn bad: Sequences of redemption and contamination in life narrative and their relation to psychosocial adaptation in midlife adults and in students'. *Pers Soc Psychol Bull.* 2001; 27(4):474–85.

12 McAdams D. P., Logan R. L., Reischer H. N. 'Beyond the redemptive self: Narratives of acceptance in later life (and in other contexts)'. *J Res Pers.* 2022; 100:104286.

13 Ibid.

14 Seth A. K., Bayne T. 'Theories of consciousness'. *Nat Rev Neurosci.* July 2022; 23(7):439–52.

15 Fivush R., Booker J. A., Graci M. E. 'Ongoing narrative meaning-making within events and across the life span'. *Imagin Cogn Pers.* 2017; 37(2):127–52.

16 Benish-Weisman M. 'Between trauma and redemption: Story form differences in immigrant narratives of successful and nonsuccessful immigration'. *J Cross-Cult Psychol.* 2009; 40(6):953–68.

17 Pinto R. Z., Ferreira M. L., Oliveira V. C., Franco M. R., Adams R., Maher C. G., et al. 'Patient-centred communication is associated with positive therapeutic alliance: A systematic review'. *J Physiother.* 2012; 58(2):77–87.

18 Collins H. K. 'When listening is spoken'. *Curr Opin Psychol.* 2022; 47:101402.

19 Guilfoyle M. 'Listening in narrative therapy: Double listening and empathic positioning'. *S Afr J Psychol.* 2015; 45(1):36–49.

Index

Page references in *italics* indicate images.

abstinence-only sex education 139–41,
  143
acceptance
  life stories and 186–8
  social 24, 26, 27, 35, 46–7, 105, 113
adolescence
  acceptance and *see* acceptance
  bullying and *see* bullying
  closure and *see* closure
  defined 2
  image and *see* image
  loss and *see* loss
  love and *see* love, first
  memories, power of 1–4, 6–7, 8–9,
    14–15, 16, 101, 189–90
  popularity and *see* popularity
  power of 1–16
  psychology, looking at through the
    lens of 9 *see also* psychology
  redemption and *see* redemption
  risk-taking and *see* risk-taking
  sex and *see* sex
  sexual identity and *see* sexual identity
  storytelling and *see* stories
  therapy and *see* therapy
  transitions, adolescent 181–3
  understanding, power of 188
adrenal gland 7
adulthood
  acceptance and 186
  adolescent stories, adult society built
    on 192

bullying and 96, 100
first love and 101, 110
identity signalling in 51
memories of adolescence in, power of
  1–4, 6–7, 8–9, 14–15, 16, 101, 189–90
peer influence and 70, 94
popularity in school and 32–5
sensation seeking and 67–8
social risk and 71, 72
teenage girls' sexual relations with
  adult men 152–8
alcohol 10, 15
  anxiety and 82
  grief and 161–2
  parents and 9, 171, 172
  peer influence and 95
  popularity and 19, 34–5
  risk-taking and 61, 63, 65, 67, 70,
    73–5, 82
  selection and socialisation effects and
    73–5
  self-harm and 75
  sex and 130, 135
Alex 17, 19, 21, 50–52, 91–3
Alonzo, Daniel 111, 112
Amy (identical twin) 39–41
Andrews, Jack 71–2, 193
anorexia 44
anxiety/anxiety disorder 26, 41, 46, 62,
  81–3, 89, 92, 129, 177
  social anxiety disorder/prototypical
    adolescent disorder 46, 82

gender identity and *see* gender
 identity
good teenage sex example 148–52
homosexuality *see* homosexuality
masturbation 131, 143
older guys, teenage girls and 152–8
popularity and 19, 23, 34
pornography 146–8
pregnancy, teenage 15, 34, 77, 128–9,
 131–4, 136, 137–41, 145, 146, 158
regret and 127–9, 151, 152
risk-taking and 61–3, 65, 74, 76–80,
 128–30
sex-positive movement 141–4
sexual assault 128
sexual identity development
 milestones 116
sexual minority groups/
 heteronormativity 110–17
sexual self-efficacy or sexual agency
 144
sexual self-esteem 143–4
sexual wellbeing 143–4
'sexually competent' 151, 155–6
sexual desire in young adolescents
 130–31
STIs 65, 136, 140, 152
siblings 9, 24, 39–41, 63, 87, 164–5, 166
skin colour 43–4, 56–9
smartphone 15, 79–80, 146
social acceptance 24, 26, 27, 35, 46–7,
 105, 113
social anxiety disorder/prototypical
 adolescent disorder 46, 82
socialisation effects 74–5
social hierarchy 17, 19, 87
social media 9, 15–16, 18, 23, 29, 42, 80,
 179–80
social protection 35, 50
social support 18, 33, 102–3, 133,
 165–9, 185

social risk, avoiding 71–2
social sophistication 23
socioemotional system 68
sociometric popularity 19, 27, 32, 34
Son, Daye 113
South Asian ethnicity 57–8
status, social
 bullying and 85, 86–7, 89, 90–94, 96
 first love and 103, 105–6, 124, 129, 130
 image and 47, 48
 popularity and 17, 19, 20, 21, 23, 24,
  29, 30, 31, 32, 33, 34
 risk-taking and 72
 sex and 133, 141, 153
stereotypes 15, 16, 20, 62
STIs 65, 136, 140, 152
storytelling
 acceptance and 186–8
 adolescent friendships as love
  stories 35
 closure/end of 181–4
 contamination and 185–6
 grief and 174–6
 humans as storytellers 13–14
 interpretation and 188
 interviewees and 8–13
 master narrative 184
 memory and *see* memory
 origin stories 12–13
 power of understanding adolescence
  188
 redemption 184–6
stress 38, 70, 82, 134, 180
 inoculation 172–3, 174
 post-traumatic stress disorder 98,
  164
 sensitisation 173, 174
Stroebe, Margaret 162
subcultures 51–6, 59
suicide 28, 33, 74–5, 97, 114, 161, 164,
 178